Toward a self-managed life style

Houghton Mifflin Company   Boston

Dallas   Geneva, Illinois   Hopewell, New Jersey   Palo Alto   London

Toward a self-managed life style

Second Edition

Robert L. Williams   University of Tennessee

James D. Long   Appalachian State University

Printed in the U.S.A.

Library of Congress Catalog Card Number: 78-56435

ISBN: 0-395-26760-9

Credits

Cartoons in the text and on the cover by Bob Dole.

The epigraph for Chapter 2 is from "The Road Not Taken" from *The Poetry of Robert Frost* edited by Edward Connery Lathem. Copyright 1916, © 1969 by Holt, Rinehart and Winston. Copyright 1944 by Robert Frost. Reprinted by permission of Holt, Rinehart and Winston, Publishers.

Contents

CONTENTS

Chapter 5
A journey to Naif: Confronting the smoking habit   111

Chapter 6
All things in moderation: Controlling drinking   126

Chapter 7
"I am the mountain": Involvement in physical activity   138

Chapter 8
Panic in the stacks: Managing study behavior   160

Chapter 9
Looking to the future: Career planning   188

Prologue

Like the original edition, this revision of *Toward a Self-managed Life Style* is designed for persons who wish to use behavior modification techniques to change their own behavior. Instead of the traditional emphasis on how individuals *react to* their environment, the focus of this book is on how individuals *act upon* their environment to produce desired behavioral changes.

We think self-modification is the ultimate application of behavior management concepts. By teaching individuals how to modify their own behavior, we have made a permanent impact on their lives. If *we* assumed responsibility for modifying people's behavior, the quality of that behavior might continue to depend on our presence and support. But the overriding purpose of this book is to produce self-responsibility for behavior as well as the ability to achieve desired behavior changes within oneself.

Despite the similarity in focus, the current revision is substantially different from the original edition in its structure and scope. Three chapters have been added: " 'If Not Now, When?': Developing Assertive Behaviors," "Adjusting the Automatic Pilot: Domestic Self-management," and "A Familiar Aspiration: Helping Others Become Self-directing." Two chapters have been changed so extensively that they bear little similarity to the original chapters: Chapter 1, "Journey of Hope: The Philosophy of Self-management," and Chapter 3, "Directing the Inner Drama: Covert Alternatives." The original chapter dealing with health related behaviors has been divided into three shorter chapters focusing on eating control, smoking control, and drinking control.

The structure within chapters has also been changed. Several extended examples of the concepts being discussed appear in most chapters and are distinguished typographically from the running text. Reading these examples should tremendously enhance one's ability to apply the concepts discussed in the text. Many of these examples employ several different concepts, thus helping the reader integrate information from different sections in the chapter.

Another structural change within the applied chapters (Chapters 4–13) is the inclusion of a motivational section at the beginning. One will not apply the mechanics of self-management without a solid reason for doing so. Rather than assuming that an individual brings that motivation to his or her reading of the text, we have chosen to furnish information that may provide the basis for motivation.

The philosophy of self-management has been more fully covered in this edition. In the introductory chapter we describe our assumptions regarding the potential for changing one's life, the motivation for changing, the role of knowledge in the change process, and the status of will power in achieving change. The chapter also describes the potential effects of self-management on personal confidence, locus of control, personality, and spontaneity. The final section of the chapter analyzes common objections to our self-management approach, for example, its emphasis on structure, its simplicity, and its use of extrinsic payoffs. A thorough reading of Chapter 1 should add substantially to one's readiness for the information in subsequent chapters.

The next two chapters describe the mechanics of self-management. Chapter 2, "The Less Traveled Road: A Model for Self-control," is devoted entirely to the use of environmental manipulations in changing overt behaviors. Simplified from the first edition, this model now includes five steps: selecting a goal, monitoring target behavior, changing setting events, establishing effective consequences, and consolidating gains. Chapter 3 describes the use of thought processes to alter the following: (1) overt behaviors, such as excessive smoking, excessive eating, excessive alcohol consumption, aggressive behavior, assertive behavior, approval behavior, and health enhancing behaviors; (2) unpleasant physiological states, for example, tension and migraine headaches, other forms of pain, asthmatic reactions, and heart palpitations; and (3) uncomfortable psychological states, such as anxiety, stress, depression, and unwanted thoughts. Most of the book's discussion of covert control appears in this chapter. Later chapters briefly describe appropriate covert alternatives and refer the reader to Chapter 3 for a more detailed coverage.

The remaining chapters describe the application of the self-management models in areas important to most college students. Chapters 4 – 7 deal with health related issues. Chapter 4, "Battle of the Bulge: A Behavioral Approach to Weight Reduction," analyzes the concept of overweight, the role of calories in weight control, and the application of the self-management model to eating problems. Chapter 5, "A Journey to Naif: Confronting the Smoking Habit," describes rationalizations for smoking and the use of the self-management model in altering smoking habits. Chapter 6, "All Things in Moderation: Controlling Drinking," identifies roadblocks for dealing with drinking problems, procedures for recognizing that one has a drinking problem, stimuli that contribute to excessive drinking, and self-management concepts that can facilitate control of drinking behaviors. Chapter 7, " 'I Am the Mountain': Involvement in Physical Activity," includes a discussion of the payoffs for physical activity, barriers to participation in sports activity, and the use of the self-management model in increasing the quantity and quality of sports involvement.

Chapters 8 and 9 relate to academic and career planning. Chapter 8, "Panic in the Stacks: Managing Study Behavior," addresses the same topics as in the first edition: increasing study behavior, increasing reading comprehension, completing major academic projects, and becoming more creative in academic work. Closely aligned with academic work is career planning, and Chapter 9, "Looking to the Future: Career Planning," describes the type of self-understanding and knowledge of educational-occupational opportunities necessary to make judicious career decisions. The last part of the chapter illustrates how self-management procedures can be used to achieve self-understanding and knowledge of career opportunities.

The next two chapters deal with the social domain of life. Chapter 10, "Wealthier than Kings: Enhancing Interpersonal Attractions," analyzes what is involved in becoming reinforcing to others and in developing romantic relationships. Chapter 11, " 'If Not Now, When?': Developing Assertive Behaviors," begins with a description of the payoffs for assertive behaviors, proceeds to analyze barriers to behaving assertively, and then applies the self-management model to the acquisition of assertive behavior.

Chapter 12, "Adjusting the Automatic Pilot: Domestic Self-management," deals with a mundane, often neglected area of life and is based on the observation that domestic mismanagement can undermine effective control in many other areas. We have seen some very talented students become academically and socially immobilized because of domestic neglect. Discussed in the chapter are time management, household management, and money management.

The final chapter, "A Familiar Aspiration: Helping Others Become Self-directing," describes how parents and teachers can assist children to assume responsibility for their behavior, how counselors can help clients resolve their own problems, and how all of us can aid friends overcome difficulties. Most readers will eventually assume one or more of these helping roles.

To assist the reader, we have included a Glossary; however, it is not a glossary in the usual sense. Because most concepts are defined and illustrated when first introduced in the text, we have not duplicated those explanations in the Glossary. The Glossary is restricted to concepts that are not thoroughly explained when first mentioned in the text and to concepts to which we allude, but do not explain in the text itself.

As with most self-management projects, this revision was completed with considerable assistance from others. Several people read portions of the manuscript and offered editorial suggestions: Kamala Anandam, Pat Ball, James Deni, Basil Johnson, Liz Mattice, Hank Schneider, and Frank Terrant. Another group of individuals, whom we have identified as editorial consultants, gave extensive assistance in the preparation of certain chapters. These individuals, Ron Carlini, Paul Carson, Opal Fraker, Terry Howell, and Eddie Workman, did much of the literature search, wrote an initial draft, and assisted in the refinement of their respective chapters. They were chosen for this role because of their special commitment and expertise in the particular areas. The field reviewers for the revised manuscript, including Garry M. Bledsoe, DeKalb Community College, Del Brusnahan, Xavier University, David A. Eckerman, University of North Carolina, Samuel D. Gilbert, Los Angeles Valley College, Sandra D. Harrison, Mercer University, Leslie A. King, University of Minnesota—Twin Cities, and Dan G. Perkins, Richland College, have provided important feedback in our attempts to improve the text. A person whose assistance was invaluable in the preparation of the revision is Cathy Pettiford, who did most of the typing and provided important editorial suggestions. Her competence and efficiency allowed us to keep the revision process on schedule at all times.

Two people whose personal and professional support was indispensable not only in this project but in most of our endeavors are Lib Long and Jackie Williams. Much of our zest for living, which we hope is partially reflected in the text, is related to these two rare human beings. Although they played no role in the actual writing of this text, two young men, Blakeley Long and Todd Williams, have given us much personal inspiration—something that is necessary for all major projects, whether they be writing a textbook or building a tree house!

R.L.W.
J.D.L.

Toward a self-managed life style

Chapter 1
Journey of hope:

The philosophy of self-management

The grand essentials to happiness in this life
are something to do, something to love, and
something to hope for.

JOSEPH ADDISON

Hope appeared in Bob Williams's office on a penetratingly cold day in early January to request permission to add a course for that quarter. Like many of our students, Hope had been rebuffed by the university's registration machinery. Her registration difficulties typified the general tenor of her life at that time. The bitterly cold weather compounded the physical discomforts that she was already experiencing from a heavy head cold. Her physical problems were complicated by the pack of cigarettes that she smoked daily. Conversation with Hope revealed that in addition to carrying a full course load, she was working two jobs part time. Her work and academic commitments left virtually no leisure time. She was also experiencing domestic problems with her roommate, whom she described as "really letting things go around our apartment." Despite her frustration with her roommate's behavior, Hope had been unable to confront her about the domestic situation. Perhaps the most ambivalent part of Hope's life was her relationship with her boyfriend. She said that she had cared for him deeply, but that he was increasingly smothering her with his insistence on their togetherness. In a word, Hope had come to be distressed about the status of her life. There was virtually nothing in her life to which she could point with great satisfaction.

This text is written for Hope and for the multitude of others like her. Hope was not in the throes of deep depression; she was not talking suicide; and, most of all, she was not crazy. Nonetheless, her life was badly out of balance and she was taking practically no action to get herself back on track. Actually, she was spending a lot of time discussing her problems with her friends, but most of that time was devoted to rehashing the problems and making self-critical comments. She was receiving considerable attention for discussing her problems but little constructive input for dealing with them. She was spending a substantial amount of her work and study time contemplating how poorly she was managing her life.

Like most college students, Hope had some obvious assets. She was articulate, had traveled widely, and had had some valuable work experiences. She periodically flashed a charming smile, and she manifested a strong sensitivity to others' feelings. Physically, she was slender and attractive. None of these positive qualities, however, was receiving much attention in Hope's reflection on her life.

In what ways are many of us similar to Hope? For most individuals there are several areas, including the personal, physical, academic, and vocational domains, that affect their good feelings about themselves. It is not unusual for several of these domains to be out of phase at the same time. However, the problems of most people do not become severe enough to require psychiatric attention. Admittedly, many people are experiencing far less from life than they desire. Many recognize the chasm between what they intend to accomplish and what they actually get done. They sometimes feel that everything is going wrong and that they have lost their "umph."

A corollary of this immobilized feeling is the perception that there is little you can do to change the quality of your life. What you can do to stem the tide, to reverse the momentum, and to act upon your environment is the focus of our text.

People do change

The most basic assumption underlying self-management is that many human conditions can be changed. Let us quickly add that most people do not approach their fullest potential for change. This relative impotence is probably related to several factors, among which are: (1) a belief that people can't change; (2) inadequate motivation to change; (3) lack of knowledge as to how to change.   (Need)

Potential for change

Some individuals endure seemingly intolerable conditions without seriously considering how these conditions might be changed. They dismiss their states with platitudes, such as "I'm just that way" or "Whatever will be, will be." Because many human conditions, including excessive weight, strained relationships, and academic failure, are largely a product of one's behavior, these conditions could be changed by altering certain behaviors. So long as you feel that the quality of your life is mainly a product of fate or of externally controlled factors, you are unlikely to change in productive ways. If you do not systematically examine how your behaviors affect the circumstances in your life, you may be oblivious to your potential for change.

In considering your potential for change, you may find it helpful to look around and to examine changes in others' lives. From such individuals you may derive both the inspiration to change and the knowledge of how to change. You probably know someone who has lost fifty pounds, someone who has given up smoking, someone who jogs on a regular basis, someone who has dissolved an oppressive relationship, someone who has achieved a reconciliation, and, perhaps best of all, someone who has recently fallen in love.

Despite these obvious changes in others' lives, you may be tempted to conclude that you've been the way you are *too long* or that there are *too many factors* working against you for *you* to achieve such changes. In reality that is seldom the case. The seventy-year-old man whom we regularly see taking tennis lessons apparently thinks that he can still improve his game. The fifty-year-old woman who has recently started

3

People do change.

skiing every weekend, after avoiding athletic activity for most of her adult life, apparently feels that it's not too late to experience the ecstasy of gliding down a mountainside. The chain smoker who has given up cigarettes at age forty-seven to reduce the possibility of a second heart attack apparently feels that the preservation of life merits the giving up of long-standing habits. The person who has dissolved an oppressive marriage of ten years' standing is probably convinced that the reclamation of personal identity is worth the pain involved in achieving it. The young woman of twenty-seven who lost her husband in a tragic automobile accident but has lived to work, to play, to smile, and to love again is quite likely convinced that she has more potential for recovering from grief and suffering than she dared to think. Several acquaintances who have experienced extended periods of debilitating depression but eventually have come to feel that life is worthwhile — and, most of all, that they are worthwhile — symbolize the human potential for change.

Motivation to change
Motivation to change is another variable that can markedly enhance or limit personal change. In fact, some people think that altering a behavior requires nothing more than *wanting* to change that behavior. Thus, failure to change is attributed to insufficient motivation. Admittedly, desire to change is a crucial component of self-management. People may be quite knowledgeable about self-management and yet do nothing to modify their behavior. However, we disagree with the idea that desire alone will produce behavior change. A person may want to change very badly but fail because of poor self-control strategies. We contend that desire is a necessary but not an exclusive ingredient for self-control.

4

Motivation plus technique

The importance of both commitment to change and method of change was demonstrated in a study with undergraduate psychology students. The requirements for participation in the study were: (1) having had a serious problem in the area of eating, smoking, studying, or dating, and (2) having made a major effort to change the problem behavior, such as applying a specific self-management strategy for at least one week. In each of the four problem areas, twelve "successful" and twelve "unsuccessful" persons were selected via interviews. Specific criteria for "success" had been established for each problem area. For example, smokers had to have decreased the number of cigarettes per day by 50 percent and to have maintained this lower rate of smoking for at least four months prior to the interview.

In all problem areas, the successful self-controllers rated themselves as more committed to personal change than did the unsuccessful ones. However, successful students also reported using a greater number of techniques and for longer periods of time than did their unsuccessful peers. Of the various self-control techniques employed by the successful subjects, *self-reward** proved the most popular in all problem areas. The successful students arranged for special privileges and payoffs to follow attainment of their goals.

Adapted from Perri, M. G., and Richards, C. S. 1977. An investigation of naturally occurring episodes of self-controlled behaviors. *Journal of Counseling Psychology 24*, 178–183.

Many people declare they want to change, engage in behavior related to the proposed change, but are still quite unsuccessful in achieving the desired change.

The plight of the weight reducer graphically illustrates the importance of combining motivation and knowledge. Dieters generally understand that more food and more calories mean more weight. They may severely deprive themselves of food and drink for several weeks but eventually acquiesce to their hunger, cravings, and social influences. Those dieters who successfully maintain their weight-reducing behaviors have come to understand that weight loss does not mean starvation. Quite to the contrary, these individuals eat enough to satisfy their hunger completely. They achieve this by knowing how different foods affect both hunger and weight. They also know how social stimuli affect their eating behavior, and they know precisely what different exercises will do to their body structure. They know the regions of the body from which to expect early and later weight loss. In a word, they have become professionals in managing this area of their lives, and they have achieved this professionalism through a combination of motivation and knowledge.

*Terms set in italics and followed by an asterisk are defined in the Glossary.

Without a knowledge of environmental-behavioral relationships, people often put themselves in the very situations and emit the very behaviors that will negate achievement of their goals.

Since desire to change is indispensable for self-management, a crucial issue is: What produces desire? Since desire refers to an internal state known only to the individual, we can more easily identify what stimulates people *to say* that they want to change their behavior. We recognize that statements of desire are not always consistent with actual desire. Kanfer and Karoly (1972) have identified four factors that lead people to say they intend to change behavior. The first of these factors is a cue from the environment that their behavior is in conflict with the environment. For example, if Jim Long's house plants begin wilting and dying, he's likely to indicate an intention to change some aspect of his tending behavior. If a specific social behavior leads others to withdraw from him, Jim is likely to state his intention to change that behavior. Thus, cues from the physical or social environment that indicate a person's behavior is in conflict with that environment may constitute the initial impetus for an "intention to change" statement.

An added impetus for intention statements is an adverse impact of a behavior on the individual. Particularly important would be physical problems resulting from the behavior. For example, some people indicate that they want to stop smoking because of physical considerations. Although the research linking lung cancer and heart disease to smoking is motivational for some individuals, actual shortness of breath and chronic coughing are more likely to furnish an impetus for change. These symptoms should be particularly motivational to people who have previously enjoyed vigorous health and who have maintained intense respect for their physical state.

Satiation * with a behavior is another factor that may produce intention statements. Most individuals eventually get tired of behaving in a particular way. For example, some people exhibit depressed behaviors for months but then one day decide that they've had enough of being depressed. Initially they may find depressive behavior a powerful means of controlling others. Support and capitulation from others may serve as *positive reinforcers* * for depressive behaviors. Many individuals, however, get over their depression without therapeutic intervention. This ability suggests that they get tired of being depressed and begin to speak in more positive terms about their behavioral intentions.

The fourth factor supporting intention statements is the social approval they elicit. When others applaud you for saying that you want or intend to change a behavior, you *increase* the frequency of such statements. However, such an increase may not be accompanied by changes in actual behavior. Only when approval is given for actual behavioral changes should we expect approval to produce a motivation to change.

Confronting one's priorities

Roberto had made the mistake of pursuing too many commitments: maintaining a 3.0 grade point average, developing a close relationship with his son, becoming a skilled tennis player, maintaining an intense relationship with his wife, getting to know lots of other students, traveling extensively, and growing intellectually outside his academic major. Though these commitments were not inherently incompatible, they were proving to be so numerous that Roberto was feeling uncomfortable about his use of time. When he spent two hours a day playing tennis, he had less time and energy to devote to other goals. The conflict of his motives was most acutely felt in the evenings. If he played with his son, he might at the same time be worrying about course work that needed to be done.

What proved invaluable to Roberto was ranking commitments in their order of importance to him. By clearly declaring his personal priorities, he prevented his time and energy from continuing to be up for grabs. He has obtained a clearer perception of his priorities and of the time required to meet them. For example, Roberto needs to devote about two hours a day to his son in order to feel positive about *his investment* in that relationship; that time frequently comes in the evening. Because of the importance of this relationship, he can give time to his son during the evening without worrying about other obligations. This commitment means that he may not maintain his 3.0 GPA, that he will forgo long trips until he graduates, that he will play tennis for only an hour a day three times a week, that he will de-emphasize relationships with other students, and that he will reserve reading for pleasure for vacation periods. Because of their private commitments, don't try to call Roberto and his wife after 10:00 in the evening!

A conflict of motives, rather than a lack of motivation, sometimes inhibits behavioral change. You may genuinely desire results that are incompatible. You may want to lose weight but at the same time may want to appease an insatiable sweet tooth. You may desire the security of long-term relationships and yet enjoy the novelty of short-term relationships. In other instances your motives may not be incompatible but simply too numerous. You may want to be involved in twenty different activities, each of which is inherently important to you. However, attempting all twenty may result in the loss of essential rest and leisure time, in a failure to function effectively in any of the twenty areas, or in a virtual immobilization — you're so overwhelmed by your commitments that you don't know where to begin. As you proceed through the text, you will encounter various exercises that will help you to determine when motives are incompatible or too numerous to be acted upon simultaneously.

7

Method of change

This book is based on the premise that there are orderly relationships between a person's behavior and the external environment. What appears chaotic (behavior) often emerges as rather predictable when examined closely. We are fortunate because many principles of behavior that have been painstakingly derived from laboratory and applied research can be used in changing behavior. Just as a space exploration based on the principles of physics is more likely to be successful than one based on intuition, so success in the behavioral realm is apt to be based on a knowledge and application of behavioral principles.

A fundamental theme of this book is that you can change behavior by altering your environment — not simply by wanting to change or by talking about the need for change. Two major categories of environmental events must be understood and manipulated to achieve effective change: events that precede and set the stage for particular behaviors, and events that follow these behaviors, making them more or less likely to recur. Quite often, these events affect behavior without your being aware of that impact. For example, a great many eating, drinking, and smoking behaviors occur without your being conscious of them. You may eat incessantly in certain situations without realizing it. You may light up and begin smoking without being aware of what you've done. Certain emotional responses, such as crying, embarrassment, and tension, may also occur without your knowing precisely what's producing them. A basic premise of this self-management text is that environmental events controlling behavior must first be identified and then altered before many behaviors can be changed. For example, you may wish to improve your academic record, but unless you identify the specific environmental factors controlling your academic behaviors, your record is unlikely to improve.

The self-management approach described here has emerged from the general area of *applied behavior analysis.** That approach has demonstrated that a reliable way to modify behavior is to alter a person's environment. Thus, many teachers, counselors, and parents have been taught to produce appropriate behaviors in others by systematically changing environmental events. Whatever can be done to modify someone else's behavior can usually modify your own. In fact, you probably have a lot more control over events affecting your behavior. You have only limited access to the environment controlling another person's behavior, but continuous access to your own.

Our method of changing behavior is quite different from the conception of how behavior is changed held by lay persons, who often see the resources for changing behavior as being internal to the person — that is, when you want to change behavior you must apply will power. Will power supposedly involves some inner repository of strength that allows

Will power put to a test

While "will power" is extremely difficult to isolate experimentally, two researchers (Jeffrey and Christensen, 1975) attempted to appraise the impact of will power versus that of environmental manipulation on weight reduction. The environmental group employed several of the self-management strategies advocated in this text. They recorded behaviors related to weight gain and received both monetary rewards and group approval for appropriate behavior. The will-power group was informed of the procedures being used in the environmental group but did not systematically employ any of these strategies. Instead, they were told to use will power as the primary avenue to weight loss.

The environmental group lost significantly more weight than either the will-power group or a no-treatment control group. The results of the will-power group and of the no-treatment group did not differ from each other. An eighteen-week follow-up for the environmental group revealed no significant weight gain after the termination of the behavior-control procedures. While this study does not allow us to isolate the importance of any single behavior-management procedure, it does suggest that a combination of these procedures is more effective than will power in changing behavior.

Adapted from Jeffrey, D. B., and Christensen, E. R. 1975. Behavior therapy versus "will power" in the management of obesity. *Journal of Psychology* 90(2), 303–311.

---

people to withstand temptation and stay on the given task until their goal is achieved. People who reputedly use will power to change behavior seem to have certain characteristics: 1. They usually have tremendous motivation to change the behavior in question. When motivation is high, a change in the behavior is extremely rewarding. Thus, one reason why the will-power approach appears to be successful is because of powerful payoffs. Often, your health or a relationship with a person significant to you is at stake. 2. These individuals often employ some of the self-management strategies described in this text without recognizing them as such. For example, they avoid certain people and situations in order to sustain a behavioral change. 3. Those who successfully employ will power typically have a history of success in achieving other goals, which produces an expectation of success in achieving current goals.

We have just described the circumstances under which the will-power approach is likely to be successful. Our observation, however, is that dependence on will power often leads to failure. When you don't perceive the projected change as critically important, when you don't know how the environment can work for or against you, and when you don't have a history of goal attainment, the advice to use will power is likely to be ineffective.

Effects of self-management

What will self-management do in your life? Before we can reasonably expect you to continue this quest, we must provide some indication of the potential payoffs. At the very least, our self-management approach should help you change some behaviors that you really want to change — but have thus far been unsuccessful in changing. We can also alert you to new possibilities for change, to attractive behavior goals that you had not considered, particularly in the social realm where you may not be aware that your relationships could be enhanced by the introduction of new behaviors. Thus, we should help you to identify and change some specific behaviors that are adversely affecting your social relationships, physical well-being, and general zest for living.

Beyond helping to change specific behaviors, what effect will self-management have on your total life style? An ambitious (but not entirely unthinkable) goal is a higher degree of control over all aspects of your life. How far you progress with self-management depends a great deal on your initial success with it. We are alluding to the concept of momentum, so familiar in sports. If your initial attempt at self-management proves unsuccessful, you are not likely to continue using our approach. What types of circumstances will predispose you to failure in self-management? Choosing a behavior target that you don't actually want to achieve is the first mistake. People often say that they want to change a behavior ("I know I should stop smoking"; "I really need to lose weight"; "I shouldn't talk so much") to comply with social expectations and to elicit social attention. How can you identify your true motives with respect to a proposed behavioral change? If you've been talking incessantly about the need to change a behavior, stop talking about it for several days. If you continue to think about the proposed change, your statement of motives is probably authentic.

Building your confidence

You can have very genuine motives and still set yourself up for failure. After identifying the priorities in your life, you may wish to select a specific *target behavior** in your top-priority area. This approach should ensure motivation, but you may still have an ill-fated target. If you are extremely emotional about that target (if you frequently cry about it, for example, or become very hostile when you think about it), you have chosen an inappropriate *initial* target. As you will shortly see, self-management does require a considerable degree of objective analysis and control over your environment. Such objectivity is difficult to attain in a highly emotional area of life. Choose as your initial target something that matters to you but not something so crucial and painful that you fall apart whenever you focus upon it. By achieving success with the initial

First things later

Susan's relationship with her boyfriend was producing as much pain as plea-sure. Some days were filled with happiness and love, but others were fraught with extreme insecurity about the relationship. The mood swings were becom-ing exceedingly distressing to Susan. Thus, she felt the most important area to which to apply self-management would be this relationship. However, when she attempted to identify aspects of the relationship that could be changed, she often felt trapped and overwhelmed by the complexity of it all. Often, the net result of her attempts at self-analysis was more crying and more insecurity. She didn't know what to change about the relationship and even feared that trying to change it could complicate her problems.

Finally Susan decided to deal with an aspect of her life that seemed quite unrelated to the relationship — her physical condition. As a teen-ager she had enjoyed sports activity, but in college she had given most of her leisure time to social relationships — ultimately to one relationship. During this period she had not been actively involved in any sport, and her physical condition had suffered. She had gained about fifteen pounds and now became short of breath when she attempted even mild physical activity such as walking up flights of stairs. Susan decided to take a portion of the time she had been investing in lamenting her relationship and to devote that time to getting in top physical shape.

Her commitment to physical conditioning initially focused on three areas: diet control, jogging, and tennis. The first dividend of her self-management activity was the loss of four or five pounds within approximately two weeks. Then she began to experience a definite increase in stamina while jogging. She also began to rediscover the fun of playing tennis. In her track and tennis activity she began making new acquaintances — without even trying to do so. As she slimmed down and altered her measurements in appropriate directions, she was surprised at the number of people who began commenting on her physical appearance. Since her boyfriend had not been involved in her self-management activity, she felt she had achieved some self-identity apart from him. She felt much better about herself generally and was far less intimidated about dealing directly with sensitive areas in the relationship. Somewhat unex-pectedly, her boyfriend started being more attentive to her and became more willing to discuss how they could enhance their relationship.

target, you will acquire added confidence for dealing with more serious personal problems. From your first success may emerge the security and objectivity you need to deal with the more sensitive target. If certain areas continue to be overwhelmingly emotional, we would suggest the assistance of a counselor, who could help you work through emotions that otherwise might negate your potential for changing behaviors in sensitive areas. All human beings probably have deep-seated feelings about themselves that they seldom, if ever, discuss with others or that they do not even admit to themselves. Such feelings can undermine self-management efforts. If you are attempting behavioral changes in areas where you have many unresolved feelings, you are not likely to experience the full potential for self-management.

Locus of control

As you achieve behavior targets in different areas of your life, you may develop an outlook that psychologists call internal *locus of control**. This is the view that "I am in control of what happens in my life," as opposed to "What occurs in my life is a matter of chance or fate" or "Events in my life are primarily controlled by others." Individuals with an internal locus of control perceive themselves as being in control of their actions and see their actions as responsible for the rewards and punishments that follow (Clark, 1976). Researchers repeatedly affirm that an internal locus of control is a reliable indicator of good mental health. We contend that this outlook is fundamental to effective living.

A reciprocal relationship probably exists between internal locus of control and actual self-management of behavior. The more individuals effectively alter their own behaviors, the more likely they are to see themselves as in control of the events and conditions in their lives. Similarly, the more they see themselves as in control, the more likely they are to change their own behaviors. Schallow (1975) compared the locus of control of students who had been the most successful in self-modification with that of students who had been the least successful. The most successful students were initially more internal in their orientation than the least successful were. Balch and Ross (1975) found a significant relationship between initial internal locus of control and both completion of and success in a weight-control program. Although we can't infer precise cause-and-effect relationships from such studies, it does appear that internal locus of control is a good predictor of success in self-management.

Though we would like to claim that a single successful self-management project will give you an internal locus of control, change in outlook is likely to come at a much more modest rate. Many successful attempts at self-management are probably necessary to change a person's locus of control from external to internal. One experimenter (Pawlicki, 1976) systematically investigated the effect of a self-management program on locus of control. Half the subjects took the experimenter's course in self-modification; the other half took a course in community psychology. Students in the self-management course received instruction in several of the techniques to be discussed in this text and conducted their own self-modification programs. Though the self-management students changed more in the direction of internal locus of control than did the community psychology students, the difference was not *statistically significant.** Perhaps, however, a series of such projects would produce a more substantial difference in locus of control.

We also wish we could claim that achieving an internal locus of control in one area will quickly be followed by an internal locus of control in other areas. Unfortunately, we cannot. Bradley and Gaa (1977) reported on a program of weekly conferences in which students (1) received feedback regarding their attainment of previously set academic goals, (2) then set goals regarding the content and activities of the coming week, and (3) finally discussed appropriate strategies for reaching their goals. The conferences were quite effective in increasing internal locus of control in academic situations, but the program had little effect on the students' locus of control in physical and social situations. Thus, it appears that in order to alter locus of control in a specific area, activity must be conducted in that area.

To help you assess your own locus of control, we have included the Levenson Locus of Control Scale. Like most *personality inventories,** this scale is not entirely reliable; if you took the scale on separate occasions, you would not make exactly the same score each time. Thus, you should interpret your scores on the scale with some degree of caution. The scale may suggest the need for movement toward internal locus of control, but it will not give you an infallible locus of control score (see Figure 1.1).

Effect on personality

Thus far we have been looking at change in terms of specific overt behaviors. Perhaps you are more concerned about achieving generalized personality changes. We prefer to think of *personality* as a set of behaviors that a person exhibits across time and situations. Some of these behaviors may be tied together in such a way that you may change several of them by focusing on one. That is, certain responses may function as pivotal behaviors and set into motion a series of other responses. In taking a social dance course, Bob Williams soon discovered that a pivotal behavior was being able to make some type of motor response (such as tapping his foot, moving his hips, nodding his head) consistent with the beat in a piece of music. Without the beat (which all too frequently eluded him), he found it practically impossible to execute the dance patterns in a flowing fashion. (His flow was somewhat suspect even when he was with the beat!) Similarly, in social situations, being able to initiate conversation is certainly a pivotal behavior that allows all types of rapport-building responses to be set into motion.

13

Figure 1.1
Levenson locus of control scale

Using the scale $-3, -2, -1, +1, +2, +3$, indicate the extent to which you agree or disagree with each of the following items. Let -3 represent complete disagreement and $+3$ complete agreement. Put the number representing the degree of your agreement or disagreement by each item. Directions for scoring your responses are given at the conclusion of the inventory.

1. Whether or not I get to be a leader depends mostly on my ability.
2. To a great extent my life is controlled by accidental happenings.
3. I feel like what happens in my life is mostly determined by powerful people.
4. Whether or not I get into a car accident depends mostly on how good a driver I am.
5. When I make plans, I am almost certain to make them work.
6. Often there is no chance of protecting my personal interest from bad-luck happenings.
7. When I get what I want, it's usually because I'm lucky.
8. Although I might have good ability, I will not be given leadership responsibility without appealing to those in positions of power.
9. How many friends I have depends on how nice a person I am.
10. I have often found that what is going to happen will happen.
11. My life is chiefly controlled by powerful others.
12. Whether or not I get into a car accident is mostly a matter of luck.
13. People like myself have very little chance of protecting our personal interests when they conflict with those of strong pressure groups.
14. It's not always wise for me to plan too far ahead because many things turn out to be a matter of good or bad fortune.
15. Getting what I want requires pleasing those people above me.
16. Whether or not I get to be a leader depends on whether I'm lucky enough to be in the right place at the right time.
17. If important people were to decide they didn't like me, I probably wouldn't make many friends.
18. I can pretty much determine what will happen in my life.
19. I am usually able to protect my personal interests.
20. Whether or not I get into a car accident depends mostly on the other driver.
21. When I get what I want, it's usually because I worked hard for it.
22. In order to have my plans work, I make sure that they fit in with the desires of people who have power over me.
23. My life is determined by my own actions.
24. It's chiefly a matter of fate whether or not I have a few friends or many friends.

Scoring procedures for the I, P, and C scales

There are three separate scales used to measure one's locus of control: Internal Scale, Powerful Others Scale, and Chance Scale. There are eight items on each of the three scales. To score each scale add up your answers to the items appropriate for that scale. (These items are listed below.) Add to this sum $+24$. (This removes the possibility of negative scores.) The possible range on each scale is from 0 to 48. Theoretically, a person could score high or low on all three dimensions.

Figure 1.1 cont.

Scale	Items	Interpretation
Internal scale	(1, 4, 5, 9, 18, 19, 21, 23)	High score: indicates that an individual believes (s)he has control over his/her own life; Low score: indicates that an individual believes (s)he does not have much control over his/her own life.
Powerful others scale	(3, 8, 11, 13, 15, 17, 20, 22)	High score: indicates that an individual believes powerful others have control over his/her life; Low score: indicates that an individual believes powerful others do not have much control over his/her life.
Chance scale	(2, 6, 7, 10, 12, 14, 16, 24)	High score: indicates that an individual believes chance forces (luck) control his/ her life; Low score: indicates that an individual believes chance forces do not control his/ her life.

SOURCE: Levenson, H. 1974. Activism and powerful others: Distinctions within the concept of internal-external control. *Journal of Personality Assessment 38*, 381–382. Reprinted with the permission of author and publisher.

Thus, altering one response does sometimes lead to broad changes in behaviors.

Non-behavioral psychologists tend to view personality and behavior as separate spheres, personality being the inner structure on which overt behaviors are based. Thus, maladaptive behaviors are interpreted as symptomatic of more basic inner difficulties. For example, it is sometimes said that excessive eating reflects a need for affection. (In fact, numerous disorders are attributed to a need for affection.) The argument runs, "Remove the *symptom** (excessive eating) and the real problem (a need for affection) will be expressed in other ways." Though affection is undeniably important for emotional well being, it is our opinion that behavior problems do not generally reflect a need for affection, or an underlying personality disorder. A person may have many problems, some internal and some external, but there is little evidence that eliminating one maladaptive behavior will cause another to appear (Paul, 1969). Change can more easily be achieved by focusing on specific behaviors than by seeking out mysterious, deep-seated personality disorders (Paul, 1966).

Effect on spontaneity

Some individuals fear that a systematic effort to manage their own behavior might reduce spontaneity and authenticity. Such a concern fails to recognize that many "natural" behaviors are the result of earlier deliberate learning. Think of how awkward people are when first learning to dance, to drive a car, to participate in a new sport, or to perform the responsibilities of a new job. Conversing with others, introducing people to each other, and showing pleasure over a gift may initially seem mechanical and superficial; however, people become more spontaneous with practice. They eventually emit the desired behaviors without having to tell themselves what to do. There is truth in the adage, "Practice a virtue though you have it not and soon it will be yours."

If you wait for behaviors to occur in a refined, spontaneous form, your behavioral repertoire will be severely limited. People acquire behaviors at somewhat different rates, but everyone begins at a relatively awkward level. For example, the first few times Jim Long skied, he could barely get into his equipment. From this point his skills slowly evolved until he was able to negotiate even the advanced slopes. One of the major challenges of self-management is putting yourself into situations in which skills can be learned. Typically, people try to avoid all situations in which their behaviors will be awkward. The feeling of awkwardness is probably intrinsically aversive; it is doubly uncomfortable to expose your awkwardness to others. The challenge of self-management is to identify situations in which you can learn a desired skill, to put yourself into those situations, and to remain in those situations until you reach the refined level. We contend that self-management can greatly expand your repertoire of spontaneous behaviors by meeting this challenge.

The "best" you

We would be appalled if our self-management approach were to be construed as a vehicle for producing conformity. We shall examine many behavior targets, some of which will be consistent with your own personal goals. Incorporating our self-management approach into your life won't mean that you are adopting anyone else's goals. Our guess is that your uniqueness will be enhanced. Since many environmental factors induce social conformity, assuming control over the factors affecting your own behavior is likely to lessen the degree of your social conformity. Our self-management model should put more control in your hands and allow you to achieve more goals consistent with your natural endowments and private aspirations. Its effect is intended to be similar to that of a true friend:

A friend is someone who leaves you with all your freedom intact, but who obliges you to be fully what you are.

John L'Heureux

Objections to self-management

The prospect of self-management is so intrinsically appealing to us that we are always mildly shocked when others do not share our enthusiasm. However, these people are probably reacting more to *our brand* of self-management than to the basic concept of self-control. The objections to our self-management approach center in three areas: emphasis on structure, simplicity of techniques, and inclusion of extrinsic rewards.

Emphasis on structure

As you will learn from the next chapter, our approach involves *systematic* analysis of your present behaviors and *systematic* modification of your personal environment in order to change behaviors. You must identify the important areas of your life, formulate some specific goals for each area, assess where you stand relative to those goals, and develop specific strategies for reaching them. Individuals whose lives are devoid of systematic analysis and planning may be threatened by discussions dealing with structure. They may construe such discussions as a personal indictment and see structure as something they could not hope to achieve. These same individuals are prone to criticize others who are well organized. As is frequently the case, this criticism may result more from envy than from genuine disdain for a well-organized life.

Many people feel that structuring their lives will limit their personal freedom. They believe that if they set goals, formulate a schedule, and make specific commitments to themselves and others, they will curtail their flexibility in responding to each day's opportunities. Tom, for example, is so locked into his structure that he won't deviate from set plans to capitalize on a once-in-a-lifetime opportunity. If he has activity X planned for this afternoon, he does activity X despite the fact that an old friend has traveled from the Far East (would you believe across town?) to see him, or that the Bolshoi Ballet is performing in the city, or that it's a fine spring day, or that the home team is playing for the national championship for the first time in a century. This is not our idea of the structured life. In fact, if Tom employs our self-management approach, he is likely to be the freest person in town on this special afternoon. He will be free because he has planned ahead and has met academic commitments well in advance of deadlines.

Well-managed people are the ones who work diligently during the winter winds so they can play in the warm spring breezes. Thus, instead of brooding on a rainy day, they work like fury so they will have ample time for play when the sun breaks through. Unstructured people, on the other hand, are often caught without time or money when the attractive possibilities emerge. To avert failure, they will have to stay up all night studying for an exam regardless of how miserably sleepy they are. We

Goal-setting and task persistence

A salient characteristic of people with unstructured lives is their tendency to jump from one activity to another. Such individuals may appear to be on task a high percentage of the time, but their involvement with any particular task is short lived. As a consequence, they seldom complete major tasks. Their lives are a plethora of loose ends.

Two variables that appear to be related to persistence at a task are goal setting and internal locus of control. Gagné and Parshall (1975) used the Academic Achievement Accountability questionnaire to rate sixth-graders according to internal or external locus of control. The questionnaire had students attribute their school achievement to luck, to others, or to their own efforts.

All the participants were then asked to repeat a sample digit span and were given immediate feedback as to the correctness of their response. They were then given the option of trying twenty-five more digit-span tasks. Students who took the challenge were asked how many of these digit spans they thought they would recall correctly — ten, fifteen, or twenty-five. The number of digit spans the students actually attempted was used as the measure of their persistence.

Students with an internal locus of control demonstrated significantly greater persistence than those with an external orientation. The goal-setting condition notably increased the persistence of internal students but had a negligible effect on the persistence of the external subjects. We suspect the internal students were normally more inclined to set goals for themselves and thus responded more positively to that condition. The persistence of external subjects could perhaps be substantially increased only through regular experience with goal setting. Prospects for persistence are poor when individuals have limited experience in goal setting.

---

repeatedly see lack of structure lead to personal immobilization, such as loss of friendships by failing to keep commitments, exhaustion of financial resources by not planning ahead, and untenable academic positions (flunking out) by not organizing study time.

Another reason why structure is threatening to some people is that it may entail confronting unpleasant aspects of their lives. Systematically analyzing their present circumstances may not yield complimentary findings. Students on the verge of academic oblivion may in fact be spending 80 percent of their waking hours goofing off. Smokers who confront the medical and social effects of their habit may encounter some distressing feedback. Individuals who examine the social value of their behaviors may find little that is genuinely helpful to anyone. Being unsystematic may allow some people to avoid the reality of their nonproductivity. Individuals who always seem to be short of money just when they need it most may discover that most of their funds are devoted to frivolous expenditures. Thus, some individuals choose to continue without systematic analysis rather than confront uncomplimentary aspects of their lives.

We hope that the tone of our comments about structure has not been harsh or condescending. Certainly, structure has little inherent value but is useful only to the extent that it enhances productivity and free time. If you are offended by the prospect of analyzing and structuring your life, you are not likely to find this text appealing. If your nonstructured approach is producing desirable results, then your aversion to our structured approach is understandable. However, if your life has reached a level of immobility and nonproductivity that is painful to you, it might be advisable for you to explore our systematic approach a bit further.

Simplicity of self-management

Another major reservation regarding our approach pertains to its simplicity. Simple solutions tend to be insulting, because they make a person's problem behaviors look unwarranted. Complex, deep-seated causes are more appealing because they provide justification for problem behaviors. We don't deny that some of the more basic questions of human existence, such as the fundamental purpose of living, do not have simple answers. Nevertheless, many of the daily problems that may plague your existence do have simple solutions — if you are willing to confront those solutions. We base this contention on our earlier assumptions regarding the relationship between a person's behavior and environmental events. The self-management model to be described in the next chapter will give you the tools for isolating the environmental events that precede and follow your problem behaviors. Once you have identified the environmental stimuli supporting bad behaviors or negating good behaviors, you will be in a better position to change those behaviors.

Our self-management approach obviously does not emphasize existential insights, attitudinal changes, or global inner processes to resolve human problems. We are denying neither the reality nor the periodic usefulness of such inner phenomena. Our contention is that a more manageable approach to solving your problems is to change circumstances in your personal environment. Without those environmental changes your problem behaviors are likely to continue. For example, two people may agree they need to improve their relationship. However, unless they modify their environments in a way that leads to behavioral changes, their relationship is unlikely to improve. Our emphasis on environmental events and overt behaviors does not mean that *specific* covert responses do not have a place in self-management. Chapter 3 will describe a number of covert alternatives that may prove useful to you. These covert alternatives are intended to be both specific and manageable.

Extrinsic payoffs

Subsequent chapters will examine the role of *extrinsic reinforcement** in changing behaviors. Extrinsic payoffs often are said to be artificial and unnecessary *if behaviors are worth changing.* Frankly, many of our students have been quite successful in changing their behaviors without employing added external payoffs. However, if a behavior change involves the loss of an immediate satisfaction, as will happen when you reduce your eating, drinking, and smoking behaviors, you may need immediate external rewards to sustain your self-management activity. The immediate consequences of behavior, rather than the long-term ones, will have the greater controlling impact on behavior.

Others object to extrinsic payoffs on ethical grounds: To provide an external payoff for a personal achievement is to prostitute the value of that achievement. However, most people do not apply this type of reasoning to payment for their labors. As a matter of fact, most people believe that high-quality achievement deserves substantial external rewards. If it's legitimate for others to recognize your achievement through external payoffs, why is it inappropriate for *you* to recognize those achievements via external payoffs? What would be inappropriate about using a special privilege as a reward for a personal achievement? If an immediate external reward will help you change a behavior that you otherwise might not change, which procedure is more appropriate: changing the behavior through external payoffs, or leaving the behavior unchanged because you refuse to use them?

Concluding thoughts

Many treatises have been written on the subject of self-control. Philosophers, theologians, educators, and poets have spilled a considerable amount of ink on this topic. The distinction between this book and others that have dealt with the subject lies in the specificity of our procedures. Instead of using nebulous and moralistic terms, we shall attempt to describe specific procedures that can be interpreted and implemented with minimal confusion.

Self-management will not solve all your problems. We have personally explored several philosophical, religious, ethical, and social systems and have yet to find one that resolves all human difficulties. There are

Self-management in a wheelchair

On an autumn afternoon in 1970, a nationally known advocate of self-management, Israel Goldiamond, was involved in a serious automobile accident. Following surgery he spent several months in the hospital attempting to regain enough of his motor skills to resume the professional position he enjoyed so much. During that period he became an astute observer of his own behavior. He kept detailed records of his motor responses, including rather minute muscular movements. He also recorded medications, X rays, surgery, exercises, and his emotions and the environmental events to which they were related. To clarify his progress and the relationship between his behavior and environmental events, he graphed many of his responses.

During his hospitalization he participated in a rehabilitation program that focused on using eating utensils, getting from the bed to a wheelchair to a car, sitting, and standing. He also re-established his professional activities in his hospital room. Colleagues and students were constantly with him during visiting hours. Re-establishing these activities served as a powerful incentive for engaging in the hospital's physical therapy and rehabilitation program.

The hospital had told Goldiamond's wife that she should expect him to be profoundly depressed; the hospital staff treated her contention that he wasn't depressed with considerable skepticism. According to Goldiamond, the sick and disabled often become depressed because consequences that used to be powerful reinforcers are no longer available to them or are available only at great cost (both financial and physical). The principal solution to this problem is to develop reinforcement potential for other consequences or to develop alternative behaviors for achieving old reinforcers (such as learning to play basketball from a wheelchair).

Goldiamond has since reassumed his full professional position and is as vigorous as ever in charting new territory in behavioral self-analysis.

Adapted from Goldiamond, I. 1973. A diary of self-modification. *Psychology Today 7*(6), 95–102.

some problems that we believe to be inherent to human existence, problems that cannot be solved through self-management or any other approach. The tremendous problems created by physical illnesses, tragedy, old age, and death cannot be eliminated through self-management, but self-management has something to offer even in these areas. A leading psychologist (Goldiamond, 1973) has provided a moving account of his rehabilitation from a devastating automobile accident through the application of simple self-management procedures.

Beyond these profound experiences, there is a multiplicity of everyday experiences that contribute fundamentally to the quality of life. It is with these experiences that the impact of self-management can be felt most keenly. Despite your degree of success or nonsuccess with self-management, you will be *attempting to improve the quality of your existence*. This is in contrast to pitying yourself or blaming others for your problems. Thus, at the very least, self-management can be viewed as a journey of hope.

References

Balch, P., and Ross, A. W. 1975. Predicting success in weight reduction as a function of locus of control: A unidimensional and multidimensional approach. *Journal of Consulting and Clinical Psychology* 43(1), 119.

Bradley, R. H., and Gaa, J. P. 1977. Domain specific aspects of locus of control: Implications for modifying locus of control orientation. *Journal of School Psychology* 15(1), 18–24.

Clark, R. A. 1976. The I-E scale: Control of what? *Journal of Consulting and Clinical Psychology* 44(1), 154.

Gagné, E. E., and Parshall, H. 1975. The effects of locus of control and goal setting on persistence at a learning task. *Child Study Journal* 5(4), 193–199.

Goldiamond, I. 1973. A diary of self-modification. *Psychology Today* 7(6), 95–102.

Jeffrey, D. B., and Christensen, E. R. 1975. Behavior therapy versus "will power" in the management of obesity. *Journal of Psychology* 90(2), 303–311.

Kanfer, F. H., and Karoly, P. 1972. Self-control: A behavioristic excursion into the lion's den. *Behavior Therapy* 3, 398–416.

Levenson, H. 1974. Activism and powerful others: Distinctions within the concept of internal-external control. *Journal of Personality Assessment 38*, 377–383.

Paul, G. 1966. *Insight vs. desensitization in psychotherapy: An experiment in anxiety reduction*. Stanford: Stanford Univ. Press.

Paul, G. 1969, Outcome of systematic desensitization II. In C. Franks (ed.), *Behavior therapy: Appraisal and status*. New York: McGraw-Hill.

Pawlicki, R. E. 1976. Effects of self-directed behavior modification training on a measure of locus of control. *Psychological Reports 39*, 319–322.

Perri, M. G., and Richards, C. S. 1977. An investigation of naturally occurring episodes of self-controlled behaviors. *Journal of Counseling Psychology 24*, 178–183.

Schallow, J. R. 1975. Locus of control and success at self-modification. *Behavior Therapy 6*, 667–671.

Chapter 2
The less traveled road:

A model for self-control

Two roads diverged in a wood, and I —
I took the one less traveled by,
And that has made all the difference.

ROBERT FROST

When Robert Frost wrote "The Road Not Taken," he may not have had self-management in mind. Yet the message of his poem surely applies to our present quest. Our objective is to present you with the alternative of examining, planning, and conducting your life in a systematic fashion. Frankly, this alternative is infrequently chosen. It is our opinion that most people do not come close to fulfilling their potential for good self-management. They engage in behaviors that are hazardous to their health, they fail to attain important personal goals, and they generally experience much unnecessary frustration. Effective self-management is simply not the prevailing life style in this culture. Apparently most individuals either don't know what's involved in effective self-management, or they refuse to be as systematic in dealing with their personal lives as they are in attacking other kinds of problems (such as a drop in sales, or a mechanical breakdown). This chapter will describe what self-management entails; you can decide whether you want to pursue that path.

There are two major types of responses that you may wish to change through self-management and two corresponding types of strategies for achieving those changes. Behaviors and self-management strategies that relate to external, observable events are classified as *overt*. Examples of overt behaviors would be jogging, smoking, singing, talking, and laughing. Examples of overt strategies would be keeping a schedule to remind you of certain commitments, being with people who will provide approval for a particular behavior, avoiding a social situation in which an unwanted behavior might occur, and granting yourself a material payoff for completing specified chores.

Obviously events take place within us that we would also like to change — tension, depression, negative self-evaluation. Although these internal responses often have overt components (such as remaining quiet in group discussion, talking faster, letting your shoulders slump), they have other aspects that are concealed from external scrutiny. These events or states, which are identifiable only on an internal basis, are classified as *covert*. Some covert responses will be targets of change; others can be used as avenues of change. For example, you may want to stop an anxiety reaction but be able to use pleasant thoughts to strengthen other reactions. Chapter 3 will explain how both overt and covert responses can be altered through systematic application of covert processes.

Because we consider overt self-management simpler than covert self-control, this chapter will provide an overview of *overt* procedures that can be used in changing *overt* responses. Specifically, we shall discuss (1) selecting a goal, (2) monitoring target behavior, (3) changing setting events, (4) establishing effective consequences, and (5) consolidating gains. You will not need to go through all five steps in solving every problem. In fact, Steps 1 and 2 will be adequate for modifying many behaviors. When you reach the level of behavior you desire, you can skip to Step 5 and work on consolidating your improvement. (Table 2.3 showing the model appears at the end of the chapter.)

Step 1: Selecting a goal

Selection of a goal is the first step in self-management and perhaps the most critical. Many self-management attempts go awry because of inappropriate goals. You can probably think of many dimensions of your life that you would like to change, but you cannot deal with all of them simultaneously. It is usually best to establish one goal at a time. Working on a single goal maximizes your chances of success and increases the probability of your moving on to other goals. In formulating your first self-management goal, factors you should consider are (1) importance of the goal, (2) measurability of the goal, (3) level of the goal, and (4) positive versus negative quality of the goal.

Importance of the goal

To begin with, you must select a goal that you care about attaining. Self-management may involve doing things that are foreign to you. You are not going to expend much effort unless you are working toward something that really matters. If a behavior is causing you pain (anxiety, guilt, fear, embarrassment), then you will probably work to change it. Any sign of progress will be reinforcing to you and will provide further impetus to your self-management efforts. However, as we suggested in the first chapter, it is quite possible to care *too* much about a problem. Effective self-management demands a high degree of objectivity, something difficult to achieve while overwhelmed by a problem. Therefore, an initial focus of self-management should be something that is causing you pain, but not the most excruciating problem in your life. Getting to work on time would probably be a better first goal than re-establishing a badly strained relationship.

You must be cautious about selecting an initial goal that requires the elimination of long-standing behaviors. One of our students almost became a self-management dropout by choosing such a goal. Her objective was to reduce the frequency of her sarcastic comments. On the surface this goal seemed reasonable, but in reality it jeopardized a well-honed mechanism for producing subtle social reinforcement. For quite some time her sarcasm had been eliciting reactions, such as laughter, that she found reinforcing. In attempting to limit her sarcasm, she inadvertently began to withdraw from social situations or to remain silent when otherwise she would have made cutting remarks. In achieving her goal, she felt she had lost her spontaneity and fighting spirit. That is not the way self-management is supposed to work. Her mistake was in choosing a goal that took away a powerful source of social reinforcement and left nothing in its place but grim virtue!

Measurability of the goal

Another consideration in formulating an initial self-management goal is to define that goal in measurable behavioral terms. You can easily measure overt behaviors such as talking, smiling, walking, crying, smoking, and eating. In contrast, you might have extreme difficulty in determining whether you have met nonbehavioral goals such as "becoming less anxious," "developing a more positive attitude," and "being a better person" — all are certainly worthwhile considerations, but they must be translated into measurable, behavioral terms before they will be amenable to self-control. To illustrate the point, suppose your problem is excessive anxiety. Ask yourself, "What are some ways in which I manifest my anxiety?" or "What kinds of things does my anxiety prevent me from doing?" It might, for example, keep you from participating in class discussion. Let us say that you presently make few, if any, comments during class. A possible first goal might be to make at least one comment per class period in a particular course. By stating your goal in these terms, you identify something that can be measured. Had you said that your goal was to remove pangs of anxiety, there could have been considerable confusion, even in your own mind, as to exactly what constitutes a pang of anxiety — one heart flutter? a twinge? two gulps? a combination? You can see the mess — and the anxiety — this method would create. Objectivity in measuring the frequency of goal-related behavior is fundamental to self-management. Confusion as to the meaning of a goal can strike a death blow to that objectivity.

Level of the goal

You can identify a goal that is important to you, state that goal in measurable terms, but still have an inappropriately defined goal. Many self-management neophytes get too bold in the formulation of goals. Instead of aiming for one comment per class period, they aspire to be the class orator. You should set your first goal only slightly higher than your present level of operation. If you never comment in class, your initial goal might be one comment per week. It is imperative to begin with a goal that is readily attainable. When you can consistently meet that goal, you can move your expectations up a notch (a comment every two class

26

An early self-management advocate

Though self-management research is relatively young, primarily dating back to the 1960s, its principles were being systematically applied in the 1700s by one Benjamin Franklin. To accomplish his somewhat ambitious goal of living "without committing any fault at any time," Franklin first compiled a list of thirteen virtues that he wished to cultivate. Although his virtues were very global (for example, temperance, cleanliness, humility), he specified measurable behaviors for each one. For example, humility meant avoiding such words as "obviously," "certainly," and "undoubtedly." These undesirable words Franklin would replace by more tentative declarations: "It so appears to me at present," "I imagine," and "I conceive." Though Franklin never quite attained the goals he had set for himself (especially humility), he did provide an excellent example of how to translate broad (but legitimate) concerns into precise, measurable goals.

Adapted from Snortum, J. R. 1976. Self-modification: Ben Franklin's pursuit of perfection. *Psychology Today 9*, 80–83.

sessions). People rarely change their whole being in one dynamic, creative moment. What we call personality includes a multitude of overt and covert reactions. Therefore, the effective method for producing change is to deal with these small units of behavior. When enough bits and pieces have been changed, possibly the whole person will be transformed.

Positive versus negative goals

It is usually best to state goals in terms of positive behaviors. What we are aiming for is not just the absence of negative responses, but the presence of positive ones. You can refrain from many negative behaviors and still have an unsatisfactory existence. Besides, one of the best ways to eliminate negative behavior is to strengthen a positive behavior that is *incompatible** with the negative. A teacher who was trying to limit her use of the expression "okay" made a list of terms she might use in its place: "excellent," "great," "that's better," "you're improving," "remarkable," "terrific," "fantastic," and "I like that." When she increased the frequency of these responses, she decreased the likelihood of saying "okay." If you cannot find a positive response that is incompatible with the negative, perhaps you can initially replace the negative response with a behavior that is not quite so undesirable. For example, one girl

*Terms set in italics and followed by an asterisk are defined in the Glossary.

reduced the frequency of scratching her skin disorder by substituting stroking and then patting for the scratching behavior (Watson et al., 1972).

There is another reason for stating goals in positive terms, which will become clearer as you explore the section on recording behavior. The act of recording must be reinforced in order to be sustained, and you will find that logging positive events is much more rewarding than logging negative. You may be eager to record the days you get to work on time but disinclined to record the times you are tardy. If your record-keeping system focuses primarily on negative behaviors, you will be more likely to let it slip.

The practice of stating goals in positive terms can easily be implemented when you're trying to change a behavioral deficiency such as in exercising or studying. However, when the problem consists of a behavioral excess, such as in eating and smoking, you will have more difficulty in identifying and monitoring positive behavior. One researcher (McFall, 1970) attempted to overcome this problem in the case of smoking by having subjects record their urges to smoke that were successfully resisted. This approach worked well in McFall's study, but others (for example, Hanna, 1977) have not been able to replicate the effect. Hanna found that for both behavior deficits and behavior excesses, it is better to record overt occurrences of behavior. As expected, he also found that subjects are more likely to continue recording an overt positive behavior than an overt negative behavior.

Step 2: Monitoring target behavior

Importance of recording

It is important to appraise the precise nature and extent of your problem before attempting to solve that problem — for several reasons. People frequently launch massive self-management attempts without making provisions for monitoring the target behavior. A major reason for recording behavior before beginning a self-management strategy is to provide a reference point for evaluating progress. You may feel that you can recognize changes in your behavior without elaborate record keeping. However, behavior does not usually change abruptly; it may evolve so gradually that you become habituated to the change. Yet these slight day-to-day changes can add up to significant improvement over an extended time period. For example, you might reduce your smoking by one or two cigarettes per day, which would not give you an overwhelming sense of accomplishment, but continuing this rate of reduction for

Some of the more intimate moments of life certainly do not lend themselves to on-the-spot behavior recording!

several days would produce a substantial cut. Keeping precise records of the target behavior maximizes your knowledge of progress.

We call the initial appraisal of behavior the *baseline assessment*. Although there is no "right" length of time for the baseline period, we do suggest that it span several days; a week would be adequate for most behaviors. If you record the behavior for only a day or so, the behavior may be atypically high or low for that period. Recording the behavior over a period of several days will allow you to see cycles in your responses. Variation in behavior is the result of the many biological and environmental factors that affect every person. A baseline assessment of several days will allow you to evaluate more fully the variations that may occur later during the *treatment period.** Often you will find not only that the average level of the behavior changes from baseline to treatment, but also that the behavior becomes more stable during the treatment phase. The latter phenomenon is probable because you have identified and altered the principal factors controlling the behavior.

By recording events that immediately precede and follow occurrences of the target behavior, you may be able to identify factors controlling that response. This kind of assessment may reveal key factors accounting for cycles in your behavior. You may not initially know that certain events consistently trigger an undesirable response. Smokers, for example, may not be aware that they light cigarettes more frequently when drinking or talking. They are probably even more oblivious to the *specific events* within drinking and conversing situations that precipitate lighting up. You may be equally unaware of what is producing certain of your social behaviors. You may have had the experience of expecting to behave one way (laughing, talking) in a social situation but actually behaving in an opposite manner. Perhaps you began an evening expecting to be the life of the party but wound up hardly saying a word. Maybe the subdued laughter to your first joke, the involvement of your favorite people in conversations with others, someone's comments about your not looking well, or even the temperature of the room contributed to your depressed responses. As you will see in later sections, identifying the specific stimuli that precede and follow a behavior makes it easier to do something about that behavior. As long as you do not know what is setting the stage for an undesired behavior or what might be reinforcing that behavior, you have little chance to modify it.

Although self-recording is very valuable in self-management, one problem in using this device is that it may disrupt ongoing behavior. Thus, what you record is not a realistic picture of what normally occurs. For example, consider how the process of self-recording a particular verbal expression might alter the flow of your conversation. First, you would have to realize that you had used the expression before you could record it. Attempting to be aware of when you use a particular term — "you know," "okay," or "uh" — will drastically alter the nature of your typical conversation. Furthermore, some behaviors (such as unconscious nonverbal responses) simply cannot be recorded accurately on a self-monitoring basis. Perhaps you've already realized that you may need an external observer to establish an accurate baseline for some kinds of behaviors. Knowing that someone else is recording a particular behavior may have some impact on the incidence of that behavior, but usually not to the degree as with self-recording. For example, Nelson et al. (1976) found that external monitoring of face touching by college students minimally affected that behavior, but that self-monitoring substantially altered the response.

Methods of recording

Behavior records tend to be most accurate when you record responses as they occur. Attempting to reconstruct your behavior several hours later will introduce an intolerable degree of subjectivity into your self-management efforts. People selectively remember and forget. Unless you record behavior immediately, you may never be able to determine precisely the effects of your self-management program. Naturally, you have reservations about the feasibility of recording behavior immediately after it occurs. You cannot imagine always having paper and pencil conveniently available or being able to record behavior unobtrusively in all situations. Some of the more intimate moments of life certainly do not

Table 2.1
Card for recording swearing behavior directed toward roommate

Behavior episode	Precipitating event	Follow-up event
1. "Go to _____"	Roommate told me to turn down stereo.	Roommate didn't speak to me rest of day.
2. "I'll be _____"	Fell over books left in front of door — possibly by roommate.	Roommate, hiding in bathroom, broke into laughter.
3. "_____ you"	Roommate asked me to vacate the room so he could spend the evening with girlfriend.	Roommate physically removed me from room.
4. "You're both _____"	Roommate's girlfriend called me an S.O.B. as I left room.	Both roommate and his girlfriend threw shoes at me as I was running down the hall.
5. "Open that _____ _____ door"	Locked out of my room at 7:00 A.M.	Resident hall assistant gave me a demerit.
6. "What the _____?"	Found salt between sheets of my bed.	Roommate rolled on floor with laughter.
7. (Censored!)	Found my recently completed term project in commode.	Roommate informed me that project should have been flushed.
8. "You're an incredible _____hole."	Roommate called my parents to inform them that I had flunked out of school.	Roommate presented me with my packed bags.
9. "Holy _____!!"	Roommate came at me with a karate chop.	Huh?

Project temporarily discontinued during hospital recovery. So far roommate has not sent flowers.

lend themselves to on-the-spot behavior recording! However, many situations do. For example, most academic behaviors occur in situations where paper and pencil are available. The number of times you speak up in class, the amount of time you devote to study, and the number of assignments you complete are quite easily recorded. All you need is a sheet on which to record instances of the behavior and events preceding and following those instances (see Table 2.1).

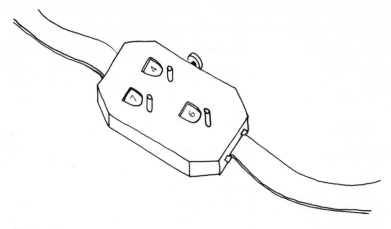

Figure 2.1   The wrist counter shown above is available from most sporting goods shops and general merchandise stores for between one and three dollars.

Figure 2.2   The knitting-stitch counter shown above can be purchased from knitting shops for less than one dollar.

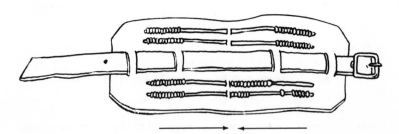

Figure 2.3   This bead counter allows you to monitor eight behaviors concurrently. When a particular behavior occurs, you move a bead to the opposite end of that strand. In the drawing, six of the eight behaviors have not occurred, one has occurred twelve times, and one six times. The arrows indicate the direction in which the beads are moved when a behavior occurs. A counter similar to this one can be obtained from Behaviordelia, P.O. Box 1044–17, Kalamazoo, Michigan 49005, for approximately eleven dollars.

You might be surprised at the versatility of paper-and-pencil recording strategies. One of our students (Gilmore, 1973) set as his self-management goal the consistent buckling of his seat belt whenever he entered his car. To establish the baseline level of his behavior and the circumstances (besides just getting in the car) that might be contributing to that behavior, he devised a card on which he indicated the time of seat-belt application or nonapplication, whether family or friends were in the car with him, and mileage traveled (a mileage counter was mounted on the front dashboard). He put the card on the console of the car, where it was readily accessible.

In situations where paper-and-pencil recording would be obtrusive, alternative devices are available. Two of these are a wrist counter and a knitting-stitch counter (see Figures 2.1 and 2.2), both of which you can manipulate without interrupting other activities. With the wrist counter, you can record three behaviors concurrently, or you can record occurrences of a particular behavior as well as opportunities for that behavior. For example, you might record the times that you behave assertively as well as the times that you want to behave assertively. If you want to know how frequently a specific behavior is occurring in different situations, you can use the separate dials to record instances of the behavior in those situations. At a party you might record the frequency of your swearing when you are talking with different people. We have found the knitting-stitch counter most useful for teachers. It fits snugly over the end of a pencil and allows the individual to continue teaching functions while recording behaviors.

Perhaps even more versatile than either of these counters is a bead counter, presently being used at the University of Tennessee's Counseling Center. As shown in Figure 2.3, the bead counter is worn around the wrist and allows you to monitor up to eight behaviors at once. The beads are tightly strung so they will not accidentally slip back and forth. Each strand has twelve beads, but the number of strands and of beads per strand can be increased. If you want to record behavior across a host of situations to determine precipitating stimuli, the bead counter would be an excellent device.

Types of records

As we have already suggested in our discussion of modes of record keeping, there are three major types of behavior records that can be used in self-management: *frequency count, time duration,* and *product assessment.* A frequency count involves nothing more than tabulating the number of times a particular behavior occurs. This is the easiest and most widely used method of assessing behavior. Any behavior that can be defined in terms of discrete instances can be assessed by a frequency count. Comments in class, sit-ups, nasty remarks to your spouse, and obscene gestures can all be subjected to frequency-count assessment.

33

Any behavior that occurs over a short time period and has a definable beginning and end can be recorded by a frequency count.

Many behaviors, such as crying, sleeping, and studying, tend to occur over extended time periods and therefore cannot be separated into discrete behavioral events. The most accurate way of assessing behaviors of this kind is to record the amount of time devoted to the behavior. You can use a stopwatch, activating it each time the behavior starts and deactivating it when the behavior stops. If the stopwatch approach reminds you too much of your track coach, you could simply use a regular watch, jotting down starting and stopping times for different episodes of a behavior. From this information you can later compute total time devoted to a behavior. This procedure is more laborious than the stopwatch approach, but it does indicate the times during the day when the specified behavior has occurred — information that may be important in determining where to begin in modifying that behavior.

In many cases you can get an accurate record of behavior by examining the products of that behavior. Completed assignments, a clean room, and weight on the scale are products that can be used to establish the efficacy of a self-management strategy. In fact, products often provide the ultimate verification that a self-management program has worked. However, products do not usually tell you where to begin in changing your behavior. Finding out that you turned in only one homework assignment last week or that you have weighed 312 pounds for ten consecutive days does not tell you how to solve your problem. Instead, you first have to identify behaviors that are interfering with completion of assignments or contributing to excessive weight and then change those behaviors. In other words, your behavior-change strategies should be applied to the *process behaviors*** (eating, napping) that contribute to the behavior product. For example, one of our students wanted to lose five pounds over a two-week period. She hypothesized that between-meal snacking was the principal barrier to reaching that goal. Therefore, her reinforcement conditions were primarily tied to nonsnacking behavior (process) rather than to loss of weight (product). As normally happens with this arrangement, the process behavior evidenced a change before the behavior product. The relationship between these dimensions is shown in Figure 2.4.

Regardless of which recording system you use, you will find that graphing behavior helps to clarify the current status of your actions and provides a reference point for evaluating future performance. The vertical axis on a self-management graph generally denotes level of behavior (frequency, duration, amount, or percentage), and the horizontal axis represents baseline and treatment days (refer to Figure 2.4). In addition to clarifying the status of the target behavior, graphing can provide

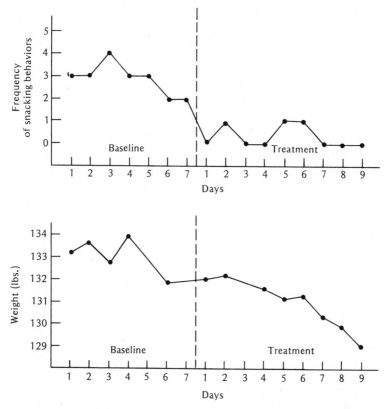

Figure 2.4 Magnitude of process and product behavior changes during baseline and treatment days. (Reprinted with the permission of the author from: Kornrumph, C. 1973. Self-management of snacking behavior. Unpublished manuscript, University of Tennessee.)

significant reinforcement for your self-management endeavors. There are few things more reinforcing than seeing desired behaviors begin to increase or undesired ones decrease. Some researchers (Broden et al., 1971; Johnson and White, 1971; Kanfer, 1970; Mahoney et al., 1973) report that the mere act of recording and graphing a behavior frequently leads to improvement in that behavior. This is particularly true of behaviors that you are highly motivated to change. Recording and graphing cause you to be aware of the target behavior, when it occurs, how often it's occurring, and the circumstances under which it's occurring. That's all the highly motivated person may need to alter a problem behavior.

Self-recording of studying and dating

The effects of self-recording on behavior were demonstrated in an investigation among undergraduates during an introductory psychology course. One group of students recorded their study time on cards that they returned to the instructor each week. In addition, they graphed their daily and their weekly study behavior. A second group of students recorded and graphed their dating activity during the course. Dating activity meant any recreational experience involving a person of the opposite sex. These students also submitted their weekly records to the instructor. (Lest you become alarmed, they were recording only the amount of dating activity, not the specifics of that activity.) The grades of these two groups were compared to those of a third group, which did not record and graph anything. All participants had been randomly assigned to one of the three groups. Grading of weekly quizzes and student projects was done by graduate students in psychology who didn't know the experiment was being conducted.

Analysis of the results indicated that the students who recorded their study behavior performed at a significantly higher level than students who did no recording. Students who recorded their dating behavior fell between these two groups in course achievement. The results indicate that systematically assessing one's behavior in an area (studying) can by itself enhance performance in that area. The findings also suggest that recording behavior in one area (dating) can increase performance in another area (course achievement). Apparently if individuals self-record occurrences of one important life activity, they are confronted with how they are spending time and energy. This type of self-confrontation may produce insights that affect several areas of life. Another possible explanation of the findings is that the "dating" observers saw the value of self-recording and applied that skill to studying. In fact, a few of the "dating" students voluntarily told the experimenters they had begun to record their studying behavior during the course.

Adapted from Johnson, S. M., and White, G. 1971. Self-observation as an agent of behavioral change. *Behavior Therapy 2,* 488–497.

Your graph may reflect only the amount of the target behavior that you exhibit each day as in Figure 2.4, or it may indicate the total amount of target behavior you have exhibited to any particular point in your self-management project. In the latter case, the plot for any given day would reflect the quantity of target behavior for that day plus the total for all preceding days. For obvious reasons, this type of system is called _cumulative graphing_. You should employ the type of graphing system that will maximize your sense of progress. If the nature of the target behavior is such that you are likely to reach a plateau in the amount exhibited each

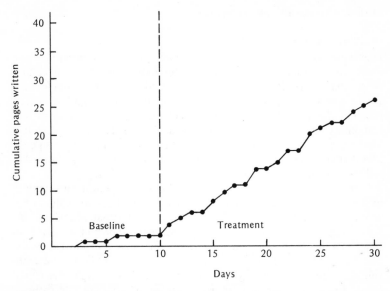

Figure 2.5 Cumulative graph of pages written for *Toward a Self-managed Life Style*.

day, you may prefer a cumulative graph. You may be able to read only so many books, swim so many laps, and spend so much time studying. Thus, if you are only recording the amount achieved during a given time period, it will appear that you have ceased to progress. In contrast, a cumulative graph will show that you are continuing to add to your total of "good" behaviors (see Figure 2.5).

This section has given you a general overview of procedures for recording behavior. We must emphasize that the recording of behavior is begun prior to starting other self-management procedures and is continued during the application of those procedures. Only by following this course can you determine the precise impact of your self-management strategies. As we deal with different types of personal and academic problems in subsequent chapters of the book, we shall identify specific behaviors to record and procedures for recording them. For the time being, remember that objectively measuring your behavior may reveal something far different from what you subjectively believe to be the case. Objective measurement may, in fact, be the answer to Robert Burns's plea:

O wad some Pow'r the giftie gie us
To see oursels as others see us!
It wad frae monie a blunder free us ...

Step 3: Changing setting events

Avoiding situations

Most behaviors are triggered by certain situations or by certain events within those situations. Psychologists refer to these precipitating stimuli as *setting events*. Perhaps the easiest way to deal with a troublesome situation is to avoid it. One overweight student reported that her weight problem was partially related to the fact that she passed a particular restaurant on her way to and from school each day. The delectable aroma from the restaurant invariably led to a short snack. The suggestion that she take a different route does not seem profound — but it did reduce snacking.

If you are protesting that avoiding situations does not solve anything in the long run, you have a point. It would be a pathetic individual who dealt with all problems simply by avoiding difficult situations. That individual might eventually have a severely restricted sphere of activity. The avoidance strategy is recommended only for those problem behaviors that invariably occur in given situations. You have to be honest with yourself — in certain settings you are going to imbibe, eat, get upset, and so on. In fact, these behaviors may occur quite automatically without your even being aware of what is happening. If your objective is to avoid exhibiting those behaviors at all cost, you will initially have to avoid the situations in which they habitually occur. Note that we used the word *initially*. There are a number of other strategies, which will be described later, that can help you defuse vexing circumstances. However, at the onset of your self-management endeavors, the best way to avoid some undesired behaviors may be to avoid certain situations. For example, if you are seized with an anxiety attack every time you attend an athletic contest, the most obvious way to prevent these attacks is to stay home.

Altering troublesome situations

Effective self-management primarily entails modifying bothersome situations, not completely avoiding them. Many problem behaviors are evoked by a wide range of stimuli, which also serve to increase the immediate reinforcement value of those behaviors. Sitting down to watch TV, picking up a magazine, and turning on the stereo all may lead to snacking behavior and to making snacking more enjoyable. Self-management in such situations should be directed toward accomplishing three major changes: 1. The circumstances should be arranged so that you are forced to think about the problem behavior before it occurs; the intent is to prevent behaviors from occurring reflexively and automatically. 2. The range of stimuli that produce the undesired behavior should be reduced. 3. The cues associated with the nonproductive behavior should be made as nonreinforcing as possible.

Becoming aware of behavior   "I wasn't thinking." This excuse is often used to explain away a blunder. One challenge of self-management is to identify procedures that will cause you to think about your responses before you act. You can achieve awareness of what you're about to do if you arrange circumstances so that you must take a series of actions before performing the problem behavior. For example, overweight individuals might purchase only food that requires considerable preparation before it can be eaten; this would preclude the unthinking consumption of cookies, chips, and candy. If overweight people posted pictures of obese and slender persons on their refrigerator door, they would be even more inclined to think about what they were doing. People with a smoking problem might store their cigarettes in a location difficult to get to — say in a metal safe, with the combination known only to their best friend . . . who is presently out of the country! If part of your problem is sinning before you realize what you are doing, the strategy suggested in this paragraph is a beginning step toward self-management.

Limiting the precipitating stimuli   A second step is to limit the range of stimulus situations associated with the problem behavior. Suppose you have been inclined to light a cigarette while watching TV, reading, or engaging in conversation. You should not initially expect to stop smoking completely. In all probability, that expectation would quickly fall by the wayside. A far more realistic approach is to limit the situations in which you smoke. You might identify one place in your home and one at work where you can continue to pollute yourself. That locale should be a non-TV, nonreading, and nonconversation setting. Remember the student who wanted to lose five pounds in two weeks? She allowed herself to snack only while sitting at her dressing table in the bedroom. As a consequence she had to carry the food from the kitchen (her usual snacking locale) and look at herself in the mirror as she ate.

Eliminating additional reinforcers   By following the strategy outlined above, you will discover that you require more time to get environmentally situated for the target behavior, thus causing the behavior to lose some of its reinforcement potential. You will also find that the absence of niceties such as TV, books, and conversation will further diminish the enjoyment you derive from the target behavior. The approach is quite simple: Think of all the accompanying stimuli (food, drink, sex) that embellish the undesired behavior; then require that the target behavior occur in the absence of these stimuli. The undesirable behavior subsequently decrease in frequency because of its reduced reinforcement value.

Providing supportive stimuli

If your problem can best be described as the absence of a particular behavior, you need initially to make the environmental setting as favorable
as possible for the desired response to occur. If you are unable to talk in
group settings, don't place yourself before a throng of thousands and
expect to be loquacious. Put yourself in a small-group situation, among
the warmest, most accepting people you know. If you have difficulty
talking to person A but can talk to person B forever, try first to talk to A in
B's presence. Some of the warmth and acceptance that you feel from B
should make it easier to talk to A. After establishing a high frequency of
desired behavior under the most favorable circumstances, you can then
move up one notch in difficulty; attempt to exhibit the behavior in a
slightly less favorable situation (talk to A when B is some distance away).
By moving very gradually to increasingly difficult situations, you eventually may be able to speak freely even before that throng of thousands.

Optimizing setting events is not necessarily a highly complex operation. The student who wanted to use the seat belt more often simply
made certain that the seat belt and shoulder harness were clean, that
they were properly adjusted for use, and that they were appropriately
hung after each use. People attempting to get to work on time usually
have to arrange setting events the previous night; this may include
changing the location of the alarm clock, altering the temperature of the
room, laying out clothes for the next day, getting work materials together, packing lunch, and putting the breakfast cereals on the table.
There may be some equally simple changes in setting events that would
facilitate the behaviors you want to acquire.

Step 4: Establishing effective consequences

We have now discussed the first three steps of our self-management
program: selecting a goal, monitoring target behavior, and then changing setting events for the desired behavior. If we stopped at this point, we
would have given you a modestly effective strategy for altering many
behaviors. However, the most powerful technique for producing behavior change is yet to be considered.

Most of our behaviors are governed by their consequences. Consequences that strengthen behaviors (make them more likely to occur) are
called *reinforcers,* and consequences that weaken behavior, *punishers.*
You can immediately identify some events that are reinforcing or punishing to you. Perhaps praise, money, athletic activities, and fine wine
are reinforcing to you. (They certainly are to us.) What is reinforcing or
punishing varies from person to person and from situation to situation

for the same person. There is probably no event that would be reinforcing for all persons in all situations. When you consider reinforcement and punishment, you should think in terms of how environmental consequences affect you. If an event is highly reinforcing to you, it doesn't matter that it has a neutral impact on most others. We caution only that you do not choose reinforcers that will create other problems for yourself. A slightly overweight undergraduate used ice cream and chocolate mints as the immediate reinforcers for nonsmoking behavior. She reduced her smoking but she also gained 8.25 pounds by the end of the third week of treatment!

Identifying reinforcers

Identifying reinforcers can be more baffling than you think. For example, we have found that primary- and junior-high-school students have considerable difficulty predicting how particular consequences will affect their behavior (Atkins and Williams, 1972; Runyon and Williams, 1972). This is especially true for consequences that they have not encountered frequently. We suspect that adults are equally unaware of many potential reinforcers. A principal component of your self-management quest is expanding the list of consequences that you can use as reinforcers. Developing this list will require some systematic investigation. You might carry a note pad with you for a few days and jot down the especially pleasant or unpleasant events that occur. Ordinary actions may be significant reinforcers; consuming a cold drink of water, having a cup of coffee, looking through a magazine, eating ice, reading a newspaper, going on evening walks, and sitting in a particular chair are some of the short-term consequences used by our students as reinforcers for appropriate behaviors. New phonograph records, stereo tapes, and items of clothing have been the long-term payoffs most frequently used by our students.

Your present sphere of activities may not include many *obvious* reinforcement possibilities. There may be activities that you've experienced in the past that you would still enjoy. It's not unusual to rediscover an activity after years away from it. Jim Long rediscovered tennis through a new acquaintance. Though he hadn't played at all for several years, he now plays on a regular basis. To help you identify past and present reinforcers, we have included the Reinforcement Survey Schedule (Table 2.2).

There are probably many activities in which you've never engaged that could be tremendously enjoyable to you. Most individuals can think of several things that they would like to be able to do (skiing, dancing, tennis, bridge), but they may not like the process of acquiring the necessary skills. To learn a new set of skills, you may have to put yourself into an awkward situation both physically and socially. You probably know

41

Table 2.2
Reinforcement survey schedule

The items in this questionnaire refer to things and experiences that may give joy or other pleasurable feelings. Check each item in the column that describes how much pleasure you derive from it.

		None at all	A little	A fair amount	Much	Very much
1.	Eating					
	a. Ice cream	___	___	___	___	___
	b. Candy	___	___	___	___	___
	c. Fruit	___	___	___	___	___
	d. Pastry	___	___	___	___	___
	e. Nuts	___	___	___	___	___
	f. Cookies	___	___	___	___	___
	g. Salad	___	___	___	___	___
	h. Steak	___	___	___	___	___
	i. Lobster	___	___	___	___	___
	j _____	___	___	___	___	___
2.	Drinking beverages					
	a. Water	___	___	___	___	___
	b. Milk	___	___	___	___	___
	c. Soft drink	___	___	___	___	___
	d. Tea	___	___	___	___	___
	e. Coffee	___	___	___	___	___
	f. _____	___	___	___	___	___
3.	Drinking alcoholic beverages					
	a. Beer	___	___	___	___	___
	b. Wine	___	___	___	___	___
	c. Hard liquor	___	___	___	___	___
4.	Solving problems					
	a. Crossword puzzles	___	___	___	___	___
	b. Math problems	___	___	___	___	___
	c. Figuring out how something works	___	___	___	___	___
5.	Listening to music					
	a. Classical	___	___	___	___	___
	b. Country western	___	___	___	___	___
	c. Jazz	___	___	___	___	___
	d. Show tunes	___	___	___	___	___
	e. Rhythm and blues	___	___	___	___	___
	f. Rock and roll	___	___	___	___	___
	g. Folk	___	___	___	___	___
	h. Popular	___	___	___	___	___
6.	Petting animals					
	a. Dogs	___	___	___	___	___
	b. Cats	___	___	___	___	___
	c. Horses	___	___	___	___	___
	d. _____	___	___	___	___	___

Table 2.2 cont.

	None at all	A little	A fair amount	Much	Very much
7. Watching sports					
a. Football	___	___	___	___	___
b. Baseball	___	___	___	___	___
c. Basketball	___	___	___	___	___
d. Track	___	___	___	___	___
e. Golf	___	___	___	___	___
f. Swimming	___	___	___	___	___
g. Running	___	___	___	___	___
h. Tennis	___	___	___	___	___
i. Pool	___	___	___	___	___
j. Other	___	___	___	___	___
8. Reading					
a. Adventure	___	___	___	___	___
b. Mystery	___	___	___	___	___
c. Famous people	___	___	___	___	___
d. Poetry	___	___	___	___	___
e. Travel	___	___	___	___	___
f. True confessions	___	___	___	___	___
g. Politics and history	___	___	___	___	___
h. How-to-do-it	___	___	___	___	___
i. Humor	___	___	___	___	___
j. Comic books	___	___	___	___	___
k. Love stories	___	___	___	___	___
l. Spiritual	___	___	___	___	___
m. Sexy	___	___	___	___	___
n. Sports	___	___	___	___	___
o. Medicine	___	___	___	___	___
p. Science	___	___	___	___	___
q. Newspapers	___	___	___	___	___
9. Looking at interesting buildings	___	___	___	___	___
10. Looking at beautiful scenery	___	___	___	___	___
11. Watching TV	___	___	___	___	___
12. Attending movies	___	___	___	___	___
13. Listening to radio	___	___	___	___	___
14. Singing					
a. Alone	___	___	___	___	___
b. With others	___	___	___	___	___
15. Dancing					
a. Ballroom	___	___	___	___	___
b. Discotheque	___	___	___	___	___
c. Ballet/interpretive	___	___	___	___	___
d. Square dancing	___	___	___	___	___
e. Folk dancing	___	___	___	___	___

Table 2.2 cont.

		None at all	A little	A fair amount	Much	Very much
16.	Performing on a musical instrument	____	____	____	____	____
17.	Playing sports					
	a. Football	____	____	____	____	____
	b. Baseball	____	____	____	____	____
	c. Basketball	____	____	____	____	____
	d. Track and field	____	____	____	____	____
	e. Golf	____	____	____	____	____
	f. Swimming	____	____	____	____	____
	g. Running	____	____	____	____	____
	h. Tennis	____	____	____	____	____
	i. Pool	____	____	____	____	____
	j. Boxing	____	____	____	____	____
	k. Judo or karate	____	____	____	____	____
	l. Fishing	____	____	____	____	____
	m. Skin diving	____	____	____	____	____
	n. Auto or cycle racing	____	____	____	____	____
	o. Hunting	____	____	____	____	____
	p. Skiing	____	____	____	____	____
	q. _____	____	____	____	____	____
18.	Shopping					
	a. Clothes	____	____	____	____	____
	b. Furniture	____	____	____	____	____
	c. Auto parts and supply	____	____	____	____	____
	d. Appliances	____	____	____	____	____
	e. Food	____	____	____	____	____
	f. Sports equipment	____	____	____	____	____
	g. _____	____	____	____	____	____
19.	Gardening	____	____	____	____	____
20.	Playing cards	____	____	____	____	____
21.	Hiking or walking	____	____	____	____	____
22.	Completing a difficult job	____	____	____	____	____
23.	Camping	____	____	____	____	____
24.	Sleeping	____	____	____	____	____
25.	Taking a bath	____	____	____	____	____
26.	Taking a shower	____	____	____	____	____
27.	Being praised					
	a. About your appearance	____	____	____	____	____
	b. About your work	____	____	____	____	____
	c. About your hobbies	____	____	____	____	____

Table 2.2 cont.

	None at all	A little	A fair amount	Much	Very much
d. About your physical strength	____	____	____	____	____
e. About your athletic ability	____	____	____	____	____
f. About your mind	____	____	____	____	____
g. About your personality	____	____	____	____	____
h. About your moral strength	____	____	____	____	____
i. About your understanding of others	____	____	____	____	____
28. Having people seek you out for company	____	____	____	____	____
29. Flirting	____	____	____	____	____
30. Having somebody flirt with you	____	____	____	____	____
31. Talking with people who like you	____	____	____	____	____
32. Making somebody happy	____	____	____	____	____
33. Being around babies	____	____	____	____	____
34. Being around children	____	____	____	____	____
35. Being around elderly men	____	____	____	____	____
36. Being around elderly women	____	____	____	____	____
37. Being around people	____	____	____	____	____
38. Having people ask your advice	____	____	____	____	____
39. Watching other people	____	____	____	____	____
40. Somebody smiling at you	____	____	____	____	____
41. Making love	____	____	____	____	____
42. Being close to an attractive person	____	____	____	____	____
43. Talking about the opposite sex	____	____	____	____	____
44. Talking to friends	____	____	____	____	____
45. Being in church or temple	____	____	____	____	____
46. _____	____	____	____	____	____

SOURCE: Reprinted with permission of author and publisher from: Cautela, Joseph R., and Kastenbaum, Robert 1967. A reinforcement survey schedule for use in therapy, training, and research. *Psychological Reports* 20, 1115–1130.

Don't go near the water!

Bob Williams is attempting to make swimming a reinforcing activity for himself. He is convinced that swimming can be excellent exercise and extremely refreshing on a hot summer day. Not having been around water as a child, he experiences much intimidation about getting into the water. He finds it much easier to lie on a comfortable lounge chair and sunbathe. Knowing that swimming can never become reinforcing unless he gets into the water, he has arranged some contingencies to increase that probability. The neighborhood pool where he swims has a twenty-minute adult swim period every hour. At that point the hordes of children clear the pool and he has adequate space to work on his swimming strokes. He must participate in one of these twenty-minute periods in order to play an hour of tennis (a very high-priority activity) on the courts located enticingly near the swimming pool. While in the swimming pool, he does not require himself to engage in any particular activity except to keep his head above water a certain amount of time! Though wading is presently his preferred pool activity, he also spends considerable time working on basic strokes and rotary breathing. At this point he is experiencing less intimidation about getting into the water, but he cannot honestly claim that swimming represents the zenith of his day's activity. So far no one has suggested that he consider lifesaving as a career alternative.

the uncomfortable feeling of not knowing what to do or, even if you've been told what to do, not being able to do it. Unless you possess considerable capacity for laughing at yourself, you will need some additional reinforcement to remain in the right situations long enough to learn the necessary skills. For example, college males who reported difficulty in relating to females gave themselves points for putting themselves in situations involving females, such as calling up girls for dates (Rehm and Marston, 1968). Note that they did not set as their initial goals actually getting dates or feeling confident in the presence of females. Thus your initial target behaviors may be taking tennis lessons, spending time on skis, and attending a dance class. Later, when your skills are refined, you may be able to use these activities as reinforcers for other target behaviors.

Establishing reinforcement contingencies

Having formulated a list of consequences that are reinforcing to you, you are now ready to use these consequences to modify your behavior. The strategy here is straightforward — make yourself exhibit the desired target behavior before you partake of the reinforcing consequences. If your problem is failing to work on assignments, then allow yourself a highly reinforcing privilege, conditional upon working on assignments. However, there are behaviors other than the target that you should also reinforce. These behaviors are what Skinner (1953) called *controlling responses* — the behaviors involved in implementing a self-management strategy. Recording behavior and rearranging setting events are controlling behaviors that are fundamental to the success of self-management. Therefore, these behaviors should be rewarded regardless of what is happening to the target behaviors. For example, you should earn certain privileges simply for recording behavior and for making specified changes in setting events (such as buying low-calorie foods). Thus you will earn some reinforcers from the very beginning of your self-management efforts, even before you begin to change the target behavior.

Although you have identified target and nontarget behaviors to reinforce and privileges to use as reinforcers, your excursion into self-management can still be less than ecstatic. Two things can bring your self-management program to naught: not applying the reinforcers immediately after the desired behaviors occur, or setting the requirements for reinforcement too high.

Immediacy of reinforcement Suppose you have chosen attending a movie as the principal reinforcer for completing academic assignments. You probably cannot go off to a movie immediately after completing each assignment. What you might do is set up a credit system in which you reward yourself with points or tokens whenever you finish an assignment. For example, you might decide that you will earn five points for each completed assignment and that when you have earned twenty points, you can go to a movie of your choice. Five immediate points will not be so pleasant as an immediate movie, but because points are associated with movies, they will assume increasing reinforcement value as you proceed with self-management. Most important, points will allow you to bridge the time gap between target behaviors and certain reinforcement privileges.

In addition to using points to bridge this delay, some students use visual representations of the desired long-term reinforcer. One student, who was earning reinforcement points toward extra serving pieces for her china and silver, prominently displayed pictures of these pieces in the place where the undesired behavior (snacking) was likely to occur. Another student, who had gained 50 pounds in two and a half years, put a picture of herself at 118 pounds on the table where she ate. Since these pictures served as prompts for good behavior, they would technically be classified as setting events. Nevertheless, they also gave immediate relevance to long-term reinforcers.

Don't interpret the preceding paragraphs to mean that most rewards will be of a long-term nature. Where possible, actual rewards should be applied immediately after the desired behavior. Our student with the seat-belt problem applied four types of reinforcement to seat-belt application. He placed a bag of large jelly gumdrops on his car console and ate one as soon as he had fastened the seat belt. He also placed on the console a bag containing five dollars' worth of dimes and immediately took a dime each time he put on his seat belt. He used the dime for coffee during his midmorning break — no dime, no coffee; money that remained at the end of the treatment phase was to be given to his wife. As a third *contingency*,* he turned on his cool-air vent after he had applied the seat belt. Finally, since his wife walked to the car with him each morning, he received an immediate kiss for fastening the seat belt at that time. Whenever he applied the seat belt away from home, this type of reinforcement was deferred until he returned home in the afternoon. Following the study this student reported that he found the candy and the kiss the most reinforcing consequences. He attributed their strength to their immediacy. The money could not be used until midmorning, and the air vent generated no cool air until the car was moving.

Requirements for reinforcement With the very best of intentions, newcomers to self-management often impose exceedingly stringent reinforcement requirements upon themselves. Their rationale is that a difficult goal will make them work harder to change. Unfortunately, things usually work in the opposite direction. In your virgin attempts at self-management, it is imperative that you experience success early and frequently. The more success you have, the more likely you will be to maintain your program. The probability of success can be directly altered by manipulating the criteria of success. The initial criterion for reinforcement should be only slightly above your present level of operation. If you are presently accomplishing nothing on your assignments, doing perfect assignments every day of the week would not be an appropriate initial criterion for reinforcement. A better starting point would be to reward yourself for just getting out your academic materials. The next criterion level might be to complete some small part (any part) of an assignment. By very gradually raising your criterion for reinforcement, you may eventually reach the point of completing assignments every night. In all probability you would never achieve that degree of productivity if perfect performance were your initial criterion for success.

Mobilizing social reinforcement

Thus far we have suggested pleasant activities and tangible payoffs as possible reinforcers for appropriate behavior. It is apparent that some of the more potent reinforcers are social in nature. A compliment or criticism from a person you like can change the course of the day's events. If you can arrange the circumstances of your life so that you receive social support for appropriate behavior, your self-management efforts will be markedly enhanced. In attempting to accomplish this objective, you

A self-management failure!

Figure 2.6 shows the fate of a self-management exercise program conducted without any social support by a college professor named Wes. The first ten data points provide a baseline of his mile-running behavior; the baseline data were plotted retrospectively. The behavior was highly stable at the zero level during this period, where it had been for the previous six months, since the demise of his earlier exercise program. After the ten-day baseline period, Wes decided that daily graphing might serve to strengthen his running behavior. The miles accumulated during his first month of graphing, but then his frequency of running began to wane. By early March he was back to his original level of inactivity.

In late March, Wes decided to make watching the evening news on TV (a high-probability event) contingent on running a mile each day. That contingency produced an abrupt increase in his running behavior, an increment that lasted for about two months and then rapidly diminished. He was a little embarrassed to admit that in June he started cheating on the contingencies. He began letting himself watch TV even when he had not run his mile. Unfortunately, this is the destiny of many self-management projects that are undertaken without external support.

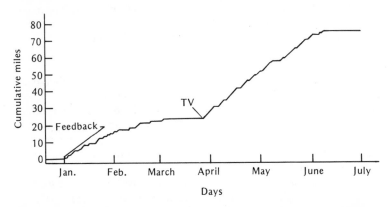

Figure 2.6 Cumulative graph depicting running behavior. (Morgan, W. G., and Bass, B. A. 1973. Self-control through self-mediated rewards. In R. D. Rubin, J. P. Brady, and J. D. Henderson [eds.], *Advances in behavior therapy*. New York: Academic Press, pp. 117–126.

should first be careful not to establish reinforcement contingencies that are aversive to others; that will invariably result in nonsupport for your efforts. If what is ecstatically reinforcing to you is excruciatingly abrasive to others (for example, playing acid rock throughout the night), you will not experience profound social approval from your neighbors.

Some type of social support may be indispensable to the long-term effectiveness of self-arranged reinforcement contingencies. If the reinforcement contingencies involve payoffs that are known only to you, controlled by you, and administered by you, you may find yourself cheating on the contingencies. Once the contingencies are nullified, control over the target behavior is likely to evaporate. We recommend, therefore, that you make your goals and reinforcement contingencies known to some people who care about your progress. Display your graphs publicly so these people can readily see whether you're self-recording, whether the behavior is changing, and whether you're administering the reinforcers on the prearranged basis. When others have similar behaviors they wish to change, participate together in activities related to your common goal (exercise together, meet each other at the library). When the company of others is especially reinforcing, use socializing as a reward for goal attainment.

Occasionally you may wish to put tangible payoffs in the hands of others who will provide reinforcement at appropriate times. Several of our students employ this strategy to getting to work on time. They give a specified amount of money to a colleague and ask this person to provide money for the coffee break only if they have arrived on time that day. If they have not, the money for the day goes to the other person. The major hazard of this arrangement is that you may come to dislike the other person if that person has to withhold a great many payoffs.

Applying aversive consequences

Inducement of physical pain Positive events are not the only type of consequences that can be used in modifying behavior. Some people apply aversive consequences to their undesirable responses. For example, one of our persistent nail biters applied a commercial preparation of cayenne pepper to his nails each morning. When he put his fingers to his lips, the cayenne produced a burning sensation. This strategy completely eliminated the nail biting.

Despite the success of our nail biter, we have ambivalent feelings about using punishment to modify behavior. Since a person rarely derives intrinsic satisfaction from self-inflicted pain, there will have to be powerful external reinforcers to maintain that behavior. If your target behavior changes drastically or if you receive international acclaim for your self-administered punishment, you may continue your punishment contingencies. Otherwise, a strategy that requires you to flip yourself with a rubber band, shock yourself, or slap yourself could lead not only to the termination of that strategy but to avoidance of other self-management strategies.

Stimulus satiation Satiation is another way to use aversive consequences to alter undesired behavior. In using this approach, you repeatedly emit the target behavior until you simply tire of whatever made the response reinforcing. Everyone is familiar with the idea of tiring of a good thing or of keeping so much company with a friend that the friendship wanes. Forcing yourself to smoke one cigarette after another or to consume several bowls of banana pudding could cause you to become sick of those activities. Presumably you would eventually choose to do something else. The major hazard of a satiation strategy is that if satiation does not occur, the behavior becomes more firmly instilled because of all that reinforcement.

Step 5: Consolidating gains

Though self-recording, changing setting events, and designing reinforcement contingencies are exceedingly important in initially changing behavior, no one is willing to continue these activities indefinitely. The time comes when the umbilical cord must be severed and the behavior change must stand on its own in the natural environment. Whether the change survives depends very much on what happens in this final phase of the self-management model.

The first strategy in making the transition from artificial support to natural support is to do it gradually. If you have self-recorded the target behavior on a daily basis during a five-week project, now record every other day for a week or so. If you maintain the target behavior at the desired level, you can then self-record every third day, then every fourth day, and so on. Later you may be able to sustain the behavior through monthly or bimonthly spot checks; eventually you may drop out self-recording altogether. However, if at some later point you perceive that the behavior is slipping, don't hesitate to return to self-recording as an objective means of reassessing the target behavior and the events precipitating or impeding it.

Fortunately, most changes in setting events can easily be maintained on a permanent basis. You may not want to display a picture of a slender person on your refrigerator door from now on, but you will want to have nourishing low-calorie foods in your home. The time won't come when you can keep the candy and cookie jars overflowing and yet maintain appropriate eating habits. You must also continue to provide a conducive time and place for exercise if you want exercise to remain a regular part of your life. Thus, a key to the long-term maintenance of the target behavior is to incorporate supportive setting events into your natural environment.

If you have employed special reinforcement contingencies in your project, first determine whether you can maintain any of these as a natural part of your daily routine. You might find it easy to continue the

Sustaining exercise

M. L. Kau tried to establish an exercise routine by using tooth brushing at night as the payoff for completing a series of calisthenics. However, she was initially unsuccessful because she was ignoring the tooth-brushing contingency. She then identified some reinforcers, monetary and social, that could be controlled by her husband. A contract was agreed upon and signed by both. Immediately after jogging one mile Ms. Kau was to receive 25 cents from her husband. At the end of each week in which she jogged every day, she could select and engage in one of several reinforcing activities (such as eating at a restaurant or going to a movie) with her husband. Since her jogging was also monitored through an *aerobics** point system, she was later required to earn at least 25 points a week under this system to qualify for the social activity. Her husband not only dispensed the reinforcers but tabulated the points she had earned. When the natural consequences of jogging (increased energy, loss of weight, greater stamina while running) began to be reinforcing, she dropped the monetary contingency. Later she also eliminated the social-activity contingency. We have no long-term follow-up data on this subject, but don't be surprised if Ms. Kau shows up for the next Boston Marathon.

Adapted from Kau, M. L., and Fischer, J. 1974. Self-modification of exercise behavior. *Journal of Behavior Therapy and Experimental Psychiatry 5*, 213–214.

practice of completing your daily work assignments before taking your daily swim, to continue running your mile before viewing the evening news, or to continue cleaning up the evening dishes before curling up by the fire with a good book or whatever or whomever. However, if your reward contingencies involved the awarding of points and *back-up rewards** based on those points, you will most likely not continue this practice indefinitely. You can phase out these artificial contingencies in the same way you phase out self-recording. Gradually decrease the frequency of points and back-up rewards. Actually, such a decrease may occur naturally as you increase the criteria for reinforcement in Step 4 of our model. Simply require yourself to go longer and longer before applying your artificial consequences.

Another way to extricate yourself from artificial contingencies is to create social support for your changed behavior. As mentioned under Step 4, let others know what you're attempting to accomplish or have accomplished. If you feel uncomfortable making outright statements such as "I've lost twenty pounds," "I'm now running two miles a day," "I've cut my smoking in half," or "I've completed all of my projects for the quarter," simply guide the conversation toward a discussion of the target behavior. You can mention an article you just read about a special diet, or the fact that you saw so and so on the track; you can mention how much better you've felt recently, or how friendly your psychology professor was when you dropped by his office. Many individuals report that over an extended period, social support is much more important than artificially developed contingencies in maintaining desired behavior.

After applying the self-management model to several different domains, you will find that effective management in one area provides support in other areas. For example, effective management of domestic behaviors may at least partially sustain effective management in academic work, recreational activity, or an exercise program. One self-management project will not revolutionize your life, but the more areas you successfully manage, the easier it becomes both to change behavior and to sustain changes in additional areas.

Concluding thoughts

After this rapid excursion through the mechanics of self-management, you may be quite concerned about the difficulty of it all. Sometimes our students ask, "Wouldn't it be easier just to change your behavior than to do all the things you recommend?" It would certainly be easier to tell yourself that you are going to change than to go through the many steps we have outlined. However, how far does "telling yourself" usually take you? A major difference between self-management and the conventional "telling" approach is that self-management does not require you to change a behavior directly. With self-management you modify the factors that are controlling the behavior. Once you alter these factors, the behavior changes automatically.

Students are sometimes distressed by the sheer number of techniques included in our model. However, no self-management project ever involves all of these procedures, or even a majority of them. The mere identification of a problem (Step 1) is occasionally sufficient to produce behavior change — an individual may become sensitized to a difficulty and consequently behave differently. Appreciable changes in behavior may also occur when individuals begin recording a behavior and get their first objective look at that behavior. In certain cases, therefore, Step 1 or a combination of Steps 1 and 2 is all that a person needs to alter a behavior. Most problems, however, require more effort. Our third strategy — changing setting events — should be especially useful in coping with such problems as overweight and poor study habits. Step 4 recognizes that individuals behave for a reason, that is they seek rewards and attempt to avoid punishment. Most problems cannot be solved without altering the consequences of problem and nonproblem behaviors. Step 5

Table 2.3
Self-management model

Step 1 Selecting a goal	Step 2 Monitoring target behavior	Step 3 Changing setting events	Step 4 Establishing effective consequences	Step 5 Consolidating gains
		Continue recording the target behavior.		
A. Establish one goal at a time.	A. Start recording target behaviors before implementing behavior-change strategies.	A. Initially avoid situations that are certain to produce undesirable behaviors.	Maintain changes in setting events.	
B. Goal should be: 1. important 2. measurable 3. attainable 4. positive	B. Record behavior immediately after it occurs.	B. Alter situations so as to: 1. become aware of what you're doing; 2. limit the stimuli that evoke the bad behaviors; 3. eliminate additional reinforcers for bad behaviors; 4. make it easy to emit desired behaviors.	A. Identify consequences that would be reinforcing or punishing.	Maintain natural consequences.
	C. Use paper and pencil, wrist counter, knitting-stitch counter, bead counter, stopwatch, or wrist watch to record behavior.		B. Arrange reinforcement contingencies such that: 1. appropriate behavior is immediately reinforced; 2. criteria for reinforcement are readily attainable; 3. other people will support attainment of behavioral goals.	A. Phase out self-recording.
	D. Do a frequency-count, time-duration, or product assessment of the behavior.		C. Possibly use aversive consequences if reinforcement contingencies fail to produce desired changes in behavior: 1. mechanically induced pain, 2. stimulus satiation.	B. Maintain most changes in setting events.
				C. Maintain natural reinforcement contingencies.
				D. Phase out artificial reinforcement contingencies.
				E. Enlist social support.
				F. Apply self-management in other areas.

— consolidating your gains — allows you to remove most of the artificial support systems while sustaining the behavior in less contrived ways.

This chapter is talking about more than solving just one problem through self-management. This is the starting point, but our long-range hope is that you will develop a self-management orientation to life. Instead of acquiescing to self-pity, the self-manager looks for the factors that contribute to a problem and alters them (see Table 2.3). Not many people manage their lives in this way, but you are not averse to taking the less-traveled road this time, are you? It could make all the difference.

References

Atkins, J., and Williams, R. L. 1972. The utility of self-report in determining reinforcement priorities of primary school children. *Journal of Educational Research 65*, 324–328.

Broden, M., Hall, R. V., and Mitts, B. 1971. The effect of self-recording on the classroom behavior of two eighth-grade students. *Journal of Applied Behavior Analysis 4*, 191–199.

Cautela, J. R., and Kastenbaum, R. 1967. A reinforcement survey schedule for use in therapy, training, and research. *Psychological Reports 20*, 1115–1130.

Gilmore, G. D. 1973. Report of self-management project. Unpublished manuscript, University of Tennessee.

Hanna, R. 1977. Parameters affecting the reactivity of behavioral self-monitoring. Paper presented at the Canadian Psychological Association, Vancouver.

Johnson, S. M., and White, G. 1971. Self-observation as an agent of behavior change. *Behavior Therapy 2*, 488–497.

Kanfer, F. H. 1970. Self-monitoring: Methodological limitations and chemical applications. *Journal of Consulting and Clinical Psychology 35*, 148–152.

Kau, M. L., and Fischer, J. 1974. Self-modification of exercise behavior. *Journal of Behavior Therapy and Experimental Psychiatry 5*, 213–214.

Kornrumph, C. 1973. Self-management of snacking behavior. Unpublished manuscript, University of Tennessee.

McFall, R. M. 1970. The effects of self-monitoring on normal smoking behavior. *Journal of Consulting and Clinical Psychology 56*, 135–142.

Mahoney, M. J., Moore, B. S., Wade, T. C., and Moura, N. G. M. 1973. Effects of continuous and intermittent self-monitoring on academic behavior. *Journal of Consulting and Clinical Psychology 41*, 65–69.

Morgan, W. G., and Bass, B. S. 1973. Self-control through self-mediated rewards. In R. D. Rubin, J. P. Brady, and J. D. Henderson (eds.), *Advances in behavior therapy*. New York: Academic Press, pp. 117–126.

Nelson, R. O., Lipinski, D. P., and Black, J. L. 1976. The relative reactivity of external observations and self-monitoring. *Behavior Therapy 7*, 314–321.

Rehm, L. P., and Marston, A. R. 1968. Reduction of social anxiety through modification of self-reinforcement: An instigation therapy technique. *Journal of
Consulting and Clinical Psychology 32*, 565–574.

Runyon, H. L., and Williams, R. L. 1972. Differentiating reinforcement priorities
of junior high school students. *Journal of Experimental Education 40*, 76–80.

Skinner, B. F. 1953. *Science and human behavior.* New York: Macmillan.

Snortum, J. R. 1976. Self-modification: Ben Franklin's pursuit of perfection. *Psychology Today 9*, 80–83.

Watson, D. L., Tharp, R. G., and Krisberg, J. 1972. Case study in self-
modification: Suppression of inflammatory scratching while awake and asleep.
Journal of Behavior Therapy and Experimental Psychiatry 3, 213–215.

Chapter 3
Directing the inner drama:

Covert alternatives

The pleasantest things in the world are pleasant thoughts; and the art of life is to have as many of them as possible.

MICHEL DE MONTAIGNE

Within each person there exists a hidden stage.[1] Of that stage and its accompanying drama, most acquaintances are allowed only brief glances; only in the presence of a few trustworthy and intimate companions are the curtains drawn. Even then, the curtains may abruptly stop short of points of embarrassment and self-consciousness, precipitating a quick retreat into socially acceptable "external" behavior. At times the scenes on your inner stage induce calm and pleasurable responses, as when you imagine the embrace of a loved one. On other occasions, however, your internal dramas become battle scenes that result in inner turmoil and self-defeating behavior. This chapter discusses how your thoughts and feelings (covert events) can be self-managed to change behaviors and alleviate unpleasant inner states. And now the curtain opens!

For several years, behavioral psychologists (such as Skinner, 1953) have believed that covert events follow the same principles or rules as overt events. For example, these psychologists believe that thoughts are affected by their consequences in much the same manner as are behaviors (Mahoney, 1974). Imagined rewards and punishments are now being used to manage thoughts as well as behaviors. It has been demonstrated that as people change the nature and frequency of their thoughts, their corresponding overt behaviors also change in nature and frequency. Thus, the major question to be explored in this chapter is how to focus the expanse of inner events in order to produce desirable overt and covert responses.

Using covert self-control procedures requires a vivid imagination — that is, the ability to visualize scenes in great detail. Most individuals can produce mental _imagery_* quite readily. In fact, you may already devote considerable time to fantasizing. There is a malicious rumor that some college students are so skilled in covert self-control that they engage in nonacademic imagery during some of their less exciting classes! The major prerequisites, then, for effectively using covert strategies are that you can voluntarily imagine a specific scene and that you can maintain that image for around twenty to thirty seconds (Haney and Euse, 1976; Tondo and Cautela, 1974).

Both the physical setting and your physical state contribute to the maintenance and clarity of your imagery. First, you should find a quiet place in which to engage in that imagery. Baron (1974) found that sometimes even the slightest sound, such as a faint electronic beep, can

---

[1] Eddie Workman, School Psychologist/Director for the Interpersonal Development Project of the Little Tennessee Valley Educational Cooperative, served as editorial consultant for this chapter. Eddie has employed covert strategies in changing his own behaviors, in working with children who are experiencing adjustment problems, and in conducting his doctoral dissertation research.

*Terms set in italics and followed by an asterisk are defined in the Glossary.

completely disrupt an image. Quite obviously, you should not practice these procedures while sitting in front of your TV set and simultaneously listening to the latest rock album! Second, before using most covert strategies you will need to achieve a calm and relaxed physical state; this should enhance both the clarity and the duration of the scenes you imagine. To achieve such a state, you may want to use the relaxation procedures discussed later in this chapter.

It is important to note that when you're using covert alternatives you will be using two components of the overt-control model. Thus, covert self-management typically involves (1) selecting a goal, (2) monitoring target behavior, and (3) implementing a covert strategy. As with the overt-control model, you continuously monitor your progress toward the goal. In the following sections we shall explore how you can use covert strategies to change both overt and covert responses.

Overt target behaviors

Excessive behaviors

The major type of overt responses to which covert strategies have been applied is excessive behaviors. These are behaviors in which you engage too often and which you would like to *decrease* in frequency (such as smoking, overeating, and problem drinking). Most people have a few vices that could legitimately be put in this category.

Smoking   The hazards of smoking and the misconceptions many smokers have about this behavior are discussed in Chapter 5. Our discussion here is devoted entirely to the use of covert procedures to change smoking behavior. If you don't know whether you really want to decrease your smoking, perhaps you should read Chapter 5 before attempting any of the covert strategies described in this section.

The major covert procedure that has been used in modifying smoking behavior is *covert sensitization* (Cautela, 1966; Tooley and Pratt, 1967). In this procedure an individual becomes "sensitized" to the unpleasant qualities of a stimulus and subsequently avoids that stimulus. In using covert sensitization, you first imagine yourself engaging in an excessive behavior and then you imagine yourself experiencing an unpleasant event, such as becoming nauseated and starting to vomit. Use any event that is highly distasteful to you, including events involving feces and spiders, as long as the thought of the event elicits negative sensations. Finally, you imagine yourself terminating the target behavior and immediately thereafter feeling relaxed and comfortable. Although this procedure may not sound enticing, there is a large amount of research data demonstrating its effectiveness (Cautela, 1973).

In using covert sensitization to decrease smoking, you would first imagine a situation that you have found to result in smoking, such as finishing a meal, watching TV, or drinking alcohol. Then imagine yourself feeling the urge to smoke, reaching for a cigarette, putting it in your mouth, lighting it, and becoming nauseated and vomiting. During the scene in which you become nauseated, you might also imagine some form of social ridicule: people being shocked upon seeing you vomit. You would then imagine taking the cigarette from your mouth, putting it out, and subsequently feeling calm, relaxed, and refreshed. For optimal results, you should "hold" the scene in which you reach for the cigarette, put it in your mouth, and light it for about fifteen seconds, and the scene in which you become nauseated and vomit for at least twenty to thirty seconds. The scene in which you are putting the cigarette down should last for ten to fifteen seconds, while the scene in which you are calm and relaxed should last for twenty to thirty seconds.

Cautela (1967) suggests that you should carry out the covert sensitization procedure ten to twenty times per day, as well as any time you feel the urge to smoke. He also suggests (1966) that you should focus these covert sensitization trials on several different situations in order to covertly sensitize yourself to a cross-section of events that precipitate your smoking. Recording the events that precede smoking, as suggested in Chapter 2, will let you know which situations to emphasize.

Another covert alternative that you can use to reduce smoking is called coverant conditioning (Homme, 1965; Tooley and Pratt, 1967).[2] The best time to use this procedure is at the moment you are tempted to engage in an excessive behavior. When used to reduce smoking, coverant conditioning involves two steps: 1. When you first feel the urge to smoke, focus on a negative thought (negative coverant) that is incompatible with smoking: "Smoking causes me to have bad breath and tarnished teeth," or "Smoking resulted in Uncle Bill's having to have his larynx removed." 2. Following the negative coverant, produce a thought that emphasizes the positive consequences of *not* smoking: "Not smoking will allow me to save forty-five dollars per month," or "I'll have really shiny teeth if I don't smoke." After you've completed the sequence of negative-positive coverants (*coverant pair*), you should do something that is highly reinforcing to you (read a risqué magazine, for example, or eat a favorite food) that takes you out of the smoking situation. This pleasant overt activity should increase the frequency of your using cover-

[2]Coverant is a contraction for the term *covert operant*. An operant is a behavior that operates on the environment and results in a change in the environment. For example, placing a coin in a candy machine is an operant that usually results in your receiving candy. An example of a possible covert operant is silently telling yourself how good a candy bar would taste. This thought may set into motion a series of events that result in your acquiring a candy bar.

The fantasy route to smoking control

In response to comments from respected colleagues, Eddie Workman began to question the appropriateness of his smoking habit. As the first step in analyzing his problem, he established a one-week baseline of his smoking frequency. He did this by inspecting his cigarette pack each night. Surprisingly, he discovered he was smoking an average of thirty cigarettes per day. Upon calculating the monthly cost of this behavior (a whopping twenty-seven dollars), he decided to apply some self-management strategies to smoking.

For one week following baseline, he self-recorded his smoking by making a tally mark on an index card each time he smoked. During this week his average rate of smoking dropped to twenty cigarettes per day. Following this self-recording phase, he implemented covert sensitization. In the covert sensitization procedure he imagined himself (1) having an urge to smoke in a specific situation, such as after a meal, (2) picking up a cigarette and lighting it, and then (3) seeing a green slime pour out of the cigarette onto his face, resulting in violent vomiting. (What an imagination!) He then imagined himself putting the cigarette out and subsequently feeling calm and refreshed. He carried out this procedure five times each day, with trials interspersed throughout the day, for approximately three weeks. During this period he reduced his smoking to approximately seven cigarettes per day. During a subsequent three-week period, he increased the daily number of covert sensitization trials to ten, and his smoking rate dropped to approximately two cigarettes per day.

Covert sensitization alone did not completely eliminate Eddie's smoking behavior, so he added to the covert sensitization program a smoking-reduction device, a sequence of filters that progressively reduced nicotine intake, and he eventually stopped smoking altogether. Bravo! A follow-up approximately three months later indicated that Eddie had maintained these effects without either covert sensitization or the smoking-reduction device. It appears that, thanks to a little bit of aversive imagery and American technological ingenuity, our colleague Eddie Workman may never partake of demon tobacco again.

ant pairs, which in turn should eventually decrease the frequency of smoking.

Excessive eating   As Stuart (1971) has pointed out, at least one in every five Americans is substantially overweight. Obesity is typically a result of overeating, and self-control procedures for reducing obesity should therefore focus primarily on eating smaller quantities of certain foods. (We shall have much more to say about calories and food selection in Chapter 4.)

Of the covert alternatives that are applied to eating behavior, covert sensitization is the most commonly used. Using this procedure, you might imagine yourself (1) approaching a food that you plan to eliminate from your diet, (2) beginning to feel nauseous, and then (3) vomiting all over the food as you bring it to your mouth. Following this sequence of unpleasant events, imagine yourself (4) turning away from the food that you plan to eliminate, and (5) being refreshed and relaxed. Use the same rules regarding timing of scenes and number of trials that we suggested for covert sensitization with smoking.

Available research indicates that covert sensitization is moderately effective in losing weight. One study (Manno and Marston, 1972) showed that covert sensitization produced an average weight loss of 4.13 pounds over a four-week period, whereas a control condition resulted in a loss of only .83 pounds. Using subjects approximately forty pounds overweight, Janda and Rimm (1972) found that covert sensitization resulted in an average weight loss of 9.5 pounds over a six-week period, and 11.7 pounds over a twelve-week period. The control procedures resulted in no such weight losses over the same periods. It appears that an excessively overweight person can expect to lose about one pound per week when using covert sensitization. Although there is little definitive research on how long you can expect to maintain these losses, our experience indicates that you can maintain them indefinitely if you give yourself covert sensitization "boosters," periodically reimplementing the procedure after you've reached your desired weight.

Homme's (1965) coverant conditioning can also be used to control overeating. Whenever you feel the urge to eat a forbidden food, focus on a negative thought (coverant) that is incompatible with eating that food: "If I eat those French fries I'm going to look like a blimp," or "Eating those cookies will make my flab even thicker." You should follow this negative coverant with a positive thought, focusing on the advantages of not eating that food: "If I don't eat French fries, my body will look better and better," or "People will find me more attractive if I quit drinking milkshakes and lose weight." After you've emitted the negative-positive coverant pair, be sure to reward yourself by engaging in some behavior that is highly reinforcing to you and that takes you out of the eating situation — going for a short walk in the park, or relaxing in the sun for a few moments.

The limited research on coverant pairs as a vehicle for weight control is fairly optimistic. One study (Horan and Johnson, 1971) showed that students who were 20 to 30 percent overweight lost about six pounds in eight weeks by practicing the coverant-pairs procedure several times a day. Individuals who were not instructed to follow the coverant pairs with a reinforcing activity lost only half as much over the same period. Thus, engaging in a nonfood-related pleasant activity following the coverant pair may be a crucial step in applying this procedure to eating problems.

"What's a roach doing in my cola can?"

In order to reduce her consumption of a famous brand-name cola, our friend Brooks Workman implemented a covert sensitization procedure that capitalized on a long-standing insect phobia. In each trial she imagined herself opening a can of the soft drink, bringing the can to her mouth and placing her lips on the can, and having hordes of roaches run out of the can and into her mouth. Ugh!! She carried out this trial approximately five times each day.

After a couple of days, Brooks found that her consumption of the canned cola had dropped to zero. She could not even tolerate the thought of drinking a can of it. However, this strategy had not affected her enjoyment of the cola drink from a cup. This result underscores Cautela's (1966) suggestion that covert sensitization be used with a wide array of stimuli related to the behavior to be decreased.

Excessive alcohol consumption   This section is not intended to be a lecture on the evils of alcohol. Instead, it will suggest how individuals can use covert alternatives to *limit* their drinking if they think they're drinking excessively. By excessive drinking we mean drinking that is heavy enough to interfere with what you believe is your optimal level of interpersonal, academic, or vocational functioning. For a discussion of the motivational aspects of drinking control, see Chapter 6.

The covert procedure that is probably most commonly applied to drinking is covert sensitization, a procedure with which you are becoming quite familiar. Each trial would consist of visualizing (1) being in a situation in which you frequently drink, (2) approaching an alcoholic beverage and bringing it to your lips, and (3) promptly becoming nauseous and vomiting into the glass or bottle. To complete this merry sequence, you would imagine yourself turning away from the drink and feeling relaxed and calm. For the best results, you should carry out ten to twenty trials per day. The trials, of course, should sample a wide array of situations that (according to your self-observation records) trigger drinking. If you are interested only in limiting your drinking, rather than in stopping it completely, you should use covert sensitization only with images of yourself having your second or third drink.

Ashem and Donner (1968) have investigated the effects of covert sensitization on the drinking patterns of alcoholics. Over a six-month period following treatment, 40 percent of the individuals who used this procedure totally abstained from alcohol. None of the individuals in a control group was abstinent. Several other studies have indicated similar successes with covert sensitization in the management of alcohol consumption (for example, Anant, 1968; Cautela, 1966, 1971).

If your behavioral records indicate that your drinking occurs most commonly in anxiety-provoking situations, then the relaxation procedures we describe later in this chapter may serve as your first step in drinking control. If you drink primarily when you're feeling uneasy, the major purpose for drinking is probably to reduce anxiety; learning to relax in situations in which you feel anxious will pre-empt that particular payoff. Relaxation training will also provide more permanent relief from anxiety than does drinking. Consumption of alcohol only relaxes you temporarily and may lead to behaviors that cause added anxiety.

Most of the procedures we've described for controlling alcohol consumption could also be used to decrease the consumption of other drugs. For example, many drugs are directed toward the reduction of tension; learning to relax through covert procedures diminishes that particular reinforcement for drug use.

Aggressive behavior The person who habitually exhibits aggressive behavior generally creates serious interpersonal problems (Berkowitz, 1963; Lazarus, 1973). Aggressive behavior is any behavior that results in either physical harm or emotional abuse of another individual: hitting others, threatening to hit others, shouting obscenities at another, calling names, or verbally ridiculing another person. Although you may engage in very little physically aggressive behavior, you may have some socially aggressive tendencies (such as conveying subtle put-downs) that you would like to minimize. In identifying both a target behavior and a strategy for change, you might want to develop a baseline assessment of various aggressive responses and the accompanying environmental events.

Covert sensitization (we hope you've not had too much of this term) can be applied in the control of aggression. The procedure would involve: (1) imagining a situation in which you frequently behave aggressively, (2) picturing yourself engaging in the aggressive response, and then (3) imagining the occurrence of an unpleasant event. For example, if the target response involves verbal aggression, you might visualize yourself verbally attacking another student in class and your being ridiculed by peers and feeling very embarrassed.

Another procedure that you can use to decrease aggressive behavior is coverant conditioning. Whenever you feel provoked, you can formulate a thought emphasizing the negative aspects of responding aggressively and follow it with a thought related to the positive aspects of keeping your cool. After reflecting on this negative-positive combination for a few moments, reward yourself by engaging in some highly pleasant activity that, ideally, would remove you from the upsetting situation. Thus, when you feel antagonized because someone ridicules you in class, you would first say to yourself, "If I tell this guy off, everyone will think I'm

Yes, talking to yourself can be rational and productive!

really uptight"; then say to yourself, "If I just ignore that comment, they will see me as having good self-control"; and finally you would take out a piece of gum, chew it, and savor its delectable flavor while covertly praising yourself for having such highly developed self-management skills.

Deficient behaviors

Deficient behaviors are those responses that you want to increase in frequency. They may be positive behaviors in their own right, such as exercising, speaking up in class, or showing affection, or they may be behaviors that you deem important because they're incompatible with behaviors you want to eliminate. As we emphasized in Chapter 2, one of the quickest ways to weaken a negative behavior is to strengthen a positive response incompatible with that behavior.

Behaviors incompatible with aggression *Covert positive reinforcement* appears to be the most applicable covert procedure for increasing pro-social behaviors incompatible with aggression (Cautela, 1970). In this procedure, you imagine yourself (1) engaging in some behavior you want to *increase* and then (2) experiencing a very pleasant stimulus. You should imagine the target behavior for approximately fifteen seconds on each trial and the reinforcing scene for at least twenty seconds. Ten to twenty trials each day should result in an actual change in the target behavior (Scott and Rosenstiel, 1975).

An adolescent's self-management of aggression

John was a bright fifteen-year-old boy who was referred to a school psychologist by his parents. The initial referral problem was that he was having extreme difficulty "getting along with family members." A series of interviews with John and his parents revealed a cluster of aggressive behaviors and several setting events that seemed to provoke those responses. The behaviors were occurring at a rate of approximately two per day; they included hitting or kicking the walls or furniture and screaming at one of his parents or at his sister. Setting events included such things as John's being asked to do a chore, his parents' refusing to take him somewhere as soon as he asked, and his sister's playing her piccolo.

Following an initial period of counseling, during which John recorded the frequency of the target behaviors, ten covert positive reinforcement (CPR) trials were incorporated into his weekly sessions. In each trial John was instructed to close his eyes and to imagine that he was: (1) encountering one of the setting events, (2) responding to that event in a calm and relaxed manner while saying to himself that there is no reason to get angry, and (3) experiencing a highly pleasant event. He was instructed to imagine the first two scenes for fifteen seconds each and the third scene for thirty seconds. Pleasant events included winning ten thousand dollars, catching a very large bass, and having a travel trailer of his own.

After this procedure was introduced into John's counseling sessions, his aggressive behaviors dropped by almost 70 percent. When John began carrying out at least one CPR trial at home each day, aggressive behaviors were practically eliminated. John's success suggests that the more often trials are carried out, the stronger is their effect on behavior. A one-month follow-up report from John's mother indicated that during that month the target behaviors had occurred only twice.

Adapted from Workman, E. 1977. The use of covert behavioral self control procedures in a program for gifted children and adolescents. Presented at the 9th Annual Convention of the National Association of School Psychologists, Cincinnati.

To use covert positive reinforcement to control aggressive behavior, you would first need to identify behaviors that are incompatible with the aggressive response you want to weaken. Say, for example, that the behavior you want to decrease is physically threatening and verbally ridiculing your child for not making straight As and Bs. You might imagine yourself confronted with a C-and-D report card and saying, "I see that you have several Cs. That's not bad! Now, why don't you try to think of some things that you can do to raise all your grades to Cs." When you are imagining the behavior that you want to increase, imagine it taking place in the same situation where the aggressive behavior usually occurs. After you imagine the behavior to be increased, immediately shift to imagery that is highly pleasant to you. Objects of such imagery can be chosen from the Reinforcement Survey Schedule (see Table 2.2 in Chapter 2), or you can make up your own. We find scenes that relate to lying on the beach in the Bahamas, skiing effortlessly down a mountainside, and submerging in cool water on a hot day especially pleasant. Designing reinforcement scenes can be an exercise in creative imagination, the only rule being the more pleasant the scene, the better.

Assertive behavior   The most appropriate way to react when your needs are not being met is to respond assertively. Assertive behavior means expressing your needs, feelings, preferences, and opinions in a nonthreatening, nonpunitive manner (Hollandsworth, 1977). Examples include telling your spouse that you'd rather see movie X than movie Y, asking your boss to make changes in your work schedule, expressing your opinions in a classroom discussion, and saying no to something you don't want to do. Although these behaviors may sound easy, many people find it hard to do *some* of them in *some* situations. This section describes covert procedures that you can use to increase the frequency of assertive behaviors in any situation you desire.

The first procedure, *covert modeling* (Cautela, 1973, 1976), is based on the principle that you can learn complex behaviors by observing someone else exhibit them. If you use covert modeling to increase assertive behavior, each trial would consist of visualizing a situation in which the assertive behavior would be appropriate and then imagining another person (the model) engaging in the assertive response in that situation. Recent research suggests that covert modeling will be most effective when you use different types of covert models throughout the trials (Kazdin, 1976). For example, on the first day of your program you might imagine a model who is similar to you in age and sex, but on each of the next three days you might imagine models who are younger or older and of the opposite sex. You could alternate these types of models in your trials. Behavioral research (Kazdin, 1974, 1976) also indicates that covert modeling is most effective in increasing assertive behavior if the covert model's assertive behaviors produce positive consequences.

Say that you want to increase the number of times that you express your ideas during a mental health course. You decide to put Williams and Long to a test by finding out what covert modeling would contribute to the target behavior. The steps in each of ten daily covert modeling trials might consist of imagining the following scenes: 1. There is a class discussion going on in the seminar. The professor brings up the issue of how locus of control is related to mental health. 2. A student who is similar to you in age and sex speaks up and describes several critical studies on locus of control. 3. Immediately after the student speaks, the professor smiles and says, "Those were very pertinent examples. I wasn't even familiar with the second study you mentioned. I must make a note of that." You should have three or four different events that you can use as positive consequences for the model, and each of these should be highly pleasant to you personally.

Another covert procedure that could alter assertive behavior is covert positive reinforcement. On each trial you would simply imagine yourself being in a situation calling for a particular assertive response, engaging in the target behavior, and then experiencing a highly pleasant event. By using this strategy several times a day, you will reinforce your assertive behaviors far more frequently than if you were reinforcing only *overt* assertive behavior.

Giving verbal approval to others   The behavior-modification literature is replete with examples of the positive effects of verbal approval on the behavior of others. Probably one reason for this effectiveness is that our society is basically punishment oriented (Skinner, 1971). You can doubtless think of many situations in which good performance is ignored while poor performance is quickly punished! Thus, it seems that being able to praise the behavior of others would be a highly desirable interpersonal skill. According to Aronson (1972), individuals are most attracted to people who praise them for their behavior.

Covert positive reinforcement might be an effective procedure for increasing your frequency of giving praise. In using this approach you would picture (1) another person engaging in a desirable behavior, (2) your verbally praising that person for engaging in the behavior, and (3) your partaking of a highly pleasant event. For example, suppose that parents want to increase their frequency of praising their children for playing cooperatively. In a series of ten to twenty trials per day, the parents could imagine themselves (1) walking into the den and seeing their children playing cooperatively, (2) praising each child for such behavior, and then (3) experiencing one of several highly pleasant events, such as their children's smiling at them or hugging them. If you have difficulty picturing yourself giving approval to others, you might initially employ covert modeling rather than covert positive reinforcement.

Health-enhancing behaviors   A behavior that is presently receiving tremendous emphasis in our society is exercise. Yet there are numerous college students and teachers who still lead virtually sedentary lives. In attacking the problem of exercise, you might use either covert positive reinforcement or covert modeling. Which of these covert alternatives is best for you will depend on whether or not you have difficulty visualizing yourself engaging in exercise. If you can visualize yourself on the track, in the weight room, or on the flying trapeze, then use covert positive reinforcement. On each trial you would picture yourself engaging in the desired exercise (such as running one mile each day) and then visualize a highly pleasant scene (being in excellent physical condition and others praising you for it). In using the covert modeling procedure you would simply imagine a model, instead of yourself, engaging in the behavior and receiving reinforcement for it.

The procedures described above might also be used to increase the eating of healthful foods. The procedures for carrying out the trials would be identical to those described for increasing exercise except that the target behaviors would be eating various healthful foods — apples, oranges, fresh green vegetables — and drinking milk, water, and fruit juices.

Summary

In this section we have explored the use of covert self-control procedures in the self-management of a variety of overt behaviors. These behaviors included excessive behaviors such as smoking, overeating, problem drinking, and aggressive acts. We also explored the use of covert self-control with deficient behaviors such as pro-social responses, assertive behavior, praising others, and health-enhancing responses. Now that you know how to use covert processes to alter overt behaviors, let's turn our attention to the changing of covert target responses.

Covert target responses

Covert alternatives can be used to modify other covert responses. As you remember, covert responses refer to events that take place within *you*. Thus, most covert responses are *directly* observable and measurable by only one person — you. This section will describe how to use covert resources to alter unpleasant physical reactions and uncomfortable psychological states not involving specifiable physical pain.[3] Examples of unpleasant physical reactions would be migraine headaches and nausea; examples of uncomfortable psychological states would be depression, anxiety, and low self-esteem.

Unpleasant physical reactions

Tension and migraine headache A tension headache is apparently caused by the prolonged contraction of the muscles of the head and neck

---

[3]We're not proposing a dichotomy between physiological and psychological events. All unpleasant responses have a physiological basis but may not entail identifiable physical pain.

(Wolff, 1963). It is probably the most common type of headache and one to which most people periodically succumb. Among the covert procedures that may relieve this problem, relaxation training appears to be the most effective (Haynes et al., 1975).

The major strategy for muscular relaxation is the repeated tensing and relaxing of various muscle groups, such as hand and forearm, upper arm, forehead, eyes and nose, cheeks and mouth. The traditional approach is to tense a specific set of muscles for five to seven seconds and then relax them for twenty to thirty seconds (Paul and Bernstein, 1973), focusing your attention on the differences in how the muscles feel in the two states. Using this procedure, you should cover all the major muscle groups, moving from the lower to the upper extremities and using about two tension-release cycles per muscle group.[4] In our estimation the sequence in which you relax muscle groups is relatively unimportant. Goldfried and Davison (1976, pp. 88–93) provide a complete description of muscle-relaxation exercises.

Since this relaxation procedure takes twenty to thirty minutes to complete, some researchers (Russell and Sipich, 1973) have suggested a way to shorten the process. You initially go through the muscle groups to achieve deep muscle relaxation and then pair that relaxation with a self-produced cue word such as "calm" or "control." When you are totally relaxed, focus all your attention on breathing and silently repeat the cue word with each exhalation. The obvious objective is to associate relaxation with a specific cue. Henceforth when you begin to experience anxiety, begin to breathe deeply and silently repeat the cue word.

Bugg (1972) has proposed an even simpler method. He advocates that you do three things to relieve stress: 1. Take a deep breath and let it go suddenly. According to Bugg this procedure forces relaxation at least for a split second. 2. Tell yourself to relax. 3. Focus for a few seconds on something very pleasant. After completing these steps, redirect your attention to the problem situation. If the anxiety recurs, repeat the three-step model. Because this procedure is so easy, it can be applied hundreds of times to both imagined and actual situations.

Perhaps the least complex procedure for producing relaxation has been developed by Beary et al. (1974). In this relaxation sequence, you go to a very quiet place with minimal external distractions, get into a comfortable position with eyes closed, and silently or audibly repeat a sound, word, or phrase with each exhalation. You might try repeating the word "relax" so you can use this word as a relaxation cue when you sense the early signs of a headache. You could also focus your verbal cue

---

[4]A relaxation tape following this procedure is available from Instructional Dynamics, Inc., 116 East Superior Street, Chicago, Illinois 60611.

on specific body regions, for example, "My forehead is relaxed," "My neck is relaxed."

After practicing your relaxation exercises for several days, simply saying the word "relax" to yourself several times in succession should induce a state of relaxation. Whenever you detect the early signs of a tension headache, you can use this verbal cue to counteract the headache. After the word "relax" becomes a cue for relaxation, you should periodically use the complete relaxation instructions in order to maintain the association between the cue word and the actual relaxation response.

Somewhat less common than the tension headache is the migraine. Migraine headaches occur on a periodic basis and are frequently accompanied by irritability, visual disturbances, nausea, and vomiting (Lutker, 1971), symptoms that could also be related to problems other than the migraine. Migraines are thought to involve stretching of the cerebral and cranial arteries because of increased blood flow to the head (Alexander and Flagg, 1965). According to Lutker (1971), relaxation training may also be effective in inhibiting migraine headaches.

Other pain   Cautela (1977) has developed a package of covert procedures that you can use to self-manage a wide variety of pain symptoms. This package includes _thought stopping_,* relaxation, and covert positive reinforcement. Whenever you feel pain, or pain intensifying, yell, "Stop, relax," and then imagine a highly pleasant scene. In addition, you identify situations that typically produce pain and apply covert positive reinforcement to *each* of these situations several times a day. In using this procedure you imagine being in a situation that is usually painful, feeling very comfortable and free from pain, and then experiencing a highly pleasant event. If you have pain that is confined to a particular part of the body, apply the relaxation techniques to that area. Cautela also says not to complain about pain to anyone, lest social attention reinforces those pain reactions.

Other physiological responses   Relaxation training could potentially be used in controlling many types of physical discomfort. Sirota and Mahoney (1974) successfully trained a forty-one-year-old asthmatic woman to control her breathing difficulties through relaxation. After the client had identified several events that seemed to trigger asthmatic attacks, she was taught to relax herself in these situations. Her respiratory functioning improved so dramatically that she was able to discontinue most of her medication and the respiratory-assistance device on which she had become dependent. She maintained these gains over a six-month follow-up period.

Mind over body?

The client was a thirty-seven-year-old married female with three children. She was referred for treatment because of severe arthritic pain, particularly in her knees and toes, and depression. Five years of psychotherapy had not alleviated either problem. Before the client began covert conditioning treatment, her pain had become so severe that she had to use a wheelchair in situations that required much walking.

The treatment took the following form: 1. The client was given relaxation training as a means of reducing general stress and pain. 2. She was told to shout "stop" to herself whenever she was especially aware of pain. 3. She was taught to use covert positive reinforcement, in which she imagined herself painlessly getting in and out of chairs, walking, writing, and so on, followed by a pleasant image. She used this procedure five times each day for each pain-producing situation. 4. She was told not to complain to anyone about her pain. 5. Her husband and children were asked to ignore her when she complained of pain.

After one week of treatment the client reported that her pain was minimal. After three weeks she had no more pain in her knees and feet. (Occasionally, she experienced wrist pain following prolonged writing.) A follow-up indicated that she had maintained these gains over an eight-month period. Could this procedure help you overcome any of your aches and pains?

Adapted from Cautela, J. 1977. The use of covert conditioning in modifying pain behavior. *Journal of Behavior Therapy and Experimental Psychiatry 8*, 45–51.

According to Chinnian et al. (1975), relaxation training results in a reliable decrease in both blood pressure and heart rate. When you find yourself in situations that tend to increase your blood pressure and cause heart palpitations, you might prevent these responses by relaxing yourself, using the cue-controlled procedures described earlier.

Relaxation procedures have also proved quite useful in alleviating insomnia (Knapp et al., 1976; Lick and Heffler, 1977), probably because a major cause of insomnia is an inability to reduce muscle tension (Knapp et al., 1976). For insomnia, you should carry out the relaxation exercises for *all* muscle groups and then let yourself drift off to sleep as you become more and more relaxed. As you are tensing and relaxing your muscles, you might also use the cue word "sleep" each time you exhale. Focusing on the word "sleep" may help you control the racing thoughts that often accompany insomnia.

Uncomfortable psychological states

Anxiety Webster's dictionary defines anxiety as a "painful or apprehensive uneasiness of mind over an impending or anticipated ill." You are probably familiar with feelings of anxiety and with its characteristic responses such as tenseness of certain muscles, subjective sense of panic, and queasiness in the stomach. This section explores the use of covert self-control in the self-management of such responses. There are three types of anxiety that are perhaps most common to college students: test anxiety, which is produced when an individual thinks about or is exposed to a test (evaluation situation); social-contact anxiety, produced when an individual approaches others; and public-speaking anxiety, manifested when an individual gives presentations to groups or participates in class discussions.

Several covert self-control strategies can be applied to these types of anxiety, the most prominent procedure being *covert desensitization* (Wolpe, 1969). Of all behavior-therapy procedures, covert desensitization is considered the best established (Marshall et al., 1974). The basic principle behind covert desensitization is relatively simple. If you expose yourself to progressively more threatening covert images of a stimulus while you're relaxed, the anxiety response to the stimulus will eventually be neutralized (desensitized).

The steps in this procedure usually include: (1) constructing an anxiety hierarchy, (2) training yourself to relax, and then (3) imagining items on the hierarchy while you're relaxed (Marquis et al., 1971). To construct an anxiety hierarchy, you should first list about ten situations that are related to the object or event that makes you anxious. You then rank the items in terms of how much anxiety they produce, the first item in your hierarchy being the most threatening and the last item being the least threatening (see Figure 3.1). The items should represent real experiences that you've had or experiences you expect to have in the near future. They should also include details of each situation, such as people, and places.

The second step in covert desensitization is relaxation training, using the relaxation procedures we described earlier. To be sure that you are maximally relaxed, you should carry out the tense-and-relax sequence for *each* muscle group every time you use covert desensitization. Once you've relaxed your entire body, you should imagine the least threatening item in your hierarchy (for example, Item 10 in Figure 3.1). When you begin to feel anxious during the visualization, stop imagining that event and re-establish relaxation. Keep reintroducing the item until you can visualize it without feeling any anxiety. If you continue experiencing anxiety after repeating this procedure fifteen or twenty times, you may need to make the initial scene less threatening. Remember, the first scene should evoke only a very mild anxiety response.

When you're able to visualize the initial scene without any anxiety, you can move to the next item in your hierarchy. You then progress up the hierarchy until you can imagine the most threatening item without

Figure 3.1
Examples of anxiety hierarchies

A. Test anxiety hierarchy[a]

1. Taking a test in a calculus class, not being able to answer *any* of the items, and panicking
2. Taking a test in calculus and being able to answer only abut half the items
3. Sitting in the calculus classroom as the professor gives the test instructions and passes out the test
4. Sitting in the classroom before the test and watching the other students walk in
5. Walking in the door of the classroom about ten minutes before class
6. Walking down the hall toward the calculus class
7. Entering the building in which the calculus test is going to be given
8. Walking out of your apartment on the morning of the calculus test and heading toward campus
9. Waking up in the morning before the test and seeing your calculus text lying on your desk
10. Thinking about your calculus test just before you go to bed the night before the test

B. Social-contact anxiety hierarchy[a]

1. Asking a specific member of the opposite sex to go to a movie this weekend
2. Talking with that person about school
3. Walking up to that person and initiating a conversation
4. Saying hello from ten or fifteen feet away
5. Being thirty to fifty feet away and walking toward that person
6. Being fifty to one hundred feet away from that person
7. Starting to walk toward that person
8. Seeing that person walk out of a campus building
9. Walking to class on the day you plan to ask that person out
10. Waking up the morning of the day you plan to ask that person out and remembering that this is the day

C. Public-speaking anxiety hierarchy[a]

1. Presenting a report alone in front of the mental health class while the professor and students fire one hostile question after another at you
2. Presenting a report alone in front of the class and several people asking supportive questions
3. Presenting a report alone in front of two or three of your best friends
4. Being an active, verbal participant in a group that is presenting a report to class
5. Being a member of a group that is presenting a report, but making no comments
6. Watching another single individual report to the class
7. Watching a group present to the class

---

[a] Items are arranged in descending order of threat — that is, Item 1 is the most threatening.

becoming anxious. If you have difficulty reducing your anxiety to any of the items, the steps between the particular items may be too large. You should then insert additional items in order to reduce the increment between items. When you've completed your hierarchy, you will very likely find that you no longer experience anxiety in the situation that originally troubled you.

A large number of investigations have indicated that covert desensitization is effective in reducing test anxiety (Freeling and Shemberg, 1970; McManus, 1971), social-contact anxiety (Dawley et al., 1973), and public-speaking anxiety (Migler and Wolpe, 1967). Several studies suggest that self-administered covert desensitization procedures can be as effective as the same procedures administered by a therapist (Baker et al., 1973; Phillips et al., 1972). However, professional assistance may be helpful in the initial stages of learning to relax and constructing an anxiety hierarchy.

In-vivo relaxation has also been used to successfully self-manage anxiety. In this case you relax yourself in the actual situation whenever you begin to feel anxious. You do this by saying the word "relax" (or "calm") to yourself after you have paired this cue with muscular relaxation a sufficient number of times. Deffenbacher (1976) investigated the effect of in-vivo relaxation on the test anxiety of two secretaries and two college students. Use of this procedure led to gains on a civil service test by the secretaries, improved GPAs by the students, and reduced anxiety ratings for all four subjects.

Another covert strategy for self-managing anxiety is covert positive reinforcement. Using this approach to decrease anxiety, you imagine yourself being in a situation that usually produces anxiety, engaging in a behavior that is incompatible with anxiety, and then experiencing a highly pleasant event. Suppose, for example, that you have enrolled in a new school and don't know anyone. Furthermore, the prospect of making acquaintances is very intimidating to you. So you decide to manage your anxiety by using covert positive reinforcement. On each of ten to twenty daily trials, you might imagine yourself meeting someone for the first time at the student center, initiating a conversation with that person, all the while feeling calm and self-assured, and then having that person respond very warmly to you.

Wisocki (1973) showed that covert positive reinforcement can significantly decrease the test anxiety of college students — the more vivid the student's imagery, the greater the reductions in test anxiety. Guidry and Randolph (1974) also found that this approach resulted in significant decreases in test anxiety. In a landmark study, Kostka and Galassi (1974) found that covert positive reinforcement was as effective as covert desensitization in the management of test anxiety.

Calming the tempest

One young executive was absolutely petrified at the thought of attending staff meetings at work. His anxiety stemmed primarily from the possibility that he might be called upon to speak. At previous staff meetings during which he had been called upon, he had experienced symptoms of extreme anxiety (heart pounding, sweating, light-headedness). He also reported being very much concerned about what the audience might think of him (their saying to themselves, "He's wasting our time," or their laughing at him mockingly).

The first step in this client's anxiety-management program was to construct a hierarchy. Items ranged from very low anxiety events such as sitting in the conference room before anyone had arrived, to very high anxiety events such as two people laughing openly at what he was saying. After he had constructed the hierarchy, he made a relaxation tape using his own voice. He also taped instructions to himself for visualizing the scenes in his hierarchy. He visualized each scene until it no longer produced anxiety, at which time he moved to the next scene.

After seven self-desensitization sessions, the client reported that he could calmly attend staff meetings and did not get anxious even when called on to speak. In fact, he reported feeling elated and proud of himself. An eight-month follow-up indicated that the client had continued to speak in public without anxiety.

Adapted from Migler, B., and Wolpe, J. 1967. Automated self-desensitization: A case report. *Behaviour Research and Therapy 5*, 133–135.

Stress Somewhat related to anxiety is a reaction called stress. According to the eminent physician Hans Selye (McQuade, 1972), stress is the nonspecific response of the body to any demand made on it (stressor). Stressors might include loss of a loved one, a move to a new community, a change in jobs, and unexpected bills. Some theorists contend that any type of change in an individual's life serves as a stressor. Since college students have to adjust to new classes, new professors, new peers, and often new living conditions, they are prime prospects for stress. As our society moves into an era of extremely rapid cultural change, stress will probably become an increasingly common aspect of modern life (Toffler, 1970). For this reason, it is important for individuals to learn procedures that will help them cope with the stresses of living.

One of these procedures is called stress inoculation training (Meichenbaum, 1976; Meichenbaum and Turk, 1976). It is based on the same principles as those behind medical inoculation against disease. That is, if someone is exposed to a stressor that is powerful enough to arouse defenses, but *not* powerful enough to be overwhelming and damaging, this exposure will prepare the person to deal with that stressor in greater intensity. The first step in this procedure is to learn what Meichenbaum and Turk (1976) call *direct action* and *cognitive coping* strategies for dealing with stress. Direct action strategies include: (1) collecting information about the stressor against which you are inoculating yourself, (2) identifying ways to escape from the stressor when you are confronted with it, and (3) learning relaxation exercises, such as those described in the previous section, in order to relax yourself immediately when confronted with the stressor.

The cognitive coping strategies are ways of talking to yourself that will prepare you to cope with the stressor. Yes, talking to yourself can be rational and productive! The first step in mobilizing positive self-talk is to record the negative, anxiety-provoking, and self-defeating comments that you make when confronted with a stressor. Comments such as "Oh, no! I can't handle this," and "Why did I ever get into this?" may sound familiar to you. Whenever you catch yourself making such statements in a stressful situation, you should stop them and immediately replace them with positive coping statements. Examples of positive coping statements are shown in Figure 3.2, categorized by stages in the process of coping with stress. These stages include (1) preparing for a stressor, (2) confronting the stressor, (3) coping with the feeling of being overwhelmed, and (4) reinforcing yourself for having successfully coped. You should select statements from each stage that are most appropriate for the particular kind of stress you're experiencing.

The second major phase in stress inoculation training involves the use of covert positive reinforcement. On each covert positive reinforcement trial you might imagine the following scenes: (1) finding yourself confronting a highly stressful event against which you'd like to inoculate yourself (such as a situation in which you become extremely embarrassed); (2) giving yourself information about the situation (describing to yourself why this situation is embarrassing to you); (3) making self-confident statements about your ability to cope with the stressor ("Relax, you're in control," "This situation is not really anything to be embarrassed about," or "It will be over in just a second"); (4) coping with the situation while feeling calm and relaxed; and (5) partaking of a highly pleasant activity. You can use this procedure to inoculate yourself against any number of stressors, such as embarrassment, verbal abuse, and fear-provoking situations.

Depression   Depression refers to a set of responses to which people usually assign such labels as "the blahs" or "the blues." This set of responses includes loss of sense of humor, feelings of worthlessness, guilt about your shortcomings, and loss of pleasure from previously enjoyable activities (Seligman, 1975). According to Shearer (1977),

Figure 3.2
Examples of self-statements rehearsed in stress inoculation training

1. *Preparing for a stressor*
   What is it you have to do?
   You can develop a plan to deal with it.
   Just think about what you can do about it. That's better than getting anxious.
   No negative self-statements; just think rationally.
   Don't worry; worry won't help anything.
   Maybe what you think is anxiety is eagerness to confront the situation.

2. *Confronting and handling a stressor*
   Just psych yourself up — you can meet this challenge.
   One step at a time; you can handle the situation.
   Don't think about fear; just think about what you have to do. Stay relevant.
   This tenseness can be an ally, a cue to cope.
   Relax; you're in control. Take a slow deep breath. Ah, good.

3. *Coping with the feeling of being overwhelmed*
   When fear comes, just pause.
   Keep the focus on the present; what is it you have to do?
   Rate your fear on a scale of 0 to 10 and watch it change.
   Don't try to eliminate fear totally; just keep it manageable.
   You can convince yourself to do it. You can reason your fear away.
   It will be over shortly.
   It's not the worst thing that can happen.
   Just think about something else.
   Do something that will prevent you from thinking about fear.
   Describe what is around you. That way you won't think about worrying.

4. *Reinforcing self-statements*
   It worked, you did it.
   Wait until you tell your friend about this.
   It wasn't as bad as you expected.
   You made more out of the fear than it was worth.
   It's getting better each time you use the procedures.
   You can be pleased with the progress you're making.

SOURCE: Meichenbaum, Donald. *Cognitive Behavior Modification*. © 1978 General Learning Corporation (General Learning Press, Morristown, N.J.). Reprinted by permission of Silver Burdett Company.

recent research suggests that 15 percent of all adults between the ages of seventeen and seventy-four periodically suffer from serious depression. However, the focus of this section is the use of covert alternatives with milder forms of depression such as temporary "down" periods. Serious depression may require the application of both medication and psychotherapy.

Fuchs and Rehm (1977) have recently analyzed depression in terms of self-management. Specifically, they view depression as a distortion in self-monitoring; depressed persons selectively attend to their negative characteristics and experiences. They also tend to set unrealistic and global standards for themselves, making success very improbable and increasing their tendency to evaluate themselves negatively. These individuals also appear to be characterized by low rates of self-reward and high rates of self-punishment. For example, Rozensky et al. (1977) found that on a memory task, highly depressed persons punished themselves significantly more and rewarded themselves significantly less than did nondepressed persons.

The self-management approach offers several procedures that might be effective in reversing a depressive orientation. One promising procedure is Fuchs and Rehm's (1977) package consisting of (1) the daily self-monitoring of positive events (including positive self-statements), (2) specific goal setting, and (3) self-reinforcement for goal attainment (including self-praise and covert positive reinforcement). In using this package you should make a special effort to set goals that are *clearly* attainable. We would suggest setting small daily goals such as completing an assignment, washing your clothes, or calling a friend.

Since a low rate of self-reinforcement appears to be a key element in depression, procedures that increase the frequency of positive self-statements may serve to inhibit depression. Mahoney (1971) used a modified form of coverant conditioning to increase a client's positive self-statements. Four cards bearing positive self-statements (such as "I'm proud of being in good physical trim") were placed on the client's cigarette pack. Each time he took a cigarette, he had to read one of the cards. This procedure increased the weekly incidence of positive self-thoughts from near zero to more than fifty-six. Following the implementation of this strategy, the client also reported positive mood changes.

Johnson (1971) used a modified coverant conditioning procedure to increase the positive self-statements of a depressed seventeen-year-old college student. Before urinating (a high-probability behavior), the client was required to read a positive self-statement from an index card (low-probability behavior). After several days he no longer had to use the index card, but spontaneously emitted the positive self-statements whenever he urinated. After two weeks the client reported that his depressive episodes had completely disappeared.

As Seligman (1975) has suggested, depression may also be related to a highly external locus of control. That is, depression might stem, in part, from the belief that you have little or no control over your experiences and actions. If this is the case, you might change that orientation by verbalizing statements of self-responsibility. For example, you might precede a high-probability activity with such verbalizations as "I can do something about feeling bad," "Others don't make me feel bad — I allow myself to feel that way," "I have more control over my life than anyone else," and "I'm going to do something about my situation." The premise underlying all of these self-verbalization strategies is that the way you talk to yourself affects the way you feel about yourself.

Unwanted thoughts   There are three categories of unwanted thoughts to which covert control would be especially applicable: catastrophic expectations, personally unacceptable thoughts, and thoughts that precipitate unacceptable behaviors. Catastrophic expectations are those recurring thoughts that dwell upon the possibility of some highly aversive event. Personally unacceptable thoughts are those that you deem inappropriate because they're inherently unpleasant or because they distract you from performing tasks. The third category of thoughts includes those that result in behaviors you want to decrease, such as angry thoughts that result in your verbally abusing a loved one.

You can minimize unwanted thoughts through several covert self-control strategies. The first of these is Cautela's (1969) thought-stopping procedure. The principle behind this procedure is that if a behavior is consistently interrupted whenever it occurs, its occurrence will eventually be inhibited. Each trial of thought stopping involves these two steps: 1. Close your eyes and deliberately think the unwanted thought. 2. As soon as you begin to think the target thought, shout "stop!" It would obviously be a good idea to be in an isolated place or at home when you carry out this phase of thought stopping! After you've carried out ten to twenty trials per day for two or three days, modify the procedure by saying "stop" covertly rather than aloud on every other trial for two or three days. Then in the final phase say "stop" covertly on *every* trial. After several days of practicing this procedure, you should be able to stop unwanted thoughts whenever they begin to occur.

One example of thought stopping to manage catastrophic expectations involved a sixteen-year-old high-school student. This student frequently worried about making statements in a group situation that would result in the female students' snickering at him and perceiving him as a "klutz."[5] In order to eliminate these thoughts the student carried out approximately fifteen thought-stopping trials per day. On each trial he would imagine himself saying something that made the girls laugh at him; he would then shout "stop" to himself. After several days he shouted "stop" only covertly, and he reported being able to control the target thoughts whenever they occurred.

Several researchers (Daniels, 1976; Yamagami, 1971) suggest that you might increase the effectiveness of thought stopping by imagining a

---

[5] Our analysis suggests that a klutz is a person who is perceived as uncoordinated, silly, or socially unacceptable.

pleasant scene after you have shouted "stop" and have terminated the target thoughts. For example, Yamagami used this approach in reducing a color-naming obsession in a twenty-four-year-old male graduate student. The student compulsively named colors approximately 100 to 120 times per day, usually after looking at colors and traffic signals. The student was taught a thought-stopping procedure and instructed to follow each trial with an image of a pleasant event. This approach resulted in a 95 percent decrease in the frequency of color naming, and these gains were maintained over a seven-month follow-up period.

Hays and Waddell (1976) used a procedure similar to Yamagami's in the control of self-degrading thoughts. Three students were individually instructed to shout "stop" subvocally whenever they engaged in such thoughts and to follow up their thought stopping with two or three favorable self-statements. For example, the student might think "I'm a bum," shout "Stop" until the self-degrading thought stopped, and then say to himself "But I can keep a job." Through this procedure the three students achieved a 40 percent average decrease in self-degrading statements.

Another covert self-control procedure that can be used to manage unwanted thoughts is rapidly counting backwards from ten to one whenever the target thought occurs (Campbell, 1973). Campbell successfully used this procedure with a twelve-year-old boy who was obsessed with thoughts of his sister's violent death. Prior to self-management training, the boy reflected on this event about fifteen times a day. He was trained to evoke a target thought, stop the thought pattern by loudly counting backwards from ten to one as rapidly as possible, and then switch to a scene of a highly pleasant event. After he could eliminate the thoughts by counting aloud, he learned to count to himself whenever one of the thoughts occurred. The boy was instructed to practice this procedure each night at bedtime and to use the procedure whenever a target thought occurred. A two-week application of the counting procedure reduced the frequency of the boy's target thoughts to three per day. An additional two weeks reduced the frequency to zero, where it remained during a three-year follow-up period.

Another procedure that you can use to manage unwanted thoughts is covert sensitization. In using this procedure you generate the thought that you want to eliminate and then imagine a highly unpleasant event. Workman (1977) applied this approach with a thirteen-year-old student whose obsessive thoughts about guns were interfering with his school work. In each covert sensitization trial the boy evoked a common daydream about guns (such as getting a rifle for Christmas) and then imagined an unpleasant occurrence (such as someone vomiting or his science teacher snickering at him). He was instructed to carry out five trials per day on his own, and after eleven days he had reduced the frequency of the target thoughts by 99 percent. He maintained this gain over a two-month follow-up period.

Concluding thoughts

This chapter has discussed the role of covert procedures in managing both overt and covert reponses. (A summary of these covert procedures is provided in Table 3.1.) The major advantage of covert strategies is their convenience; they allow maximum flexibility in terms of the time and setting in which they can be applied. You can engage in covert positive reinforcement in the midst of a dull dinner party! Another advantage of covert procedures is that they are not limited by external reality (Cautela, 1973). When using external self-reinforcement, for example, you must have certain reinforcers available to present to yourself whenever you emit a given behavior. With covert reinforcement, however, the reinforcer is imagined and thus is available practically any time. The availability of these reinforcers is limited only by your imagination, not by your wallet! Covert procedures can also give you more opportunities to work on a particular reaction than might be the case with overt management. You may become extremely anxious in a situation that you encounter only twice a year. However, there is no limit to the number of times you can encounter that situation in covert exercises.

The major disadvantage of covert self-management procedures is that they are not as well established in empirical research as are overt procedures. Research on covert control has been more limited and has dealt with processes (internal events) that are less accessible to scientific scrutiny. Covert procedures would probably also be less effective than overt strategies whenever the problem behavior is clearly tied to stimuli in the external environment. However, very little research has dealt with this particular issue.

A final point is that although covert and overt procedures can and usually have been implemented on a separate basis, there is no reason that they can't be combined to manage the same target behavior. An example of such a combination might be to use covert positive reinforcement trials to increase the number of times that you praise others, while at the same time giving yourself points (exchangeable for some valued article or event) each time praising behavior *actually* occurs. Perhaps it's through a combination of overt and covert strategies that you will be able to achieve your fullest measure of self-control.

Table 3.1
Summary of covert strategies

Target behavior	Covert strategy
I. Overt responses	
A. Excessive behaviors	
1. Smoking	Covert sensitization
	Coverant conditioning
2. Excessive eating	Covert sensitization
	Coverant conditioning
3. Excessive drinking	Covert sensitization
	Relaxation training
4. Aggressive responses	Covert sensitization
	Relaxation training
B. Deficient behaviors	
1. Behaviors incompatible with aggression	Covert positive reinforcement
2. Assertive behavior	Covert modeling
	Covert positive reinforcement
3. Approving others	Covert positive reinforcement
	Covert modeling
4. Healthful behaviors	Covert positive reinforcement
	Covert modeling
II. Covert responses	
A. Physical discomfort	
1. Headaches	Relaxation training
2. Other pain	Combination of thought stopping, relaxation, and covert positive reinforcement
3. Physiological responses, such as asthma, high blood pressure, heart palpitations, and insomnia	Relaxation training
B. Uncomfortable psychological states	
1. Anxiety	Covert desensitization
	Relaxation training
	Covert positive reinforcement
2. Stress	Stress inoculation training
3. Depression	Combination of monitoring positive self-statements, setting specific goals, and self-reinforcing goal attainment
4. Unwanted thoughts	Combination of thought stopping, counting backwards, and covert sensitization

References

Alexander, F., and Flagg, G. 1965. The psychosomatic approach. In B. G. Wolman (ed.), *Handbook of clinical psychology*. New York: McGraw-Hill, pp. 855–947.

Anant, S. 1968. Comment on "A follow-up of alcoholics treated by behaviour therapy." *Behaviour Research and Therapy 6*, 133.

Aronson, E. 1972. *The social animal*. San Francisco: W. H. Freeman and Co.

Ashem, B., and Donner, L. 1968. Covert sensitization with alcoholics: A controlled replication. *Behaviour Research and Therapy 6*, 7–12.

Baker, B., Cohen, D., and Saunders, J. 1973. Self-directed desensitization for acrophobia. *Behaviour Research and Therapy 11*, 79–89.

Baron, M. 1974. The experimental analysis of imagery: The parameters of covert reinforcement. Unpublished doctoral dissertation, Boston College.

Beary, J., Benson, H., and Klemchuk, H. 1974. A simple psychophysiologic technique which elicits the hypometabolic changes of the relaxation response. *Psychosomatic Medicine 36*, 115–120.

Berkowitz, L. 1963. *Aggression: A social psychological analysis*. Englewood Cliffs, N.J.: Prentice-Hall.

Bugg, C. A. 1972. Systematic desensitization: A technique worth trying. *Personnel and Guidance Journal 50*, 823–828.

Campbell, L. 1973. A variation of thought stopping in a twelve-year-old boy: A case report. *Journal of Behavior Therapy and Experimental Psychiatry 4*, 69–70.

Cautela, J. 1966. Treatment of compulsive behavior by covert sensitization. *Psychological Record 16*, 33–41.

Cautela, J. 1967. Covert sensitization, *Psychological Reports 20*, 459–468.

Cautela, J. 1969. Behavior therapy and self-control: Techniques and implications. In C. M. Franks (ed.), *Behavior therapy: Appraisal and status*. New York: McGraw-Hill. Pp. 323–340.

Cautela, J. 1970. Covert reinforcement. *Behavior Therapy 1*, 33–50.

Cautela, J. 1971. Covert conditioning. In A. Jacobs and L. Sachs (eds.), *The psychology of private events*. New York: Academic Press.

Cautela, J. 1973. Covert processes and behavior modification. *The Journal of Nervous and Mental Disease 157*, 27–36.

Cautela, J. 1976. The present status of covert modeling. *Journal of Behavior Therapy and Experimental Psychiatry 6*, 323–326.

Cautela, J. 1977. The use of covert conditioning in modifying pain behavior. *Journal of Behavior Therapy and Experimental Psychiatry 8*, 45–52.

Chinnian, R., Nammalver, N., and Rao, A. 1975. Physiological changes during progressive relaxation. *Indiana Journal of Clinical Psychology 2*, 188–190.

Daniels, L. 1976. An extension of thought stopping in the treatment of obsessional thinking. *Behavior Therapy 7*, 131.

Dawley, H., Guidry, L., and Curtis, E. 1973. Self-administered desensitization on a psychiatric ward: A case report. *Journal of Behavior Therapy and Experimental Psychiatry 4*, 301–303.

Deffenbacher, J. 1976. Relaxation in vivo in the treatment of test anxiety. *Journal of Behavior Therapy and Experimental Psychiatry 7*, 289–292.

Freeling, N., and Shemberg, K. 1970. The alleviation of test anxiety by systematic desensitization. *Behaviour Research and Therapy 8*, 293–299.

Fuchs, C., and Rehm, L. 1977. A self-control behavior therapy program for depression. *Journal of Consulting and Clinical Psychology 45*, 206–215.

Goldfried, M. R., and Davison, G. C. 1976. *Clinical behavior therapy*. New York: Holt, Rinehart and Winston.

Guidry, L., and Randolph, D. 1974. Covert reinforcement in the treatment of test anxiety. *Journal of Counseling Psychology 21*, 260–264.

Haney, J., and Euse, F. 1976. Skin conductance and heart rate response to neutral, positive, and negative imagery: Implications for covert behavior therapy procedures. *Behavior Therapy 7*, 494–503.

Haynes, S., Griffin, P., Mooney, D., and Parise, M. 1975. Electromyographic biofeedback and relaxation instructions in the treatment of muscle contraction headaches. *Behavior Therapy 6*, 672–678.

Hays, V., and Waddell, K. 1976. A self-reinforcing procedure for thought-stopping. *Behavior Therapy 7*, 559.

Hollandsworth, J. 1977. Differentiating assertion and aggression: Some behavioral guidelines. *Behavior Therapy 8*, 347–352.

Homme, L. 1965. Perspectives in psychology: XXIV. Control of coverants, the operants of the mind. *Psychological Record 15*, 501–511.

Horan, J., and Johnson, R. 1971. Covert conditioning through a self-management application of the Premack principle: Its effect on weight reduction. *Journal of Behavior Therapy and Experimental Psychiatry 2*, 243–249.

Janda, L., and Rimm, D. 1972. Covert sensitization in the treatment of obesity. *Journal of Abnormal Psychology 80*, 37–42.

Johnson, W. 1971. Some applications of Homme's coverant control therapy: Two case reports. *Behavior Therapy 2*, 240–248.

Kazdin, A. 1974. Covert modeling, model similarity, and reduction of avoidance behavior. *Behavior Therapy 5*, 325–340.

Kazdin, A. 1976. Effects of covert modeling, multiple models, and model reinforcement on assertive behavior. *Behavior Therapy 7*, 211–222.

Knapp, T., Downs, D., and Alperson, J. 1976. Behavior therapy for insomnia: A review. *Behavior Therapy 7*, 614–625.

Kostka, M., and Galassi, J. 1974. Group systematic desensitization versus covert positive reinforcement in the reduction of test anxiety. *Journal of Counseling Psychology 21*, 464–468.

Lazarus, A. 1973. On assertive behavior: A brief note. *Behavior Therapy 4*, 697–699.

Lick, J., and Heffler, D. 1977. Relaxation training and attention placebo in the treatment of severe insomnia. *Journal of Consulting and Clinical Psychology* 45, 153–161.

Lutker, E. 1971. Treatment of migraine headache by conditioned relaxation: A case study. *Behavior Therapy* 2, 592–593.

McManus, M. 1971. Group desensitization of test anxiety. *Behaviour Research and Therapy 9*, 51–56.

McQuade, W. 1972. What stress can do to you. *Fortune 85,* 102ff.

Mahoney, M. 1971. The self-management of covert behavior: A case study. *Behavior Therapy 2*, 575–578.

Mahoney, M. 1974. *Cognition and behavior modification.* Cambridge, Mass.: Ballinger Publishing Co.

Manno, B., and Marston, A. 1972. Weight reduction as a function of negative covert reinforcement (sensitization) versus positive covert reinforcement. *Behaviour Research and Therapy 10*, 201–207.

Marquis, J., Morgan, W., and Piaget, G. 1971. *A guidebook for systematic desensitization,* 2nd ed. Palo Alto, Calif.: Veteran's Workshop, VA Hospital.

Marshall, W., Boutilier, J., and Minnes, P. 1974. The modification of phobic behavior by covert reinforcement. *Behavior Therapy 5*, 469–480.

Meichenbaum, D. 1976. A self-instructional approach to stress management: A proposal for stress inoculation training. In C. Spielberger and I. Sarason (eds.), *Stress and anxiety in modern life.* New York: Winston and Sons.

Meichenbaum, D. 1978. *Cognitive behavior modification.* Morristown, N.J.: General Learning Press.

Meichenbaum, D., and Turk, D. 1976. The cognitive-behavioral management of anxiety, anger, and pain. In P. Davidson (ed.), *The behavioral management of anxiety, depression, and pain.* New York: Brunner/Mazel.

Migler, B., and Wolpe, J. 1967. Automated self-desensitization: A case report. *Behaviour Research and Therapy 5*, 133–135.

Paul, G., and Bernstein, D. 1973. *Anxiety and Clinical Problems: Systematic desensitization and related techniques.* Morristown, N.J.: General Learning Corp.

Phillips, R., Johnson, G., and Geyer, A. 1972. Self-administered systematic desensitization. *Behaviour Research and Therapy 10*, 93–96.

Rozensky, R., Rehm, L., Pry, G., and Roth, D. 1977. Depression and self-reinforcement in hospitalized patients. *Journal of Behavior Therapy and Experimental Psychiatry 8*, 35–38.

Russell, R., and Sipich, J. 1973. Cue-controlled relaxation in the treatment of test anxiety. *Journal of Behavior Therapy and Experimental Psychiatry 4*, 47–49.

Scott, D., and Rosenstiel, A. 1975. Covert positive reinforcement studies: Review, critique, and guidelines. *Psychotherapy: Theory, Research and Practice 12*, 374–384.

Seligman, M. 1975. *Helplessness: On depression, development, and death.* San Francisco: W. H. Freeman and Co.

Shearer, L. 1977. Depression is common. *Parade*, July 17, p. 4.

Sirota, A., and Mahoney, M. 1974. Relaxing on cue: The self-regulation of asthma. *Journal of Behavior Therapy and Experimental Psychiatry 5*, 65–66.

Skinner, B. F. 1953. *Science and human behavior*. New York: Macmillan.

Skinner, B. F. 1971. *Beyond freedom and dignity*. New York: Alfred A. Knopf.

Stuart, R. 1971. A three-dimensional program for the treatment of obesity. *Behaviour Research and Therapy 9*, 177–186.

Toffler, A. 1970. *Future shock*. New York: Random House.

Tondo, T., and Cautela, J. 1974. Assessment of imagery in covert reinforcement. *Psychological Reports 34*, 1271–1280.

Tooley, J., and Pratt, S. 1967. An experimental procedure for the extinction of smoking behavior. *Psychological Record 17*, 209–218.

Wisocki, P. 1973. A covert reinforcement program for the treatment of test anxiety: Brief report. *Behavior Therapy 4*, 264–266.

Wolff, H. 1963. *Headache and other pain*. New York: Oxford Univ. Press.

Wolpe, J. 1969. *The practice of behavior therapy*. New York: Pergamon Press.

Workman, E. 1977. The use of covert behaviorial self-control procedures in a program for gifted children and adolescents. Proceedings of the Ninth Annual Convention of the National Association of School Psychologists, Cincinnati.

Yamagami, T. 1971. The treatment of an obsession by thought stopping. *Journal of Behavior Therapy and Experimental Psychiatry 2*, 133–135.

Chapter 4
Battle of the bulge:

A behavioral approach to weight reduction

To lengthen thy life, lessen thy meals.

BENJAMIN FRANKLIN.

Interested in shedding a few excess pounds? Join the crowd. An estimated 70 million Americans are overweight; of these, some 20 million are trying to lose weight (Jeffrey, 1976). Many of these people will undoubtedly be lured by diet plans that promise quick, painless, and dramatic results. "Eat-all-you-want" and "effortless" diet fads never seem to lose their appeal. Unfortunately, such plans seldom produce long-lasting results. "Wonder cures" are no more attainable in the weight-control area than in most other spheres of human endeavor.

Our own strategy for weight reduction is based primarily on the behavioral model described in Chapter 2. The application of that model requires personal effort and a long-term commitment. In a word, your style of eating must be changed. Any plan that fails to seek a permanent change in life style — a change you and your body can accept indefinitely — will produce, at best, only temporary results. Although our approach is far from infallible (we have had a few overweight dropouts), it has been used successfully by a number of students. In fact, weight reduction leads the list of self-management projects undertaken and successfully completed by our students. We have confidence that you, too, can control your weight.

Understanding the problem

Definition of "overweight"

Weight on the scale has traditionally been used to determine whether individuals are overweight. In using this standard, you compare your weight to the desirable weight of persons with your height and frame. You can get a general idea of what is meant by desirable weight from Table 4.1. This table gives the average weight of people of small, medium, and large frames who are between twenty and thirty years old. Your desirable weight during your twenties is generally considered to be the preferred weight for later years. Does examination of this table suggest a need to continue reading a few more pages?

A more precise way of defining overweight is in terms of body fat. A physician can determine the exact amount of your body fat by measuring with skin calipers. This procedure involves grasping the skin between two fingers, applying the calipers to hold the skin fold in place, and then measuring the thickness of the fold. You can get an approximation of your amount of body fat by pinching the skin underneath the upper arm, at the side of the waist, or in the abdominal region. If the skin fold is more than one inch thick, you have excessive fat (Berland, 1974). In making this test, you will find that skin and fatty tissue readily fold whereas muscle tissue does not. If exercise is to be a part of your weight-control program, pinching the skin in various areas will indicate where to focus your exercise efforts.

Table 4.1

Desirable weights for designated heights and body builds

Weights of persons 20 to 30 years old

Height (without shoes)	Weight in pounds (without clothing)		
	Small frame	Medium frame	Large frame
Men			
5 feet 3 inches	118	129	141
5 feet 4 inches	122	133	145
5 feet 5 inches	126	137	149
5 feet 6 inches	130	142	155
5 feet 7 inches	134	147	161
5 feet 8 inches	139	151	166
5 feet 9 inches	143	155	170
5 feet 10 inches	147	159	174
5 feet 11 inches	150	163	178
6 feet	154	167	183
6 feet 1 inch	158	171	188
6 feet 2 inches	162	175	192
6 feet 3 inches	165	178	195
Women			
5 feet	100	109	118
5 feet 1 inch	104	112	121
5 feet 2 inches	107	115	125
5 feet 3 inches	110	118	128
5 feet 4 inches	113	122	132
5 feet 5 inches	116	125	135
5 feet 6 inches	120	129	139
5 feet 7 inches	123	132	142
5 feet 8 inches	126	136	146
5 feet 9 inches	130	140	151
5 feet 10 inches	133	144	156
5 feet 11 inches	137	148	161
6 feet	141	152	166

SOURCE: *Food and Your Weight*. 1973. Washington, D.C.: U.S. Department of Agriculture.

Role of calories

A precise measurement of your caloric intake is a prerequisite to a healthful, permanent weight-control program. A calorie is a basic unit of measurement that tells you how much energy you get from food. For every 3,500 calories you get that you do not use up, you gain approximately one pound. That pound is stored in the form of fat. You can lose that pound of fat by eating less (getting fewer calories), by increased activity, or by a combination of both. For example, if your present weight is maintained by 2,800 calories each day, you would have to cut back to

2,300 calories in order to lose one pound per week, unless you also increased physical activities.

There are several ways to determine your daily caloric needs. First, you can keep a record of your physical activities and of the approximate number of calories you expend in those activities. Table 4.2 indicates the approximate number of calories expended in five major activity categories. These figures are based on three considerations: 1. People approach the same activity in very different ways. Some people, for example, get more physically involved watching TV than others, especially if their favorite team is playing a "crucial" game! 2. The calories expended in activities within a given category also vary. Sewing, for instance, will probably use more calories than listening to the radio, although both are sedentary activities. 3. Even when approaching the same activity in a similar fashion, different people use different numbers of calories. The basic rate at which different people use calories is sufficiently different that three people could eat the same amount of food and engage in the same amount of exercise yet one would gain weight, one would stay at the same weight, and one would lose weight. Despite all these variables, however, you can get a relatively accurate measure of the calories you need to continue your present activities by totaling across the relevant categories in Table 4.2. Calories above that total will result in added pounds.

There is a second procedure for calculating calorie needs that is less time consuming but also less exact than the procedure described above. The first step in this procedure is to determine your desired weight. Then, if you're a relatively inactive person, you multiply that weight by twelve; twelve represents the number of calories you would need each day to maintain each pound of body weight. If you engage in a moderate amount of physical activity, you need approximately fifteen calories to maintain that pound, and if you are heavily involved in daily physical activity (loading trucks, running ten miles, playing four sets of advanced tennis), you would need eighteen or more calories per pound of body weight (Berland, 1977). Thus, if your desired weight is 160 pounds and you engage in a moderate amount of physical activity, you multiply 160 by 15, which tells you that you need 2,400 calories per day to maintain that weight.

Before you can identify what foods to eat to meet your caloric needs, you must first determine the caloric values for various foods. Food calorie charts are indispensable in choosing diet foods. Comprehensive charts of this type are provided in *Slim Chance in a Fat World: Behavioral Control of Obesity* by R. B. Stuart and B. Davis (Champaign, Ill.: Research Press Company, 1972). Another useful resource that gives the exact caloric values for brand-name foods is *The Brand Name Calorie Counter* by C. T. Netzer and E. Chaback (New York: Dell Publishing

91

Table 4.2

Calories expended in various types of activities

Type of activity	Calories per hour
Sedentary activities, such as: reading; writing; eating; watching television or movies; listening to the radio; sewing; playing cards; and typing, officework, and other activities done while sitting that require little or no arm movement.	80 to 100
Light activities, such as: preparing and cooking food; doing dishes; dusting; handwashing small articles of clothing; ironing; walking slowly; personal care; officework and other activities done while standing that require some arm movement; and rapid typing and other activities done while sitting that are more strenuous.	110 to 160
Moderate activities, such as: making beds, mopping and scrubbing; sweeping; light polishing and waxing; laundering by machine, light gardening and carpentry work: walking moderately fast; other activities done while standing that require moderate arm movement; and activities done while sitting that require more vigorous arm movement.	170 to 240
Vigorous activities, such as: heavy scrubbing and waxing; handwashing large articles of clothing; hanging out clothes; stripping beds; walking fast; bowling; golfing; and gardening.	250 to 350
Strenuous activities, such as: swimming; playing tennis; running; bicycling; dancing; skiing; and playing football.	350 or more

SOURCE: *Food and Your Weight.* 1973. Washington, D.C: U.S. Department of Agriculture.

Company, 1971). If you want to know the calories you consume at your favorite eating places, you need look no further than Table 4.3!

Seeking a solution

Determining the appropriate foods to eat is essential to weight control, but knowing what to eat obviously does not insure that you will actually eat it. Behavioral attempts to change eating patterns have usually involved some effort to control setting events. These attempts have evolved from the early work of Ferster et al. (1962), Goldiamond (1965), and Schachter (1971), who demonstrated that overeating is maintained by a wide range of stimuli. In other words, fat people do not eat simply because they are hungry. In fact, many fat people seldom experience a

Table 4.3
Fast-food nutrition: How it adds up

	Calories	Protein (grams)	Fat (grams)	Carbo-hydrates (grams)
McDonald's				
2 hamburgers, fries, shake	1,030	40	37	135
Big Mac, fries, shake	1,100	40	41	143
Big Mac	550	21	32	45
Quarter Pounder	420	25	19	37
Hamburger	260	14	9	30
French fries	180	3	10	20
Chocolate shake	315	9	8	51
Burger King				
Whopper, fries, shake	1,200	40	47	147
Whopper	630	29	35	50
Whopper, Jr.	285	16	15	21
Double hamburger	325	24	15	24
Hamburger	230	14	10	21
French fries	220	2	12	10
Chocolate shake	365	8	8	65
Pizza Hut				
10-inch Supreme (cheese, tomato sauce, sausage, pepperoni, mushrooms, etc.)	1,200	72	35	152
10-inch pizza (cheese)	1,025	65	23	140
Arthur Treacher's				
2-piece dinner (fish, chips, slaw)	900	25	45	99
3-piece dinner (fish, chips, slaw)	1,200	55	64	101
Kentucky Fried Chicken				
3-piece dinner (chicken, potatoes, roll, slaw)	1,000	55	55	71
Dairy Queen				
4-ounce serving	180	5	6	27
Arby's				
Sliced beef sandwich, 2 potato patties, slaw, shake	1,200	37	40	166

SOURCE: Reprinted with publisher's permission from "The Diet Connection" by Theodore Berland which appeared in *Insider: Ford's Continuing Series of College Newspaper Supplements* © 1977 13-30 Corporation.

state of hunger. They are more responsive to external than internal cues; their eating behavior tends to be controlled greatly by the sight, smell, taste, and accessibility of food. As Schachter puts it, they are "stimulus bound." Thus, to decrease their eating behavior, the basic approach has been to reduce the range of stimuli that precipitate eating. Additional control has been achieved by altering the consequences for appropriate and inappropriate eating behavior. Most studies stop here, but a few have attempted to control eating behavior through covert strategies. Since these various procedures fit so nicely into our basic self-control model, we shall apply the model, step by step, to the problem of weight control. Perhaps you will then be able to use the model more easily with other problems.

Selecting a goal

Losing weight is more difficult than most self-management goals. When you are trying to control a drug, cigarette, or sexual problem you *can* largely avoid external temptations, but when you are trying to lose weight you usually come into contact with food several times a day and in some measure engage in the behaviors you want to control. Therefore, you had better have some important reasons for wanting to lose weight. Otherwise you'll surely join the ranks of the "tried but failed." Just wanting to lose a few pounds probably isn't enough. Needing to fit into a smaller suit of clothing frequently falls short in incentive value. However, other considerations might motivate you to follow through on a weight-reduction program: the prospect of heart problems, the imminent possibility of diabetes, laborious breathing during even minimal exercise, inability to engage in many activities enjoyed by your peers, being markedly fatter than your close friends, a lack of heterosexual attention, or a fear of losing a lover to a trimmer person.

Because successful weight control depends on a permanent change in your eating habits, in contemplating weight reduction you should give careful consideration to your life situation. Jeffrey (1976) suggests that you should not try to lose weight if your life circumstances do not permit a long-term commitment to carry through with the program. For example, if you are experiencing problems in your studies or home life, you may have to work through these problems before committing yourself to losing weight. Many people give up on weight programs, never to resume them, because other problems are more important at the time of their initial weight-reduction efforts. How do you feel about this idea? Can *you* lose weight when you are also directing a major effort toward improving grades or earning sufficient money to stay in school? Perhaps the following questions will help you determine whether the time is right for you to lose weight.

_____ Are you at least 10 percent overweight?

_____ Does your present weight pose a health problem?

_____ Have you been receiving negative feedback about your weight?

_____ Do you attribute the absence of desired interactions to your present weight?

_____ Are you experiencing other problems that you deem more important than losing weight?

_____ Can you depend on others to offer support for weight-reducing behaviors?

If you have important reasons for wanting to lose weight and if your life situation seems conducive to such a goal, the next step may be to see a doctor. We recommend that all persons with a serious weight problem (25 percent body fat) consult a physician before undertaking any weight-reduction program. Physicians can help you determine how much weight you should lose and at what rate. They can also determine whether there is any organic basis for your excessive weight. In a word they can help you decide on a weight-reduction plan that will not jeopardize your health. Remember that a weight watcher needs the same kind of food as anyone else. You will regularly need food from the four basic food groups — dairy, meat, vegetable and fruit, and bread and cereal. You will also need at least 1,200 calories daily. Because of these basic needs, your physician would probably not suggest losing more than one to two pounds per week.

You do not have to starve yourself to produce substantial weight reduction. Starvation can undermine your health permanently. If you reduce your weight too rapidly through dieting, you will probably lose more muscle mass than body fat. Wrinkling of the skin is also far more likely with rapid than with gradual weight loss. Besides, why go on a crash diet, lose a few pounds, and then return to your old eating habits? A more realistic approach — one that your physician will probably suggest — is to establish eating habits that you can continue even after you have lost weight. Establishing eating habits that will lead to permanent rather than short-term weight reduction is the goal of self-management.

As a first goal in altering eating behavior, one researcher (Stuart, 1967) recommended that individuals interrupt their meals by putting down their utensils and sitting for two or three minutes without eating; this procedure teaches some self-control and demonstrates that eating behavior can in fact be modified. Another early goal would be to reduce between-meal snacking. In fact, a few of our students have found that the control of snacking solves their weight problem.

At some point you will probably want to alter what you eat and how much you eat during your regular meals. Most likely you'll want to start

95

A discouraging revelation in many dieting programs is that even though you're losing weight, you're not losing it in the right places.

eating more of certain foods (fruits, raw vegetables, white meat, liver) and less of others (desserts with a high sugar content, fatty foods, red meat). A 1977 government publication, *Dietary Goals for the United States,* gives some helpful hints about what changes to make in your meals. According to this report, most individuals should eat more fish and poultry and less red meat; should generally eat more fruits, vegetables, and whole grains; should eat less butter, eggs, and other high-cholesterol foods; should drink skim milk; should get no more than 15 percent of their daily calories from sugar; and should consume no more than three grams of salt a day. The report also indicates that 12 percent of a person's caloric intake should come from protein, 58 percent from carbohydrates, and 30 percent from fat. Thus, a reduction in calories should be distributed proportionately among these categories. The suggestions of this government report are worth considering when evaluating some of the more popular dieting plans (see Figure 4.1).

Dealing with desserts appears to be a major nemesis for many would-be weight reducers. Denying yourself certain desserts may seem to undermine both your morale and your concentration on work. (Surely you've lusted for a hot fudge sundae!) You may eat entire meals just to get to your favorite dessert. If there are any foods that you view as absolutely indispensable to your zest for living, try eating those foods without the additional entrées. Thus, when you choose a particular restaurant because of its banana cream pie, eat the pie without the meal

Figure 4.1
Ten diets good and bad

Diets can come in some exotic forms and make wildly incredible claims — and who are we to resist the plan that lets us eat or drink all we want of a particular food and still lose weight quickly, effortlessly and without any feelings of hunger? Most people find it difficult to pass up the quick-weight-loss promises of the fad diets for the more tedious programs of counting calories, but the fact is only few diet plans work well over the long run — and the fad diets are not among them. Here is a look at 10 popular diet plans with a discussion of why they do or do not work.

Fasting. Many people think fasting is the quickest way to lose weight, and it is true that some very overweight people can lose as much as one pound a day on a doctor-supervised fast. Any fast beyond a day or two can be dangerous, however, and even those first few days will be uncomfortable — people report feeling hungry and listless and often complain of accompanying headache.

Zen macrobiotic diet. This phony, dangerous diet has nothing to do with Zen Buddhism. Invented by the late George Ohsawa, the macrobiotic diet progresses through six increasingly severe stages, the final diet consisting of only brown rice and tea. Frederick J. Stare, M.D., of Harvard University's Department of Nutrition has called it "the most dangerous fad diet around" because it lacks most vitamins as well as the critically necessary mineral, iron.

Liquid or powdered protein diets. This fad started as a beauty-shop diet marketed as NaturSlim, a powder you add to skim milk for breakfast and lunch. When you add a sparse dinner, you eat about 750 calories a day. Then came *The Last Chance Diet* by Dr. Robert Linn and Sandra Lee Stuart and liquid "predigested" protein, *Prolinn,* originally sold only to doctors. Now it and imitators are sold in drug stores. While it can take weight off fast, it is neither complete nutrition nor the sort of food you can live on for long.

Dr. Atkins' super energy diet. This is an extension of the earlier *Dr. Atkins' Diet Revolution* which lets you eat as much protein and fat as you want but initially no carbohydrate. This high-protein diet puts your body into a state of ketosis, which can be dangerous to diabetics and hard on the kidneys. The initial weight loss is mostly a loss of body water, and eliminating carbohydrate makes most people feel lethargic.

Dr. Stillman's quick weight loss. He may be dead, but his poultry, fish, cheese and eggs diet lives on. It is called the "water diet" because you must drink at least eight glasses of water a day to flush out your kidneys. It is basically another low-carbohydrate diet that has the same risks and problems of fatigue as Atkins' diets above.

Low-carbohydrate diets. You can realize weight loss by a sensible combination of calorie-counting and low-carbohydrate eating. First, your total calories should not exceed the number necessary to lose weight. Then, in distributing those calories among protein, carbohydrate and fat, allot 50 but not more than

Figure 4.1 *continued*

60 grams to carbohydrate; limit your fat consumption to under 30 grams; and the remaining calories should be protein. Your initial loss will be water, but after several weeks, you will see real weight loss.

High-fiber diets. According to proponents, if you load your diet with high-fiber foods which include certain vegetables, fruits and grains — unprocessed miller's bran supposedly being the best source — this will speed digested foods through your intestines and thus minimize the chance your body has to absorb calorie-containing nutrients. Nonsense. But such diets do fill you up and give you "regular" bowel movements.

Acupuncture diet. The internal organs have essential nerves which form branches that emerge under the skin in different parts of the body. Acupuncture stimulates these nerve branches, sending signals through the main nerve to the organ itself. Acupuncture cannot cause you to lose weight, but it can control feelings of hunger. Treatments are usually performed by a physician.

Vegetarian diet. You can lose weight and keep it off by giving up meat. But you have to know how to mix vegetable proteins (such as rice and beans, or peanut butter and bread) and be sure you get Vitamin B_{12} to stay healthy.

Tops, Weight Watchers, Diet Workshop, Overeaters Anonymous. All of these diet groups can help you — providing you stick with them. They offer the best diets, the best advice and the best support from fellow dieters. There is an evangelical fervor at many of their meetings, but the person who is secure enough to see the praise and criticism for what it is — namely, reinforcement to keep to your diet — will not be turned off by the theatrics.

SOURCE: Reprinted with publisher's permission from "The Diet Connection" by Theodore Berland which appeared in *Insider: Ford's Continuing Series of College Newspaper Supplements* © 1977 13–30 Corporation.

that precedes it. You will appease your appetite by consuming 250 calories instead of 2,000!

Monitoring target behavior

Only through accurately recording the quantity and circumstances of your eating behavior can you establish the relationship between that behavior and your weight. For example, if you fail to record *everything* you eat, you might mistakenly convince yourself that your weight problem is due to a hormone imbalance rather than to your eating. Some people tend to underrecord their eating. Schachter (1971) found three studies in which obese individuals reported eating considerably less food than normal. Observations showed, however, that while these people ate fewer meals than others, they ate far more food per meal. Furthermore, when they were fed what they claimed to have been eating, they steadily lost weight. It is unlikely that you can deal effectively with a weight problem unless you honestly confront present eating behaviors.

Meal	Food eaten	Conditions				Calories	Weight
		Time	Place	Circumstances	Mode of preparation		
Breakfast							
Lunch							
Dinner							
Snacks							

Total daily calories _____

Figure 4.2   Daily food chart.

Now that we have stressed the importance of accurate recording, precisely what is it that you want to record? The most essential records in controlling eating behavior are: (1) a record of everything you eat, (2) a record of the caloric value of what you eat, (3) a record of conditions of your eating (time, place, mood, mode of food preparation), and (4) a record of your weight at a set time during each day. The first two records will help you see the direct relationship between your eating habits and your weight.[1] Recording the conditions of your eating behavior should provide important clues as to how to change that behavior. (More about this in the next section.) You can use a chart similar to Figure 4.2 for recording all the information in one place. You can then take your four

[1] Amount of food consumed is sometimes established by counting mouthfuls. A simple supermarket expense counter could be used for this purpose (Stuart and Davis, 1972). Also, Water Pik has a small, inexpensive hand computer that can be used in recording mouthfuls and daily bites (Teledyne Water Pik, 1730 East Prospect Street, Fort Collins, Colorado 80521).

basic records and construct graphs that will immediately tell you how changes in your behavior are affecting your weight. For example, you might graph the amount you eat, your caloric intake, and your weight. By placing your graph in a conspicuous spot (such as on the kitchen cabinet or refrigerator door), you will find that it serves not only to reinforce appropriate behavior but also to remind you of when, what, and how much to eat.

Let us examine briefly how your four basic records can be helpful with different goals. If you're trying to reduce snacking behavior, you may question the need to record everything you eat, caloric value, and so forth. Such records, however, should clarify how and to what extent snacking behavior is contributing to your weight. If you cut out snacks and simultaneously increase consumption at meals, you probably will not lose weight. Only by recording *everything* you eat can you determine whether other eating is remaining constant as you reduce snacking. Also, recording calories in your snacks will give you valuable information on how long it will take you to lose a specific number of pounds once snacking is reduced. For example, if your present weight is maintained on 3,300 calories per day and 1,000 of these calories are from snacking, you should lose two pounds per week by eliminating snacks, assuming that your activity level and other eating behaviors remain unchanged. You will also find the four basic records exceedingly useful in managing your regular meals. For instance, a record of the caloric content of foods and the mode of preparation for those foods might indicate that you could reduce your calorie intake just by preparing certain key foods in a different way.

How long should these basic records be maintained? You should keep baseline records until you see a regular eating pattern emerge on your graph. You certainly do not want to attempt any behavior changes until you know exactly what you are trying to change; to do otherwise would be to invite misinterpretation of subsequent behavior changes. A one-week baseline would probably give you an accurate picture of your eating. Once you have established a baseline, we recommend that you maintain your records until you have reached your weight goal and your control of energy intake and output has become automatic.

Continuing to record and graph your behaviors throughout the treatment phase will make it easier to transcend those inevitable plateaus in actual weight loss. The most rapid weight loss will probably come in the first few weeks, with much of this early reduction attributable to water loss. Structural changes in body tissue come more slowly. If your graph reveals an extended plateau in weight loss, you may have allowed some of your eating and exercise behaviors to slide. A detailed monitoring of eating and exercise during a long plateau period would very likely reveal

When will a fat person eat?

Schachter and his colleagues have found that obese people are less inclined than those of normal weight to expend effort in obtaining food. In one study individual subjects sat at a desk taking personality tests; a bag of almonds was prominently displayed on the desk. After the experimenter had had some almonds and had invited the subject to eat, the experimenter left the room. When the almonds were shelled, nineteen of twenty subjects indulged themselves, but when they were not shelled, only one subject ate. Whether or not the almonds were shelled had no influence on the eating patterns of the subjects of normal weight.

In a second experiment Schachter and colleagues observed that overweight eaters chose the easiest way of eating. Obese patrons at a Chinese restaurant were far more likely than patrons of normal weight to eat with flatware instead of chopsticks. Only 4.7 percent of the obese patrons ate with chopsticks, compared with 22.4 percent of those classified as normal. We conclude from these and other studies that obese persons are predisposed to eat excessively, but only if the conditions are right. What does this suggest to you?

Adapted from Schachter, S. 1971. Some extraordinary facts about obese humans and rats. *American Psychologist 26*, 129– 144.

these subtle deviations. However, some individuals temporarily stop losing weight even when they're exercising and eating judiciously. In those circumstances, a short-term measure such as a one-day fast in which you consume only fruit juices may get your body moving in the right direction again.

Changing setting events

After you've established a record-keeping system, you should be in a better position to determine ways in which you could change your behavior by altering the environment. Should your records show that you snack rather freely throughout the day, you may decide to remove snack items from your house or place of work. Don't depend on will power to resist that second potato chip. We have already noted that fat people are highly responsive to external stimuli. When food and food-related cues are available, such people are far more likely to eat excessively than are individuals of normal weight. In contrast, fat people are disinclined to expend effort in obtaining and preparing food. Not keeping ready-to-eat snack items around the house should dramatically alter their snacking behavior.

Should your records reveal that your snacking is associated with TV, reading, study, or other activities, you will want to limit the range of places where you snack. Goldiamond (1965) describes the slimming of one young man following this procedure:

He was instructed to eat to his heart's content and not repress the desire. He was, however, to treat food with the dignity it deserved. Rather than eating while he watched television or while he studied, he was to devote himself to eating when he ate. If he wished to eat a sandwich, he was to put it on a plate and sit down and devote himself exclusively to it. Thus, reinforcing consequences such as watching television or reading would be withdrawn when he engaged in the behaviors of preparing the food, eating, and cleaning up. Responding to the refrigerator in-between meals resulted in withdrawal of such consequences, as did going to the refrigerator while watching television. Television, studying, and other stimuli would lose their control of initiating the chain of behavior and conditions that terminated in eating. Within one week the young man cut out all eating between meals. "You've taken all the fun out of it," he said to me.[2]

Your records will probably reveal that you are far more likely to snack at certain times than at others. One major reason for snacking appears to be boredom. You may find that you are most inclined to snack when you are alone and have nothing to do. Other individuals report that they are most inclined to snack when they're mentally and physically tired. Having identified the hazardous periods of the day, you are in a position to schedule high-priority activities during those times. Contrary to what you might expect, eating is not the most preferred activity of obese persons. According to an outstanding authority on behavorial control of eating, fat people rank socializing, work, affectionate and/or sexual encounters, and personal nonfood pleasures ahead of eating (Stuart, 1967). Snacking behavior might therefore be replaced by any of these activities.

Perhaps the very best replacement for snacking is exercise, since it tends to dissipate hunger and give you a metabolic lift. By this time you should have an accurate idea of your own list of preferred activities. If you are inclined to snack at certain times during the day, deliberately plan for those periods high-priority activities not involving food. What you are attempting to do is to condition noneating responses to stimulus events that generally have produced eating.

In addition to helping the snacker, changing setting events can help reduce consumption at each meal. Some individuals have found that preparing smaller portions of food at each meal reduced their temptation

[2]Reprinted with permission of author and publisher: Goldiamond, I. Self-control procedures in personal behavior problems. 1965. *Psychological Reports, 17* 855. Monograph Supplement 3-V17.

to eat large amounts. If you use this strategy, make the portions of food appear as large as possible by spreading out the food on the plate. Some people find that eating from smaller plates helps reduce food intake. You might also try different modes of preparing food; a baked potato may be quite as desirable as French fries, and it contains considerably fewer calories. Even if you don't change the amount and kind of food that you eat each day, there is some evidence that portioning that food out over several small meals is more effective for weight loss than eating two or three large meals (Derby et al., 1968).

Clearly, arranging setting events for appropriate eating behavior cannot be divorced from your shopping behavior. The amount and kinds of food that you buy will affect your eating behavior at home. Be sure that you make a shopping list and that this list reflects the types and amounts of food you need to lose weight. If you are shopping for a family, you may have to buy foods that are not conducive to your weight-reduction goals. Even then, shopping from a list will reduce your chances of impulsively purchasing unnecessary items. Parking your car some distance from the store may serve as an additional deterrent to buying huge amounts of food. It may also be helpful to do your shopping just after eating a full meal.[3] Generally speaking, the more removed you are from your next eating opportunity, the more control you can exercise over your behavior. It is easier to behave rationally in the grocery store than at the dinner table. Similarly, you can exercise greater control when making out a shopping list at home than when facing an array of attractive possibilities in the store.

Establishing effective consequences

You may think that altering setting events is all that is necessary to reach your weight-reduction goals. It is true that this strategy can produce substantial weight loss. However, effective consequences can facilitate changes in setting events. If you are trying to alter setting events, you probably will be more likely to make changes if you are given an immediate payoff for that behavior (such as engaging in a pleasurable activity after buying appropriate foods). Marked changes in weight do not occur immediately; unless you receive some immediate reward for your initial efforts, you may fail to sustain appropriate setting events. Furthermore, research (Mahoney, 1974) reveals that reinforcement directed toward changes in eating habits (the conditions under which you eat) is more effective in producing weight loss than is reinforcement for weight loss per se.

[3] There is some indication, however, that fat people may buy *less* food when they shop on an empty stomach. Remember, the eating behavior of obese persons seems to be tied more to environmental cues than to actual hunger. After eating a full meal, fat people may feel more resigned to their obesity (and thus purchase more food) than when they haven't eaten.

Please, no more turkey

Barry learned rather quickly that if he was to control his weight, he must do something about feasting at parties, during weekend visits, and on special holidays. Visits home during holidays were the greatest challenge. One year during the Christmas season he gained ten pounds, completely wiping out a weight-control routine that he had faithfully practiced for several months. Barry's mother was a major contributor to his problem because she got her greatest pleasure in cooking special treats for him — and, she was always asking him to have just one more piece of pie! So Barry had to develop some special strategies for getting through festive occasions without losing his impetus for weight control.

1. He discussed his weight-control goal and strategies with his mother and friends, pointing out how he had previously been sidetracked by special occasions. He noted that he was especially prone to nibble if he remained in close proximity to food during conversation. He explained that he would need to leave the table as soon as he completed his meal and that during parties he would need to sit where he wasn't looking directly at the food. He asked for their advice on this matter and solicited their approval for his weight-control strategies.

2. Since Barry knew that his mother received so much pleasure from being with him, he concluded that he should increase the time he spent with her other than at mealtimes. He periodically reminded himself that the major purpose of his visits was to see his parents and friends rather than to eat and drink.

3. He decided to reduce caloric intake and to increase exercise time on the days preceding and following parties and dinner engagements. If the parties offered opportunity for exercise (such as dancing or swimming), he would engage in these activities enough to offset the additional calories he consumed. His participation in these activities would indicate to others that he was having a grand time.

4. He established advance limits on the number of hors d'oeuvres and treats that he would eat at parties. Previous experience told Barry it was easier to control eating if he established a limit before starting.

5. Barry spread out his food on his plate so it would look to others that he had taken a substantial quantity.

6. He ate very slowly in order to continue eating until most others had finished their meals.

7. He ate lots of fruit and raw vegetables when they were available, which served to satiate his hunger and to assure others that he was enjoying himself.

8. He talked a lot during meals and parties.

9. Barry gave his mother much affection during his home visits.

Could any of Barry's ideas work for you?

The kinds of reinforcers that can be applied to eating habits are numerous. Some of our students have set up self-administered token economies in which they earned or lost tokens (usually in the form of points) for specified behaviors.[4] When they earn enough tokens, they cash them in for such back-up reinforcers as a new sweater, a new drill press, or a weekend trip. Some students have sustained their initial weight-reducing efforts by enlisting reinforcement from others. One woman persuaded her husband to wash both the morning and the evening dishes whenever she limited herself to only one serving of each food. (Of course, the quantity of the serving had to be predefined.) Others have found that calling a friend or doing something fun following a specified behavior was enough to strengthen that behavior. Some individuals find the support of professionally organized groups such as Weight Watchers and Diet Workshop crucial in the first few months of a weight-control program. Applying any of these social consequences may give you added incentive to do the things that lead to weight reduction.

Consolidating your gains

Stunkard and McLaren-Hume's review (1959) of weight-control research showed that most individuals do not keep off the weight they lose. Unfortunately, a more recent review (Leon, 1976) confirmed that weight maintenance remains a problem for many people despite gains being made with behavioral strategies. We suspect that a combination of several factors accounts for the difficulty of weight maintenance. First, many people lose weight through crash programs that fail to alter eating habits. Once the weight is off these persons gradually return to their old ways. Since we have described a number of setting events that affect eating habits, we trust that long-term changes in eating habits will pose less of a problem for you. However, we must caution again that changes in setting events must be maintained indefinitely. For example, you should continue to disassociate snacking from TV viewing, reading, and other pleasant stimulation if you're to maintain control of snacking.

Second, many people find that a lot of reinforcement stops once changes have occurred. When you're actually losing weight, others may compliment you on your progress, you may receive reinforcement from observing the downward slope of your behavior graph or weight chart, or you may receive reinforcement from weighing yourself each day. Once you change your eating habits and have lost some weight, these reinforcers may disappear; without reinforcement the behaviors that led to the weight change could disappear as well. What you must do to consolidate your gains is to make certain that reinforcement continues until you

---

[4] Some weight watchers place pieces of pork fat in the refrigerator and remove one piece for each pound lost (Penick et al., 1971). Though this is hardly an aesthetically pleasing arrangement, it does have some symbolic significance.

have grown used to being your new self. Once you start feeling that it is natural for you to be at the new weight, extrinsic reinforcers can be markedly reduced.

Third, we suspect that many people regain lost weight because they have failed to develop alternatives to overeating. Whenever they get bored, lonely, or overlooked they revert to overeating. You probably need to develop other areas of your life in order to sustain weight control, to provide you natural reinforcement, and to make you feel more comfortable with your new self. Thus, you might maintain those behaviors that have contributed to your weight loss by expanding your involvement in other activities as your weight stabilizes. Keep in mind that participation in physical activities can markedly improve your body conditioning even after you've stopped losing weight.

Since a later chapter will discuss sports activity, we shall comment only briefly on the role of exercise in weight control. Diet control plus regular exercise definitely leads to faster weight reduction than dieting alone. Lest you think exercising makes dieting more difficult, research (Mayer, 1968) has shown that individuals who lead a sedentary life eat more than those who regularly participate in moderate activity. Overweight persons have much to gain from physical activity because they burn more calories per minute than individuals of normal weight engaged in the same activity. The first route to increased activity is to be found within your work and domestic chores. You could readily increase the amount of standing and walking that you do in your work. For example, you may choose between the elevator and the stairs several times a day. Over the course of a year, those choices could make a difference of several pounds.

Admittedly, most of us need more physical exercise than we can incorporate into our work. (Jogging in place while sitting at your desk could be misinterpreted by the instructor!) While involvement in sports is probably the best way to get that exercise, we are not opposed to sit-ups, calisthenics, and jogging. However, because these activities are not usually inherently reinforcing, you will probably need external reinforcement to maintain them. Pursuing an exercise activity with someone else not only makes the activity more reinforcing, but also allows each of you to remind the other to get out and exercise. In brief, we recommend that you develop physical activities that can reduce boredom and loneliness, that can add naturally occurring reinforcement to your life, and that can serve as a source of enjoyment *throughout* your life.

Another benefit of physical activity is that it helps you focus weight loss on specific body regions. A discouraging revelation in many dieting programs is that even though you're losing weight, you're not losing it in the right places. During early stages of weight loss, your body can look even more disproportionate than before you began. While most parts of

Expanding your knowledge base

Since effective weight management is a lifelong quest, you will periodically need to extend your knowledge in this area. Two books that you might find especially helpful are: T. Berland, 1974. *Rating the Diets*. Skokie, Ill.: Publications International, Ltd.; and M. J. and K. Mahoney, 1976. *Permanent Weight Control: A Total Solution to the Dieter's Dilemma*. New York: Norton.

Deciding what foods to eat to facilitate healthy weight control can be an extremely complex process. You are regularly exposed to a multitude of dieting plans, but some are an actual threat to survival. Berland's text will be indispensable for evaluating various dieting systems. It can also help you maintain your motivation through its description of important, but sometimes little known, benefits of weight control. For example, did you know that some insurance companies will even lower the premiums for obese people who lose and keep off substantial amounts of weight?

The Mahoney text is the most comprehensive analysis of the behavioral approach to weight control that we've seen. It has detailed descriptions of many of the concepts we've described and gives particular emphasis to the role of self-verbalizations in weight management. The book has enough specifics to help you work through most problems that you will encounter in weight control.

---

your body will probably be affected if you control your diet long enough, you can partially control the dispersion of weight loss by exercising the body regions where you most want to lose. The waistline seems to receive a lot of this selective attention!

An alternative approach

Up to this point we may have given the impression that everyone must lose weight by following steps one through five of our model. Of course, this isn't true. We personally prefer using the overt strategies of our model, but it is doubtful that everyone can lose weight through the same procedures. Perhaps some of the failures with weight maintenance have resulted from people's using strategies alien to their life style. Those who are easily aroused by mental images and who can easily visualize both positive and negative scenes may find covert processes a suitable alternative or an addition to overt procedures.

Homme's coverant pairs (Horan and Johnson, 1971) and Cautela's covert sensitization and covert positive reinforcement (Manno and Marston, 1972) are the principal covert procedures that have been used in altering eating habits. As you will recall from Chapter 3, Homme's coverant model requires the subject to visualize the negative consequences of the undesired behavior and then the positive consequences of the desired response; the consequences are typically those of an immediate nature. However, some of the early researchers on eating behavior (Ferster et al., 1962) contend that focusing on the *ultimate* consequences of obesity is essential to weight control. By pairing thoughts of those consequences with pro-eating thoughts, a person may develop an aversion to certain types of eating behavior. In developing their list of consequences, Ferster et al. had weight watchers draw primarily from personal experiences. These experiences, often related to social rejection and humiliation, were judged more aversive than statistical information on diabetes, heart disease, and high blood pressure. One of our students told us recently that he had gotten so overweight that he could hardly engage in sexual activity. Surely, that would qualify as an *ultimate aversive consequence*!*

Manno and Marston's (1972) covert sensitization strategy was designed to produce feelings of nausea in response to certain foods. This feeling of nausea was programmed to occur at progressively earlier stages in the eating process. Initially the subjects were asked to visualize the following sequence of events: seeing a specific food item, picking it up, being tempted to eat it, bringing it to the lips, and then feeling nauseated. The next sequence of images was seeing the food, picking it up (but not bringing it to the lips), wanting to eat it, feeling nauseated, putting the food down, and feeling better. The third sequence was seeing the food, reaching for it, feeling sick, withdrawing the hand, and feeling better. The last sequence of images was seeing the food, wanting to eat it, feeling ill, saying "I don't want it," and feeling much better.

Manno and Marston's covert positive reinforcement followed essentially the same sequence of images but without the feeling of nausea. At the critical moment the subjects simply imagined putting the food down and turning away; they felt very good about themselves and were applauded by their friends. In other words, they imagined positive consequences for resisting temptation. Manno and Marston found the covert sensitization and covert reinforcement strategies to be about equally effective in producing weight loss. Both were significantly superior to a control condition.

Your analysis of your eating habits may reveal a correlation between certain states of mind and inappropriate eating behaviors. For example, a recent study (Lyman and Fisher, 1977) shows that when people are depressed they prefer sweets, junk food, and cereals that convert to sugar. The inappropriate eating behaviors in which they indulge when angry, frustrated, discouraged, and anxious may continue into less emotional periods. Individuals sometimes go on eating binges when

*Terms set in italics and followed by an asterisk are defined in the Glossary.

they're upset and thereafter completely forgo their weight-control efforts. Just being aware of what moods are producing undesirable eating behaviors should give you greater control over those behaviors. In addition, you can employ the covert strategies suggested in Chapter 3 for dealing with these emotional states.

Concluding thoughts

Our analysis of excessive weight was not intended to be inclusive or exhaustive. Rather, our purpose was to demonstrate how the basic self-management model can be applied to weight control. The specific suggestions we made under each step of the model illustrated what *can* be done. Many other plans could be substituted without in any way affecting the overall approach. In fact, we hope you were stimulated to think of new ways of using goal setting, record keeping, setting events, and reinforcement contingencies to control *your* behavior.

If you are extremely obese, we recommend that before initiating an ambitious weight-reduction program, you see a physician, who can help you determine whether your weight problem is strictly a function of your eating and exercise habits. If you are particularly amenable to social approval, we suggest that you align yourself with a supportive group, such as Weight Watchers. However, despite the value of input from physicians and professional weight-reduction agencies, control of your eating and exercise behaviors ultimately lies with you. Like most personal problems, excessive weight can be dealt with in an impulsive, uninformed, and unthinking manner. This chapter has tried to present a rational approach toward controlling an area of your life that contributes to your social adjustment, recreational experiences, physical health, and basic survival.

References

Berland, T. 1974. *Rating the diets*. Skokie, Ill.: Publications International, Ltd.

Berland, T. 1977. The diet connection. *Insider: Ford's Continuing Series of College Newspaper Supplements* 13– 30 Corporation, 10– 15.

Derby, G., Rohr, R., Azouaou, G., Vassilitch, I., and Mottaz, G. 1968. Study of the effect of dividing the daily caloric intake into seven meals on weight loss in obese subjects. *Nutrito Dieta 10*, 288–296.

Ferster, C. B., Nurnberger, J. I., and Levitt, E. B. 1962. The control of eating. *Journal of Mathetics 1*(1), 87–109.

Food and your weight. 1973. Washington, D.C.: U.S. Department of Agriculture.

Goldiamond, I. 1965. Self-control procedures in personal behavior problems. *Psychological Reports 17*, 851–868.

Horan, J. J., and Johnson, R. G. 1971. Covert conditioning through a self-management application of the Premack principle: Its effect on weight reduction. *Journal of Behavior Therapy and Experimental Psychiatry 2*, 243–249.

Jeffrey, D. B. 1976. Behavioral management of obesity. In W. E. Craighead, A. E. Kazdin, and M. J. Mahoney (eds.), *Behavioral modification: Principles, issues, and applications*, pp. 394–413. Boston: Houghton Mifflin.

Leon, G. R. 1976. Current directions in the treatment of obesity. *Psychological Bulletin 83*(4), 557–578.

Lyman, B., and Fischer, I. 1977. The role of feelings and emotions in food preferences and eating behavior. Presented at the Canadian Psychological Association, Vancouver.

Mahoney, M. 1974. Self-reward and self-monitoring techniques for weight control. *Behavior Therapy 5*, 48–57.

Mahoney, M. J., and Mahoney, K. 1976. *Permanent weight control: A total solution to the dieter's dilemma*. New York: Norton.

Manno, B., and Marston, A. R. 1972. Weight reduction as a function of negative covert reinforcement (sensitization) versus positive covert reinforcement. *Behaviour Research and Therapy 10*, 201–207.

Mayer, J. 1968. *Overweight — Causes, cost, and control*. Englewood Cliffs, N.J.: Prentice-Hall.

Netzer, C. T., and Chaback, E. 1971. *The brand name calorie counter*. New York: Dell.

Penick, S. B., Filion, R., Fox, S., and Stunkard, A. J. 1971. Behavior modification in the treatment of obesity. *Psychosomatic Medicine 33*, 49–55.

Schachter, S. 1971. Some extraordinary facts about obese humans and rats. *American Psychologist 26*(1), 129–144.

Stuart, R. B. 1967. Behavioral control of overeating. *Behaviour Research and Therapy 5*, 357–365

Stuart, R. B., and Davis, B. 1972. *Slim chance in a fat world*. Champaign, Ill.: Research Press Company.

Stunkard, A., and McLaren-Hume, M. 1959. The results of treatment for obesity. *Archives Internal Medicine 103*, 79–85.

Chapter 5
A journey to Naif:

Confronting the smoking habit

Smoking is not an unbeatable foe. Millions
of Americans are former smokers.

Imagine that a new planet, the Land of Naif, has been discovered. Naif is inhabited by highly intelligent, sophisticated creatures similar to yourself, but they have access to few of the luxuries and diversions available on Earth. Imagine further that you have been offered an exclusive franchise to market a red-hot item on Naif. Millions of Earthlings are already using this product, and many of the users claim that it reduces anxiety and creates pleasant states of mood. Unfortunately (You knew it was too good to last!) your product has been tainted by scientific studies that have been publicized throughout Space. For example, your product has been linked to early death in higher organisms. Earthlings who use the product are ten times more likely to die of lung cancer than nonusers, and during any given day the risk of death is about 70 percent greater for users than for nonusers. To make matters worse, in order to market the product you personally must demonstrate it anywhere from twenty to forty times a day for your sales audiences. Would your franchise become profitable? Could you take the personal health risks? Are Naifians more intelligent than Earthlings?

Meanwhile — Rationalizing back on Earth

More than 60 million persons in the United States alone are investing enormous sums of money in using the product you could be marketing on Naif. Many use the product in a totally dependent fashion. They are especially prone to turn to it for solace in difficult situations. Most of the 60 million who use the product do not do so out of naiveté or ignorance. Its hazards are as well known to users as to nonusers. How is it that in the face of unequivocal evidence on the dangers of this product millions attempt to justify its continued use?

One group of researchers (Meyer et al., 1973) has analyzed how smokers justify their habit in the midst of a nationwide antismoking campaign. These researchers found that their sample of continuous smokers (those who had never tried quitting) ranged from those who smoked with no regrets to those who smoked with great conflict. The no-regret smokers used two basic strategies to avoid feelings of conflict about smoking: They denied the dangers of smoking, and they minimized the importance of reported dangers. The latter strategy is exemplified by smokers who stress the current pleasures of smoking, who point to their good health, and who mention the hazards of nonsmoking activities ("One can get killed crossing the street."). Those who talk about the smoker who lived to be 105 are probably trying to deny the dangers completely. No-regret smokers often create their own correlation tables, which they value over established statistical reports. One man with a seventh-grade education put it this way to Meyer et al.:

You bet your life

Many smokers question the cautionary statement that smoking leads to an early grave. Still others wonder exactly how many years they may lose. The following table clarifies the deleterious consequences of smoking. Notice that a twenty-five-year-old male who has never smoked can expect to live an additional 48.6 years, whereas his contemporary who smokes two packs a day can anticipate only another 40.3 years. In other words, the nonsmoker can expect to live 8.3 years longer than the heavy smoker. You will be encouraged to know that the life expectancy for individuals who give up smoking will eventually approach that of people who have never smoked (assuming a serious smoking disorder has not already developed).

Life expectancy (additional years) at various ages, estimated for United States males

Age	Never smoked regularly	Cigarettes smoked by daily amount			
		1–9	10–19	20–39	40+
25	48.6	44.0	43.1	42.4	40.3
30	43.9	39.3	38.4	37.8	35.8
35	39.2	34.7	33.8	33.2	31.3
40	34.5	30.2	29.3	28.7	26.9
45	30.0	25.9	25.0	24.4	23.0
50	25.6	21.8	21.0	20.5	19.3
55	21.4	17.9	17.4	17.0	16.0
60	17.6	14.5	14.1	13.7	13.2
65	14.1	11.3	11.2	11.0	10.7

SOURCE: Hammond study. Reprinted by permission of Public Health Service, Department of Health, Education, and Welfare.

. . . now I've known a couple of different men that had emphysema pretty bad but I've known men 90 years old smoking cigarettes, rolled their own when they was boys and continued on and they seem to work until they die. It maybe cuts their wind, it doesn't give them cancer. There's some young people in their 40s dying from heart attacks, cancer. Some of them never smoked. There's a man comes in here, he's a school teacher, he said he used to go around in a crowd with a fella who every time he see'd anyone light a cigarette, he'd knock it out of their mouth. He'd never smoked. A couple of years later he died of cancer, so there's the story. (p. 245)

No-regret smokers with more education often have more diversified ways of avoiding conflict. Maybe you can recognize some of your own rationalizations among those used by a young lawyer (Meyer et al.):

1. He rejects the relevance of impersonal statistics ("Doesn't mean anything about me . . .").
2. He pushes away or blocks out unpleasant thoughts ("I've blocked it to a point where I don't think about it . . .").
3. He invokes the right to privacy ("I think it's not a proper public issue . . .").
4. He finds fault with the way the reports are communicated. ("The statistics are not sufficiently focused and the reports are probably exaggerated").
5. He softens the warning ("I can't imagine that smoking can be good for you . . .").
6. He cites other risks ("Breathing other pollutants is bad for you . . .").
7. He invokes humor ("When they changed the warning on the pack I was more amused than anything").
8. He invokes medical authority ("One thing I've observed, nurses smoke"). (p. 245)

Not all smokers deny or minimize the hazards of smoking. Many believe the evidence linking smoking to dread diseases and yet continue smoking. A number of these smokers often experience great conflict. Meyer and his colleagues report that these smokers try to deal with their conflict by claiming some exemption from the hazards by reducing their smoking, claiming not to be "real" smokers, or stressing their lack of control over the problem. People who plan to quit in the future, who talk about the personal costs of quitting (such as becoming nervous, gaining weight), and who delay lighting up are probably trying to assuage their conflict without actually giving up cigarettes.

What can be made of all the rationalizing that people do regarding smoking? We have come to this conclusion: People would be far less inclined to rationalize if they believed they could overcome their problem. Lack of hope turns smokers away from real solutions to their dilemma. We think there is hope, and since you have read this far, you must think so too. Smoking is not an unbeatable foe. Millions of Americans are former smokers. Even if you smoke frequently, you can become a former smoker. Let's turn now to our self-management model and see how it can help you control your smoking.

Applying the model

Selecting a goal

In selecting a goal for smoking behavior, you must choose between total cessation or a gradual approach. In the first edition of this text we recommended the gradual approach because we believed that it gave

Smoking is not an unbeatable foe.

smokers a chance to experience early successes and that it was the surest, least painful way for *most* persons to quit smoking. Recent research (Flaxman, 1976; Lando, 1977), however, suggests that for some people total abstinence is the superior approach. At least one researcher (Mausner, 1971) hypothesizes that a gradual approach may increase the attractiveness of the habit; that is, reduced smoking still gets reinforced while the initial factors working to motivate quitting lose their appeal. Nonetheless, other researchers (such as Greenberg and Altman, 1976) have provided recent support for the gradual approach. What we have concluded is that different strategies are needed for different persons. We have found among our own students that those whose habits are least established are most likely to succeed with a gradual approach.[1] If you have a well-ingrained habit, you might be more successful with total abstinence. Also, if you have tried the gradual approach and failed, you need an alternative route.

Although some research supports total cessation of smoking, total abstinence does not have to begin "cold turkey." Cold turkey implies the immediate cessation of smoking without any attempt to alter the stimulation producing smoking. The probability of failure is great for those who go the cold-turkey route. The research that supports total abstinence is based on target-date quitting. That is, subjects spend time in treatment preparing to quit even while continuing to smoke. Flaxman's

[1]If you have just begun to experiment with smoking, now is the best time to confront your behavior. Most heavy smokers, including those dying of lung cancer, initially were light smokers. However, many have now reached a point in their smoking behavior from which they feel they cannot turn back.

Cold turkey – Hollywood style

In 1969 United Artists filmed the movie *Cold Turkey* in Greenfield, Iowa. You may remember that hilarious comedy starring Dick Van Dyke from its first release or from TV reruns. The plot focuses on the efforts of a small town to quit smoking for thirty days in order to win a $25 million prize. In truth, in an effort to attract new industry and to promote the movie, the town of Greenfield did try a cold-turkey approach to quitting smoking. For the effort the Greenfield town treasury received $6,000 from United Artists. August 8 was the date the town quit. Many people signed pledges to abstain from smoking, the evils of smoking and the benefits of not smoking were publicized, and Cold Turkey Day became a local holiday (even the fall opening of school was postponed). Of the town's 444 active smokers, 166 tried to quit beginning on Cold Turkey Day. Many merchants cooperated by removing tobacco from sale or sight, few people smoked in public, and a "No Smoking, Please" sign was erected on the outskirts of town. After thirty days, the antismoking campaign was relaxed. Ninety-two of those who tried quitting remained abstinent after one month, and seven months later forty-seven (28.3 percent) were still not smoking. Even under atypical, highly supportive group conditions, cold turkey proved only modestly successful.

Adapted from Ryan, F. J., 1973. Cold turkey in Greenfield, Iowa: A follow-up study. In W. L. Dunn, Jr. (ed.), *Smoking Behavior: Motives and Incentives*, New York: John Wiley and Sons., pp. 231–241.

(1976) subjects, for example, received instruction at four training sessions over a two-week period before they quit. Sessions were oriented toward helping subjects to establish new habits to replace smoking, to learn how to alter setting events, and to develop skill in the use of muscle relaxation, thought stopping, and self-reinforcement. Lando's (1977) subjects received six sessions in a one-week period prior to quitting smoking. They underwent aversive conditioning (rapid smoking) and received instruction on how to unlearn the smoking habit. Follow-up sessions over a two-month period included formal training in *contracting** and group support. So, whether you quit gradually or totally abstain, other tactics — besides merely stopping — are needed to maintain abstinence. Therefore, all the other steps in our model will be useful regardless of your approach.

Monitoring target behavior

Before beginning any treatment procedures, you should log the number of cigarettes you smoke, the amount of each cigarette smoked (that is,

*Terms set in italics and followed by an asterisk are defined in the Glossary.

one half, one quarter), and the conditions of smoking (time and place). This record will give you a much clearer picture of the extent of your problem and of the circumstances that you must change to deal with the problem. If you plan total abstinence, for example, your records will tell you where you may encounter the greatest temptations and will provide clues for how to deal with those situations. No matter which approach you take, your records will probably reveal some surprising relationships between your smoking behavior and setting events. For example, one student discovered that he smoked most frequently when driving his car.

You may find that the initial record keeping will itself alter your behavior. McFall (1970) found that students smoked less once they began monitoring their smoking. Before the students began their self-monitoring, their smoking behavior had been unobtrusively recorded by classmates. This reactive effect from self-recording probably results from your becoming more aware of your smoking behaviors. To maximize both the analytical and the reactive value of self-recording, you should be sure to take note of *all* the times and places that you smoke.

You should record not only the target behavior but also behaviors related to implementation of treatment (controlling responses). In what ways have you changed the setting events and consequences or applied covert strategies? How often have you used these strategies? Monitoring the treatment procedures and your smoking behaviors should reveal the relationship between changes in the controlling behaviors and the behavior product (number of cigarettes consumed). Furthermore, accurate record keeping will reveal the strengths and weaknesses of your treatment strategies should you need to adjust those strategies.

Changing setting events

Whether you gradually reduce your smoking or whether you try to abstain completely, you will undoubtedly want to make some changes in setting events. Let us consider first what you might want to alter as a gradual quitter. Since much smoking is impulsive, you may want to arrange circumstances that prevent you from thoughtlessly lighting up. One strategy known to reduce impulsive smoking is to change the place where you normally carry your cigarettes. If you normally put them in a left shirt pocket, switch them to the right pocket one day and to a coat pocket the next. Make it difficult to find a cigarette.

You could also try keeping your cigarettes in a case if that is unfamiliar to you, or you might deliberately not carry matches or a lighter so that you have to ask for a light each time you smoke. The objective is to alter setting events so that it becomes difficult for you to smoke without realizing what you're doing. Reducing your spontaneous smoking can help you in applying other strategies. For example, if you want to pair an aversive thought with lighting a cigarette, you must control spontaneous smoking.

Another way for the gradual quitter to change setting events is to reduce the range of stimuli associated with smoking. Think of all the stimuli with which you might associate smoking: smoking and eating, smoking and drinking, smoking and parties, smoking and conversation, smoking and studying, smoking and worrying, smoking and sex. It is no wonder that some people smoke heavily! Breaking these associations can reduce your tendency to smoke. We suggested earlier that you identify one place at work and one place at home in which to smoke. This suggestion is based on the concepts of self-control set forth by Ferster et al. (1962) and Goldiamond (1965). More recently Greenberg and Altman (1976) have found the strategy helpful in working with their clients.

Once you reduce smoking to one or two locations, you have a less intense (and probably less reinforcing) habit to break. However, reaching this point may require some programming of setting events. Sachs et al. (1970) had people rank the situations in which they would be most inclined to smoke. The subjects first gained control over the easy situations and then over the more difficult ones. The subjects could smoke if they wished, but they were to remove themselves from the specified situation (such as reading) before they smoked. The strategy substantially reduced smoking for the group.

In addition to eliminating the control that certain stimuli have over smoking behavior, you may want to create control for other stimuli. Upper and Meredith (1970) have provided an ingenious demonstration of this strategy. A smoker began by keeping a daily record of smoking behavior and computing the average baseline time between cigarettes. He then used a small portable timer, which he wore, initially setting it to buzz whenever the average time between cigarettes had lapsed. He smoked only when the timer buzzed. As you might guess, he gradually increased the intercigarette interval until his smoking was practically eliminated. You could use essentially the same approach with an ordinary watch or clock. You might initially let yourself smoke every fifteen minutes, then every thirty minutes, then on the hour, until you are smoking very infrequently. This approach not only controls your frequency of smoking but also supplants a host of cues (meals, conversation, stress) that previously elicited smoking.

If you have decided to stop smoking completely, you can focus on three types of changes in setting events. As with the gradual approach, you will want to reduce the cues that trigger impulsive smoking. Removing ashtrays, lighters, and other items associated with smoking from your home should reduce impulsive smoking. Next, you might try to avoid situations that are most frequently associated with smoking. Your records will prove invaluable here. Third, you will want to concentrate

Who could ask for more?

One of the most noble attempts to alter the stimulus value of smoking cues was reported by F. G. Musick. Mr. Musick had been inclined to follow his meals with coffee and cigarettes, and after thirty years of smoking he had a rather well-established habit. Under his self-management project, he would leave the table immediately after eating and start doing something that required physical activity. He began taking evening walks around the neighborhood. In addition, he carried a litter bag and started picking up debris along the street. As a result of his self-management efforts, he has stopped smoking, is getting his exercise, and is cleaning up the neighborhood. Who could ask for more?

Adapted from Musick, F. G. 1974. Thirty-year-smoker tells how he quit and retained his waistline. Knoxville *News-Sentinel*, March 2, p. 4.

on engaging in activities that serve as alternatives to smoking. One of our students found that playing tennis more frequently helped him reduce smoking; he found it awkward to smoke and play simultaneously. Developing some hobby never associated with smoking is an excellent strategy for would-be quitters. You might also identify some alternative activities that will provide some semblance of the oral gratification previously provided by smoking. Some people substitute stick candy, carrot sticks, toothpicks, or chewing gum for a cigarette.

Establishing effective consequences

Altering the consequences of smoking is one of the most widely used means of controlling the habit. While a variety of stimuli can be employed as consequences, the procedures fall into three categories: (1) applying aversive consequences, (2) positively reinforcing nonsmoking behavior, and (3) using a combination of aversive and positive strategies. The application of aversive consequences have included rapid smoking (Lichtenstein et al., 1973), electric shock (McGuire and Vallance, 1964), and satiation (Resnick, 1968).

Rapid smoking typically involves continuous smoking during experimental sessions supervised by a therapist. The subject might smoke rapidly, say, for twenty minutes. Rapid smoking should reduce the desire for cigarettes. If people can restrict smoking to treatment sessions, then, they come to associate smoking only with the negative consequences of rapid smoke inhalation. Since there are some medical questions (increase in heart rate, blood pressure, and carboxyhemoglobin) regarding the use of rapid smoking (Horan et al., 1977), we recommend it be tried only under the supervision of a physician.

If you choose to employ electric shock following smoke inhalation, you may want to use a portable shocker described by Wolpe (1971). With this hand stimulator, which is small enough to carry with you unobtrusively, you can administer shock immediately following an unwanted behavior. You can alter the intensity of the shock by turning a knob on the stimulator. However, even the most intense levels of shock from this device are not harmful.

A third strategy is to achieve satiation by initially increasing cigarette consumption. Marston and McFall (1971) found that having subjects smoke three cigarettes each time they smoked was effective in reducing smoking. (The three-for-one treatment also included self-recording of cigarettes smoked and several changes in setting events.) Six months later the group showed a relapse but was still below baseline. Although this process may work for you, you could find yourself smoking more than ever if it fails.

We confess our preference for positive techniques. They often involve getting support from others for desired behaviors. For example, you could contract to quit with another person, who would provide approval and tangible rewards for nonsmoking behavior. Tooley and Pratt (1967) have used this technique as a final strategy for reducing the smoking of a husband and wife. Tighe and Elliot (1967) got subjects to make a cash deposit (fifty to sixty-five dollars) and sign a behavior contract that provided for a weekly refund of a portion of their money for not smoking. Maybe you could strike a bargain with a friend who also wants to quit. This kind of commitment gives some people a strong incentive to reduce smoking, but if interpersonal contracts are unappealing to you, contract with yourself. One of our subjects altered setting events as the primary means of reducing smoking and bought phonograph records with the money he saved on cigarettes. If he failed to adhere to specified setting events, he had less money for records.

Combined strategies seem to be among the most effective. Delahunt and Curran (1976), for example, found that combining negative practice (increasing the number of cigarettes smoked while focusing on the negative aspects of smoking) and self-control strategies (such as applying self-reinforcement, breaking behavioral chains leading to smoking, instituting incompatible behaviors) was superior to the use of negative practice or self-control procedures alone. As reported earlier, Lando (1977) also found that combining self-management strategies with rapid smoking was highly effective. Lando's subjects achieved better than 75 percent total abstinence after six months.

You can apply any of the three basic approaches described above to either gradual quitting or total cessation. As a total abstainer you might begin with an aversive strategy, with a target date for quitting one or two weeks later. You can bestow rewards galore for your successes as well as

Dial-a-reinforcement

Does reinforcement for not smoking make a difference in whether ex-smokers return to smoking? Ron Dubren, a Ph.D. associated with the American Health Foundation, found that reinforcement has a significant effect on recidivism. Dubren compared the abstinence rates for two groups of recent ex-smokers; one group had access to a special phone number that they could call to hear prerecorded messages (taped reinforcement), and the other group did not have the number. Both groups had quit smoking as part of a television "clinic."

Upon follow-up one month later, the taped-reinforcement group had fewer recidivists (ten out of twenty-nine) than the nonreinforcement group (twenty-one out of thirty-two). Unfortunately, not everyone in the taped-reinforcement group used the telephone messages or the strategy might have been even more successful. Only twenty-three of the twenty-nine reported using the number at least once. The average number of calls was 8.4 per day for the twenty days the taped messages were available. A different message was available for each day. The messages contained social support for not smoking, pinpointed numerous benefits accruing with continued abstinence, and offered tips on how to maintain nonsmoking. The following portion of the taped reinforcement for Day 6 should give you a better idea of the content of the messages.

Money — did the man say money? You bet. Hi again. Did you ever stop to figure out how much you've spent on cigarettes since you started smoking? You may be amazed to discover that the staggering total comes to many thousands of dollars. Let's figure it out. An average of 60 cents a pack (and that's an underestimate) for a pack-and-a-half-a-day smoker comes to $6.30 a week. That's over $325 each year the average smoker spends on cigarettes and you know how many years you've been smoking . . . Each day you continue to not smoke, you are paying yourself off about a buck a day. . . .

One great way to turn these extra dollars into a way to help you continue your success is to figure out how to make these extra dollars visible . . .

Some people have got themselves a little bank and put away the money each day. Others put it in their locker or desk at work, or just find a nice cookie jar to keep it in. I also know people who have decided to start a Christmas club or vacation-club account at their savings bank with the extra money . . .

You don't need to dial a reinforcement in order to achieve success. You can write your own messages and read them to yourself as many times as you feel they are necessary.

Adapted from Dubren, R. 1977. Self-reinforcement by recorded telephone messages to maintain nonsmoking behavior. *Journal of Consulting and Clinical Psychology* 45, 358–360.

for maintaining record keeping and appropriate setting events. Or, as a gradual quitter, you can apply reinforcing and/or aversive strategies and let the treatment take its own course in reducing cigarette consumption.

Consolidating your gains

Many smokers endure considerable frustration and anxiety in their efforts to quit smoking only to resume the habit when they are on the brink of conquering it completely. We don't want that to happen to you. You must keep in mind that smoking isn't a single habit. It is many habits rolled into one. Over the years smoking may get associated with literally hundreds of stimuli. When you think you have control, an infrequent, forgotten association may leap up to tempt you. Some smokers report urges to smoke months, even years, after quitting. Most relapses, however, occur in the first weeks following treatment (Dubren, 1977). Therefore, we ask that you continue reinforcement for nonsmoking, along with the other techniques you are using, at least for several weeks after you've completely quit. You might find that calling a friend during times of temptation is helpful; an ex-smoker would be in the best position to provide empathy and support. Also, be sure to stay with hobbies, work, and nonsmoking-related activities.

Covert alternatives

Several covert processes have been evaluated for controlling smoking. Homme (1965) has achieved modest success with use of his coverant pairs. Tooley and Pratt (1967) used a treatment combination consisting of Homme's model, Cautela's (1970) covert sensitization, and a behavior contract to reduce smoking. This may represent the most judicious use of covert control — that is, as an adjunct to controlling the overt environment. Of the various covert approaches, Cautela's covert sensitization may offer the greatest potential for modifying smoking behavior. Using this strategy, Cautela first has his clients imagine scenes in which presmoking behavior leads to nausea. They escape from this nausea by putting down their cigarette and declining to smoke. Eventually the self-controlling response comes earlier in the sequence of presmoking behaviors:

You are at your desk working and you decide to smoke, and as soon as you decide to smoke you get this funny sick feeling at the pit of your stomach. You say to yourself, "The hell with it; I'm not going to smoke!" As soon as you decide not to smoke you feel fine and proud that you resisted temptation.[2]

In addition to imagining stomach nausea, you might include some very real social reactions in your covert sensitization imagery. More than

[2] Reprinted with permission of author and publisher from: Cautela, Joseph R. 1970. Treatment of smoking by covert sensitization. *Psychological Reports* 26, 417.

Between success and failure

An investigation of the attempts of forty-eight college students who on their own tried to quit smoking (twenty-four successfully and twenty-four unsuccessfully) uncovered some interesting differences between those who succeeded and those who didn't. Interviews with the students revealed that in comparison with the unsuccessful students, the successful subjects:

Rated themselves more motivated and committed to change

Used a greater number of techniques more frequently and consistently and for longer periods

Rated their techniques as more practical and useful

Reported receiving more positive feedback

Relied more on the use of positive reinforcement in their smoking-reduction efforts

Reported using more behavioral problem-solving models

Adapted from Perri, M. G., Richards, C. S., and Schultheis, K. R. 1977. Behavioral self-control and smoking reduction: A study of self-initiated attempts to reduce smoking. *Behavior Therapy 8*, 360–365.

ever, nonsmokers these days are speaking out when smoking is unpleasant to them. However, the vast majority of nonsmokers are probably still too unassertive to do so. Their eyes may be burning and they may be practically choking on smoke, but they may still be too "nice" to ask another person to stop smoking. In fact, most nonsmokers probably have difficulty saying no even when the smoker asks their permission to smoke. Please don't mistake silence for consent. Most of the time when you smoke in group situations, you are making life difficult for some members of that group. If you're sensitive to others' feelings, visualizing their covert reactions to your smoking should intensify the covert sensitization trials.

Some people say that they smoke in response to anxiety. Since attempts to reduce smoking may heighten that anxiety, you may have to employ the self-directed relaxation described in Chapter 3. By using this strategy you can learn to relax in situations in which you typically smoke and thus minimize an important source of internal stimulation for smoking.

Concluding thoughts

The problems of smoking and obesity have much in common: In each case millions of people experience the problem, millions avoid doing anything about it, and millions resolve it only to experience a relapse a few weeks later. As in our chapter on obesity, we have tried to present strategies that will increase your chances of confronting the problem, achieving success, and maintaining that success indefinitely. Specifically, we have discussed the rationalizations for smoking, presented two alternatives for quitting (the gradual approach and target-date approach), and offered our problem-solving model with optional strategies in each step. Still we cannot guarantee success or freedom from anxiety in your attempt to deal with a long-standing smoking habit. However, as Naifians will undoubtedly discover, we can affirm that the stakes are very high for yourself, your family, and your friends. Good self-management and good health!

References

Cautela, J. R. 1970. Treatment of smoking by covert sensitization. *Psychological Reports 26,* 415–420.

Delahunt, J., and Curran, J. P. 1976. Effectiveness of negative practice and self-control techniques in the reduction of smoking behavior. *Journal of Consulting and Clinical Psychology 44,* 1002–1007.

Dubren, R. 1977. Self-reinforcement by recorded telephone messages to maintain nonsmoking behavior. *Journal of Consulting and Clinical Psychology 45,* 358–360.

Ferster, C. B., Nurnberger, J. I., and Levitt, E. B. 1962. The control of eating. *Journal of Mathetics 1* (1), 87–109.

Flaxman, J. 1976. Quitting smoking. In W. E. Craighead, A. E. Kazdin, and M. J. Mahoney (eds.), *Behavior modification: Principles, issues, and applications.* Boston: Houghton Mifflin, pp. 414–430.

Goldiamond, I. 1965. Self-control procedures in personal behavior problems. *Psychological Reports 17,* 851–868.

Greenberg, I., and Altman, J. L. 1976. Modifying smoking behavior through stimulus control: A case study. *Journal of Behavior Therapy and Experimental Psychiatry 7,* 97–99.

Homme, L. E. 1965. Perspectives in psychology: XXIV. Control of coverants, the operants of the mind. *Psychological Record 15,* 501–511.

Horan, J. J., Hackett, G., Nicholas, W. C., Linberg, S. E., Stone, C. I., and Lukaski, H. C. 1977. Rapid smoking: A cautionary note. *Journal of Consulting and Clinical Psychology 45* (3), 341–343.

Lando, H. A. 1977. Successful treatment of smokers with a broad-spectrum behavioral approach. *Journal of Consulting and Clinical Psychology 45,* 361–366.

Lichtenstein, E., Harris, D. E., Birchler, G. R., Wahl, J. M., and Schmahl, D. P. 1973. Comparison of rapid smoking, warm, smoky air, and attention placebo in the modification of smoking behavior. *Journal of Consulting and Clinical Psychology 40*, 92–98.

McFall, R. M. 1970. Effects of self-monitoring on normal smoking behavior. *Journal of Consulting and Clinical Psychology 35* (2), 135–142.

McGuire, R. J., and Vallance, M. 1964. Aversion therapy by electric shock: A simple technique. *British Medical Journal 1*, 151–153.

Marston, A. R., and McFall, R. M. 1971. Comparison of behavior modification approaches to smoking reduction. *Journal of Consulting and Clinical Psychology 36*(2), 153–162.

Mausner, B. 1971. Some comments on the failure of behavior therapy as a technique for modifying cigarette smoking. *Journal of Consulting and Clinical Psychology 36*, 167–170.

Meyer, A. S., Friedman, L. N., and Lazarsfeld, P. F. 1973. Motivational conflicts engendered by the on-going discussion of cigarette smoking. In W. L. Dunn, Jr. (ed.), *Smoking behavior: Motives and incentives*. New York: John Wiley and Sons, pp. 243–254.

Musick, F. G. 1974. Thirty-year smoker tells how he quit and retained his waistline. Knoxville *News-Sentinel,* March 2, p. 4.

Perri, M. G., Richards, C. S., and Schultheis, K. R. 1977. Behavioral self-control and smoking reduction: A study of self-initiated attempts to reduce smoking. *Behavior Therapy 8*, 360–365.

Resnick, J. H. 1968. Effects of stimulus satiation on the overlearned maladaptive response of cigarette smoking. *Journal of Consulting and Clinical Psychology 32*, 501–505.

Ryan, F. J. 1973. Cold turkey in Greenfield, Iowa: A follow-up study. In W. L. Dunn, Jr. (ed.), *Smoking behavior: Motives and incentives*. New York: John Wiley and Sons, pp. 231–241.

Sachs, L. B., Bean, H., and Morrow, J. E. 1970. Comparison of smoking treatments. *Behavior Therapy 1*, 465–472.

Tighe, T. J., and Elliott, R. 1967. Breaking the cigarette habit: Effects of technique involving threatened loss of money. Washington, D.C.: paper presented at the meeting of the American Psychological Association, September.

Tooley, J. T., and Pratt, S. 1967. An experimental procedure for the extinction of smoking behavior. *Psychological Record 17*, 209–218.

Upper, D., and Meredith, L. 1970. A stimulus-control approach to the modification of smoking behavior. *Proceedings of the 78th American Psychological Association Convention 5*, 739–740. Washington, D.C.: American Psychological Association.

Wolpe, J. 1971. Dealing with resistance to thought stopping: A transcript. *Journal of Behavior Therapy and Experimental Psychiatry 2*, 121–125.

Chapter 6
All things in moderation:

Controlling drinking

One swallow doesn't make a summer but too
many swallows make a fall.

GEORGE D. PRENTICE

Alcohol abuse, like obesity and smoking, constitutes a major health problem in this society. Alcohol is by far our most widely abused drug.[1] Some ten million persons in the United States have a serious drinking problem. For them, drinking has reached the point where their own well being or that of others is jeopardized. In other words, alcohol abuse has become a *regular* part of their life. It is such abuse, not the use, of alcohol that concerns us. We are not abolitionists. We have no bias against those who use alcohol or against those who abstain from it. Our main concern is to assist those who want to *control* their drinking. Perhaps you are such a person.

Understanding the problem

Roadblocks to dealing with the problem

Any number of factors keep people from dealing with a drinking problem. First, many persons think that having a problem means being a skid row bum. Because college students can quickly recognize the differences between themselves and the stereotyped derelict, many assume they have nothing to worry about. The truth is that fewer than 5 percent of those categorized as alcoholics (chronic abusers of alcohol) are on skid row (*Alcohol and Health,* 1974). The remaining 95 percent or more come from all walks of life, college students not excluded. In fact, the proportion of drinkers classified as "heavy" increases from 6 percent among those with an elementary-school education to 15 percent among those who are college graduates.

Admitting to yourself or to others that your drinking is becoming a problem is another hurdle in understanding and dealing with that problem. You may fear that telling others you are trying to control your drinking will be perceived as a sign of weakness. Often, however, your friends may be relieved to hear you say, "No more for me, thank you. I'm trying to cut down." They may have already noticed the problem and your declaration will give them the opportunity to offer support, or they may be looking for a chance to manage their own drinking. In that case your declaration will be a source of encouragement for them. Finally, we have always felt that admitting a deficiency is a sign of strength, not of weakness.

The third reason that many people with a drinking problem are reluctant to admit it is because of the stigmas attached to being labeled an

---

[1] It is for this reason that our emphasis is on alcohol rather than on other drugs such as LSD or marijuana. Nonetheless, our discussions on the development of problem drinking and on strategies for change could also apply to most other drugs (except hard drugs like heroin).

alcoholic. Unfortunately, there is justification for this concern. Community attitudes toward alcoholism are not always based on a clear understanding of the problem or the ways of controlling it. Thus, some discriminations exist. A new public law (93-282), however, provides for the confidentiality and privacy of people who seek help for drinking problems. Also, not everyone who has a problem with drinking can legitimately be called an alcoholic. That term typically is applied to people who are chronic abusers. You can periodically abuse alcohol without being an alcoholic. You certainly need not label yourself an alcoholic just because you admit that you have a drinking problem.

Recognizing the problem

At this point you may be wondering whether you have a drinking problem or are developing one. There are a number of warning signals. For example, the National Institute on Alcohol Abuse and Alcoholism says that any one of the following signs may indicate a drinking problem. The more regularly any of these signs appears, the greater the possibility that you do need to take steps towards more responsible drinking (*From Program to People*, 1974, pp. 34–35.)

Gulping drinks for the effect that rapid drinking produces
Starting the day with a drink
Drinking alone, from a desire to escape reality or boredom or loneliness
Alcohol-taking behavior criticized by an employee, spouse, or others, and absenteeism or impaired job performance because of drinking
Rationalizing in regard to drinking behavior, characterized by such comments as: "I can stop any time I want to" or "I can take it or leave it."
Marked personality and behavioral change after taking one or more drinks
Frequent overdosing with alcohol or drunkenness.
Experiencing "blackouts" or alcohol-induced amnesia
The psychological impact of hangovers becoming as unpleasant as the physical effects, which leads to drinking to relieve discomfort and, thereby, perpetuates a vicious cycle: the more one drinks, the worse one feels, and the more one drinks
Requiring medical or hospital attention as a result of alcohol taking; frequent minor accidents or physical complaints

Learning to drink

Any number of theories have been offered to explain alcohol abuse and alcoholism. Some contend that these problems arise from lack of self-esteem, lack of love, traumatic experiences, or heredity. From a behavioral viewpoint, we believe that all drinking patterns — whether intelligent, abusive, or alcoholic — are learned. An individual with a drinking

The influence of culture

Drinking patterns may be influenced greatly by the cultural group to which an individual belongs. Some groups use alcohol regularly and in considerable quantity yet have few drinking problems; Italians, Orthodox Jews, Greeks, Spaniards, Chinese, and Lebanese have long histories of relatively safe drinking. These groups, however, share certain practices in their use of alcohol, according to the National Institute on Alcohol Abuse and Alcoholism *(Drinking Etiquette,* 1976, p. 4):

The children are exposed to alcohol early in life, within a strong family or religious group.
Parents present a consistent example of moderate drinking.
The beverage is viewed mainly as an accompaniment to food and is usually taken with meals.
The beverages commonly used are wine and beer.
Drinking has no moral connotation. It is considered neither a virtue nor a sin.
Drinking is not viewed as proof of adulthood or virility.
Abstinence is socially acceptable.
Excessive drinking or drunkenness is not condoned.
Alcohol use is not the prime focus for an activity.
Most importantly, there is wide agreement among members of the group on these "ground rules" of drinking.

Unfortunately, Americans hold ambivalent standards towards drinking. Some groups view it as proof of manliness or chicness; other groups respect heavy drinking and being able to "hold your liquor"; still other groups accept moderate drinking and detest drunkenness. What individuals in our society must do is to explore the influence of their family, friends, and societal groups and to select those beliefs and attitudes that seem most appropriate. Uncertainty about what is proper drinking can only create problem situations.

problem can conceivably learn to drink differently. The person who presently has no problem can control circumstances so that his drinking remains within acceptable bounds.

How do people learn to abuse alcohol? Behaviorally oriented psychologists say that abuse of alcohol is learned from the consequences that follow drinking. For example, Sobell and Sobell (1973) contend that heavy drinking is often a function of stress reduction. They discuss three potential reinforcers for drinking under stress. First, alcohol is a sedative. People who find themselves in a stressful situation can reduce the physiological components of stress by drinking, and they may become less inhibited about exhibiting pro-social behaviors (asking for a date, dancing, and expressing deep emotion), for which they are subsequently

The college beer blast may offer social rewards to the individual who is able to drink the most.

reinforced. Second, excessive drinking may lead to physical debilitation and subsequent removal from an unpleasant situation; a person escapes from the situation by literally passing out. Third, being drunk may serve as an excuse for otherwise unacceptable behavior. A person's flirtatious, aggressive, or sexual behavior may be excused on the grounds of intoxication. Reduced chastisement plus the inherent reinforcement value of these behaviors may indeed serve to strengthen drinking behaviors.

The foregoing rewards may not account for all alcohol abuse among college students. Other rewards are available in abundance. College students are frequently pressured by peers to drink. Maybe you've been put under pressure to drink excessively or have been a party to pressuring others. People who succumb to this pressure win the approval of their companions or at least get their companions off their backs. The college beer blast may offer social rewards to the individual who is able to drink the most. Some people find reinforcement in taking their friends to gaze at an array of empty beer cans accumulated from the previous night's fun. Excessive drinking may be learned at social gatherings for which nothing has been planned but an evening of drinking; having fun is thus equated with how much you drink. Excessive drinking may provide an escape from the thoughts of some academic failure. Thus, as you can see, many reinforcers are available to reward a pattern of drinking that may be highly detrimental to a person's best interests.

The eight-seconds drinker

John was the type of person who enjoyed a challenge. He'd challenge others on anything from canoe racing to rope climbing. He was the same way about drinking. He didn't feel comfortable unless he was trying to outdrink someone. One of his favorite drinking competitions was the chug-a-lug, in which he would wager a round of drinks that he could drink a can of beer faster than his opponent. John would interest others by pointing to his record time of downing a sixteen-ounce can of beer in eight seconds flat. He got lots of laughs and accolades for his antics, but he failed to realize that making a game of drinking posed a potential threat to himself and others. We don't know how many of the people John challenged developed a problem from gulping alcohol, but we would bet a few did. We know John did because he related the story to us along with other details of his drinking pattern.

Controlling drinking behavior

It is often said that for people with a drinking problem, control over drinking is impossible. The argument is that problem drinkers have a disease over which they have no control and that abstinence is the only solution. Abstinence can be a solution, but it may not be the only solution. We live in a drinking society. Some 100 million Americans take a drink occasionally. To expect abstinence from everyone with a drinking problem, most of whom live and work with others who drink without problems, is unrealistic. Furthermore, some people would be reluctant to do anything about their drinking if they felt that they could *never* take another drink.

Don't misunderstand us. We have nothing against abstinence. Millions of Americans abstain. (As a matter of fact, Jim Long usually abstains.) Our point is simply that moderate drinking may be a realistic alternative for some problem drinkers. This argument is based on the assumption that drinking patterns are learned. Evidence is mounting that even individuals with severe drinking problems can learn to drink moderately (Caddy and Lovibond, 1976; Hedberg and Campbell, 1974; Sobell and Sobell, 1976; Strickler et al., 1976). If environmental manipulation can help confirmed alcoholics alter their drinking patterns, it surely can work for you — which leads us once more to our model for self-control. Since we have already been through the model in detail in the two preceding chapters, we shall make the present analysis short. (Frankly, we are worried about stimulus satiation!)

To see ourselves as others see us

Dr. R. E. Vogler and several of his colleagues reasoned that if alcoholics saw videotapes of their own drunken behavior, they would find this experience aversive. So, as a part of treatment, Dr. Vogler and associates videotaped socially untoward and embarrassing behavior of alcoholics who had consumed up to sixteen ounces of 86-proof alcoholic beverages. The tapes were then replayed for the subject several times. During the first replay, the trainer made few comments in order to allow the subject an opportunity to record his subjective feelings. In subsequent showings the trainer focused on: (1) change in the subject brought on by drinking, (2) ways in which the intoxicated behavior seemed to be reinforced, (3) behaviors representative of alcohol abuse (such as gulping), and (4) personal problems mentioned by the subject while intoxicated. The hypothesis of Dr. Vogler's team was that videotaped playbacks might generate motivation to change, and the scheme seemed to have the intended effect. The group of alcoholics who saw the videotapes as part of their treatment showed more improvements in controlling their drinking than a similar group that had not seen tapes.

Have you ever thought about how you appear to others when you have drunk too much? If you can't videotape yourself, try observing someone else who is drunk. We can often see ourselves in other people.

Adapted from Vogler, R. E., Compton, J. V., and Weissbach, T. A. 1975. *Journal of Consulting and Clinical Psychology 43*, 233–243.

Selecting a goal

Perhaps you want to limit the amount of drinking you do to reduce stress — probably the most hazardous form of drinking behavior. Perhaps you also want to limit the occasions on which you drink. Drinking should be reserved for periods of relaxation, meals, and good cheer. Even on those occasions, drinking should not be the top recreational priority. One important goal would be to restrict the amount you drink on any one occasion. A person can have ten cocktails over the period of a week without experiencing any deleterious effects, but condensing those ten cocktails into one evening may reduce the individual to less than a fully functioning person.

Monitoring target behavior

Whatever your target, you will probably want to keep track of your daily consumption of alcohol. You could use a form similar to Figure 6.1 for recording the type of drink, amount consumed, conditions (time and place), time taken to consume the drink, number of sips, and occasion for drinking. You might also try to log the degree of intoxication. (This is

Day	Type of drink	Conditions		Time to consume the drink	Number of sips	Occasion for drinking
		Time	Place			
1						
2						
3						
4						
5						
6						
7						

Figure 6.1   Drinking record.

one of the few reactions that you may have to record after the fact.) Your record should tell you when, where, and how much your drinking behavior needs to be altered. If you find yourself drinking high-proof liquors, gulping your drinks, or drinking on all occasions (for example, to celebrate Washington's crossing of the Delaware), you will have some definite clues as to what needs changing. If your drinking is confined to wine, beer, or diluted beverages at dinner, an occasional drink with a friend, a moderate number of mixed drinks at parties, and other forms of socially accepted drinking, you probably will not need to alter your drinking at all. In addition to keeping a record of your drinking behavior, you should keep a record of the treatment procedures you are using. You should record how often you implement treatment strategies and whether they have the desired effect.

Changing setting events

There are any number of ways to alter setting events to control your drinking behavior. You could limit the type and amount of alcohol that you buy at any given time. Rather than picking up a pair of six-packs in preparation for a ball game on TV, you could buy yourself only two cans. Shop for liquor when you are not in a drinking mood so that you can limit the amount you consume when circumstances are conducive to drinking. Another way to change setting events is to limit the occasions or circumstances when you drink. This does not mean that you should always imbibe at a particular time and place; time or place could then serve as a stimulus for drinking regardless of what is happening on that occasion. You be the controller; do not permit trivial events to trigger unwanted drinking. To assist alcoholics, Strickler et al. (1976) provided a number of strategies for limiting the occasion and circumstances for drinking. You can judge for yourself which strategies would work best for you. The strategies are:

I. When, what
1. *Drink only in social settings, with other people – avoid drinking alone.*
2. *Wait until after 5:00* P.M. *before having a drink; never drink in the morning.*
3. *Drink only at mealtime or in the evening at parties.*
4. *During a meal, a glass of beer or wine is O.K.; not distilled liquor.*
5. *Distilled liquor is drunk only before a meal or at a party.*
6. *Drink only beer, wine, or mixed drinks — avoid straight drinks.*
7. *Avoid drinking when you are upset, anxious, worried, or angry. Find someone to talk to instead.*

II. How, how much
1. *Take at least 20–30 minutes to finish a drink.*
2. *Make a drink last for at least 6 sips.*
3. *Pause for a while between sips.*
4. *When you finish a drink, wait 5 minutes before starting another.*
5. *Limit yourself to 2 drinks at a meal.*
6. *Limit yourself to 2 drinks per hour at a party and less if it is a long party — say 5 drinks per 3 hours, or 6 drinks per 4 hours.*
7. *At parties eat something along with drinking.*
8. *Avoid drinking at parties more than 2 or 3 nights per week.*
9. *Learn how to say no when offered a drink or when someone tries to talk you into drinking.*
10. *If you are partying, drink an occasional glass of water or soda; it gives you something to sip while helping to space out your drinks. (p. 282)*

Establishing effective consequences

Establishing effective consequences should pose little problem for you. You should first establish effective consequences for all behaviors that contribute to the appropriate use of alcohol (the controlling behaviors). Most important, however, you should reward appropriate drinking behavior. A *token economy*,* a contract calling for exchange of benefits

*Terms set in italics and followed by an asterisk are defined in the Glossary.

A trip to the Keys

Harrison was a charming middle-aged man who had lived in France between the ages of twenty and forty. Returning to the United States, he was a professor of French for a number of years, then returned to graduate school to obtain a doctorate in education. At the time Harrison did his self-management study, he was living alone and experiencing considerable stress in his life. As a result, he had increased his late-afternoon and evening drinking to a degree that his personal health and career were being jeopardized. More specifically, he was consuming about a half a gallon (nine glasses) of wine each day.

Harrison's first step toward drinking control was to establish a schedule for drinking. During baseline, he had begun his drinking at about four o'clock in the afternoon and continued until his eight o'clock dinner and sometimes beyond. He decided at the beginning of the treatment phase to take no drink before six and to have dinner ready promptly at seven o'clock. He spaced his drinks by half an hour and took only two glasses with the meal. Inasmuch as he had several relapses during the first three weeks of treatment, Harrison reevaluated his schedule and decided that instead of going home in the late afternoon to a drink and dinner, he would go to a cafeteria and have a complete meal while reading. After dessert and coffee, his tension and urge to drink would largely have dissipated.

In addition to changing setting events, Harrison worked out some very potent reinforcement contingencies. He subtracted the number of glasses he drank each evening from the baseline average of nine. He calculated the money he saved by not drinking the additional glasses (50 cents per glass) and deposited that sum at the end of the week in a special savings account he had opened for a vacation trip with his ten-year-old son. Previously the trip had not seemed economically feasible.

At last accounting, Harrison was planning to spend the Christmas vacation in the Florida Keys with his son. When he returns he is extending the drinking schedule to include "days without."

Adapted from Elliot, H. 1977. Self-administered drinking control. Unpublished class project, University of Tennessee.

with a friend or spouse, the elicitation of support from others, enjoyable activities contingent upon nonabusive use of alcohol, or punishment (such as shock) for abuses — these techniques can contribute to control of your drinking behavior.

Consolidating your gains

Many people who have gained control over a problem behavior will slip occasionally. The dieter will overeat, the ex-smoker will light up, and the controlled drinker will become intoxicated. Such lapses should not be viewed as complete failures. This attitude could result in a total relapse.

Sobell and Sobell (1976) point out that few problem drinkers become permanent abstainers as a result of treatment. Similarly, few controlled drinkers maintain 100 percent control. Obviously, what you must strive for is more control. You should not give up on a plan simply because you have a temporary setback. As a matter of fact, a setback could serve as a signal to continue your record keeping, to get support from others, or to reestablish an earlier program. Too frequent slippage, of course, could mean that you need more reinforcement for your efforts or that you need alternative strategies. The whole idea of controlled drinking is to permit you to enjoy alcohol without abusing it. When you begin thinking less about alcohol, slipping less in your intended goals, and engaging in more nonalcohol-related activities, you will have gained substantial control over your drinking.

Covert alternatives

Covert sensitization is the principal covert strategy that has been applied to drinking behavior. It can be used in a variety of ways. For example, if you want to limit your drinking behavior to one or two drinks per occasion, you apply sensitization to visualization of the third drink. If you have ever been nauseated from alcohol, you might call upon those memories when you attempt to visualize nausea. There is some evidence (Ashem and Donner, 1968) that this covert sensitization procedure can affect drinking patterns over a period of several months.

We said earlier that one of the major reasons why people drink is to reduce stress. Anxiety about an upcoming test, about dating, or about a conference with the Dean may constitute a powerful stimulus for drinking. If your behavior records show that you usually drink when you're anxious, relaxation exercises — focusing on those situations that make you tense — should play a prominent role in your drinking control. (See Chapter 3 for a discussion of self-induced relaxation.)

Concluding thoughts

Although we have no bias against total abstinence, we feel that drinking can be a regular and problem-free dimension of your life. However, drinking to reduce stress or drinking heavily often spells definite trouble; this is the beginning of a behavior pattern that could eventually annihilate your chances for a productive life. Even though you discount the possibility of having a drinking problem (most people do), no harm would be done by recording the frequency, quantity, and circumstances of your present drinking. You might also seek some candid reactions from others as to how they perceive your drinking.

Perhaps their comments plus your behavior records will indicate the need for change. You can then try some of the strategies we have outlined in this chapter: to restrict the range of stimuli that elicit drinking behavior, to have available only certain types and quantities of liquor, to identify both tangible and social reinforcers for nondrinking behavior, to arrange for written and social reminders about your drinking responses, to learn to relax when you feel anxious, and to apply covert sensitization to the visualization of drinking activity. When any activity is engaged in excessively, it usually becomes a liability. Application of the self-management strategies described in this chapter will help problem drinkers apply the rule of moderation to their drinking, thus preventing something that can be very enjoyable from becoming a pernicious personal and social liability.

References

Alcohol and health. 1974. Washington, D.C.: U.S. Department of Health, Education, and Welfare.

Ashem, B., and Donner, L. 1968. Covert sensitization with alcoholics: A controlled replication, *Behaviour Research and Therapy 6*, 7– 12.

Caddy, G. R., and Lovibond, S. H. 1976. Self-regulation and discriminated aversive conditioning in the modification of alcoholic's drinking behavior. *Behavior Therapy 7*, 223 –230.

Drinking etiquette: For those who drink and those who don't. 1976. Washington, D.C.: U.S. Department of Health, Education, and Welfare, National Institute on Alcohol Abuse and Alcoholism.

Elliot, H. 1977. Self-administered drinking control. Unpublished class project, University of Tennessee.

From program to people: Towards a national policy on alcoholism services and prevention. 1974. Washington, D.C.: U.S. Department of Health, Education, and Welfare, National Institute of Alcohol Abuse and Alcoholism.

Hedberg, A. G., and Campbell, L. 1974. A comparison of four behavioral treatments of alcoholism. *Journal of Behavior Therapy and Experimental Psychiatry 5*, 251 –256.

Sobell, M. B., and Sobell, L. C. 1973. Individualized behavior therapy for alcoholics. *Behavior Therapy 4*, 49 –72.

Sobell, M. B., and Sobell, L. C. 1976. Second year treatment outcome of alcoholics treated by individualized behavior therapy: Results. *Behaviour Research and Therapy 14*, 195 –215.

Strickler, D., Bigelow, G., Lawrence, C., and Liebson, I. 1976. Moderate drinking as an alternative to alcohol abuse: A non-aversive procedure. *Behaviour Research and Therapy 14*, 279 –288.

Vogler, R. E., Compton, J. V., and Weissbach, T. A. 1975. Integrated behavior change techniques for alcoholics. *Journal of Consulting and Clinical Psychology 43*, 233 –243.

Chapter 7
"I am the mountain":

Involvement in physical activity

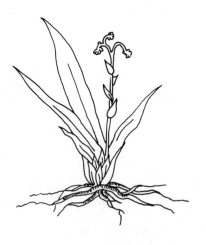

Mike said it first, somewhere up ahead, "I
am the mountain and the mountain is me!"
That cry became our song . . .

When Mike first suggested the four-mile run up the mountain to the Ramsey Cascade Falls, I couldn't believe how I responded. My mouth said, "Hey, that sounds like a great idea," while the rest of me said, "This is absolutely insane." It wasn't as if I were intimidated by running, for Mike and I had run together often. We had loped in the wee hours of the morning. We had sloshed through the snow. We had sprinted at dawn, at dusk, in packs, and alone. We had run fast and slow and a long, long way, but we had never run four miles up a hill to see water splashing over a rock!

The day proved monumental! I had forgotten the freshness of the mountain air in the early morning. I had forgotten the melody of the stream as it resonates against the solitude of the lush silent forest. And I had forgotten how it felt to be free — unencumbered by dreaded deadlines, boring books, stuffy classrooms, hostile people, grey cement, meaningless rules, latest fashions, sophisticated airs, and empty roles. By damn, we were alive and we ran.

We laughed! We screamed! We danced! We went crazy! Ever up the Mother Mountain we charged, defiant of her, until we were humbled by her awesome power and her gentle beauty. At first we cursed the pain she gave us, but as our boundaries diffused, and the blood pumped wildly through our bodies, we became engulfed by her spirit. Mike said it first, somewhere up ahead, "I am the mountain and the mountain is me!" That cry became our song as stride after stride we fought to open the shell which contained the pearl. The falls — the top . . . the pearl is expensive.

But the pearl is also delightful. We stood on the mountain top and gaped in wonder at the sights, sounds, and silence which flooded our senses. It was holy ground upon which we had earned the right to tread. We stood naked under the refreshingly cold falls and felt a kinship with all who had dared to shrug the inhibitions of the uptight, fearful, and unimaginative "civilized" world. It was all right to be alive, to be what our senses knew was good and real.[1]

What does this charge up the mountainside suggest concerning human nature? Perhaps that we can still appreciate natural beauty, that we need experiences far removed from the daily routine, and most of all that our bodies are designed to be active. The human heart and lungs, as well as the large skeletal muscles, were designed for something more than sedentary living. An earthworm is physiologically better suited than a woman or man to sit behind a desk all day, crawl into a car to get home, and lounge in front of a television set all evening. A human being must

[1]Terry Howell, the editorial consultant for this chapter, has provided this description of his mountain sojourn. Terry is now teaching at the University of Tennessee, Chattanooga, and is an avid practitioner of physical fitness.

move, work, and play. A failure to engage in such activity may produce both physical and psychological problems. We are including a chapter on physical activity not only because of these problems, but because we believe sports activity can provide moments of quality and a lifetime of pleasure.

Benefits of physical activity

Since the human body appears to be designed for vigorous activity, how is it affected by regular physical exercise? Of all the body organs, the heart and lungs appear to be affected most dramatically. The coronary arteries leading to the heart increase in size, additional capillaries develop around the heart, the heart forces more blood through the body with each beat, and it rests longer between beats (Akchin, 1977). Thus, the heart rate of a physically fit person is considerably lower in a resting state than is that of an unfit person. Over time, the acceleration in respiratory activity during exercise causes the lungs to work more efficiently, that is, with each breath to provide more oxygen for body tissues. Consequently, the breathing rate of a well-conditioned person is slower and more rhythmical than that of an unfit person.

In addition to your heart and lungs, your excretory and digestive systems also benefit from regular exercise (Michener, 1976). Elimination of waste through the skin, lungs, intestines, and kidneys is facilitated by exercise. The muscle system involved in digestion is stimulated by vigorous activity, leading to better digestion and less constipation. In fact, most of the abdominal and pelvic organs function better when the abdominal muscles are in good condition.

Participation in sports can also enhance your self-image. For example, Vincent (1976) found that female physical education majors attained higher self-concept scores than did other females. The weight control and muscle tone resulting from sports activity can produce real changes in physical appearance, which eventually will lead to changes in self-perceptions. Vigorous activity should also awaken you to aspects of your body that sedentary living may leave undiscovered. Part of this awareness comes from experiencing your body in motion. Movement sharpens your body image, while sleep and inactivity dull that image (Harris, 1972). Movement helps you to understand *that* you are, which is a prerequisite to knowing *who* you are. One of the more depressing facets of old age is the loss of body awareness resulting from immobility.

Sports activity can even have a positive emotional impact. An investigation at the University of Florida (Barger, 1968) found athletic activity to be the major avenue of stress relief for male students. The impact of

An inside view

Have you ever thought what it would be like to look into a magical mirror and see yourself without any skin? Probably not, and we can't blame you! Nevertheless, it might be a sobering experience for you. You might see things that would encourage you to alter your life style quite drastically.

Recently, Terry Howell told us of his reaction to seeing open-heart surgery for the first time. He was shocked by the enormous amount of fat revealed when the patient's chest was opened. He had noted earlier that the patient was only ten to fifteen pounds overweight for his height. Terry vividly described what he saw inside this person's body: "The fat was a pale, ugly yellow and was everywhere. Layers of it covered every organ in sight. Enveloping the muscles and organs were large connecting sacs of the substance. Piled on top of these were smaller sacs, looking like cells under a microscope." A person who works in open-heart surgery every day told Terry that the larger the sac and the deeper the sac within the body, the older the fat was. This patient had some predating World War II.

Though Terry was already an advocate of physical fitness, the experience profoundly affected him. He commented: "This operation made me realize that fat is right here," pointing to his chest, "under my skin; I may look O.K. on the outside, but there are layers of ugly, useless fat hanging on and slowing down all of my vital organs." He was seen that evening running a few additional laps around the track!

sports activity on emotionality has been most conclusively demonstrated by Ismail and Trachtman (1973). They found that four months of exercise (jogging and other athletic activity) significantly enhanced the emotional stability of middle-aged males who previously had been in poor condition. Though sports activity will not replace individual or group therapy during emotional crises, it can help mild depression, boredom, and the blues. Sports can change attitudes by giving you something to look forward to and by bolstering self-confidence. One student noted, "After conquering two miles on the track each morning, which is sometimes tough, I feel I can tackle anything that comes along the rest of the day." While some people look to drugs and alcohol to get high or to escape from the pressure of daily living, we invite you to partake of the natural "high" that sports can provide.

Physical activity may affect mental productivity. The research on this point is still inconclusive, but it appears increasingly likely that there is a connection between physical and mental functioning. Kleinman (1975) says, "In spite of the fact that many of the principles are not fully understood, sufficient evidence exists to support the contention that there is a relation between movement and ideational learning" (p. 23). Ismail et al.

(1969) believe "the evidence points to a positive relationship between some motor aptitude items, especially coordination and balance, and well established measures of intelligence and scholastic ability" (p. 91). Ismail and Trachtman (1973) report that extended periods of physical activity may stimulate the imagination. That physical exercise would enhance mental productivity is not an unreasonable physiological possibility. Exercise increases circulation to the brain, which in turn increases the quantity of glucose available for the brain's nutrition. Of course, we are not suggesting that doing fifty push-ups this afternoon will constitute adequate preparation for tomorrow's midterm exam!

The social payoffs for participating in sports are significant. Few activities provide more opportunities for meeting new people and for establishing friendships. Social interaction comes easily and naturally in the atmosphere of sports. Ismail and Trachtman suggest that sports participation can substantially improve social relationships even among old acquaintances. Discussing new techniques and acquiring new skills together can add an enriching dimension to practically any existing relationship. So if your social life is dull, consider sports as an avenue to rejuvenation. Warren (1970) says that sports may be the ideal setting for the "meeting" that, according to Martin Buber (1958), is *the* goal of all human experience.

Beyond these important benefits, sports activity provides a great deal of intrinsic reinforcement. The exhilaration that comes from rapid movement or from the correct execution of a skill usually intensifies as you progress in a sport. In the first place, your physical condition improves, allowing you to move vigorously. Also, your movements in a sport become more coordinated as a result of practice. Participation in sports can evolve into a genuinely aesthetic experience. This dimension is far more likely to emerge in some sports than in others. Aesthetic satisfaction can probably be found more readily on the basketball court than at the bottom of a football pile-up. However, aesthetic appeal varies with different value systems. The point is that experiencing rhythm and grace in your own movements can be a principal reinforcer for sustaining involvement in sports activity.

This intrinsic aesthetic satisfaction is sometimes called *flow*. In his article "The Fun in Fun," William Furlong (1976) says, "When we get totally immersed in a sport or creative act, we lose sense of time and the external world. Instead, we experience flow, the ecstatic feeling that everything is going just right" (p. 35). To feel light on your feet, to seem to float through the air, your body automatically responding to the myriad situations you encounter — the process of sports can be more meaningful than the end product. This sense of satisfaction gives new meaning to the old adage, "It's not whether you won or lost, but how you played (flowed with) the game."

The flow experience

Flow begins with total absorption in an activity. You may be oblivious to your surroundings and unaware of your past and future. You are living in the *now* and your awareness is centered on the immediate activity. Within that activity your focus is solely on what's happening at the moment. For example, as you prepare to catch the ball, you're not concerned about past catches or misses or even about the consequences of your current actions. Only you and the ball exist at that point and you are in total control of the situation. Although flow involves intense concentration on what is happening from moment to moment, you do not have to try to concentrate, nor are you aware of your concentration.

People experiencing flow typically have an altered sense of space and time. The ball may seem larger and appear to move more slowly than usual. On ordinary days people may feel rushed in executing many of the movements in a sport, but on a "flow" day they will have ample time to perform the same motions. Baseball players in hitting streaks report that they see the ball better because it seems so much larger and seems to move more slowly. There are times in sports when a moving ball appears virtually motionless.

People in flow lose a sense of distinction between themselves and the activity. Tennis players may feel that they are traveling with the ball. Mountain climbers may experience a oneness with the mountain. In flow, people may experience boundless energy to the point of almost gliding through the air, yet they are relaxed and at peace with themselves. They have no concern about how well they're doing or about the outcome of the venture. In fact, they may know the outcome of their actions even before they act. Skilled tennis players will know that they have made a good shot at the moment they hit the ball. People in flow will know that they have made a good shot *before* they hit the ball.

Adapted from Furlong, W. B. 1976. The fun in fun. *Psychology Today 10*, 35–38.

Sports provide a great opportunity for you to enhance your creativity. This may seem odd when you consider that most sports have a definite set of techniques that are correlated with success. Be that as it may, these techniques evolved through experimentation with body movements. Creative people learn the existing techniques and then add their own individuality. Basketball has never been the same since Hank Luisetti introduced the one-handed jump shot. The "Fosberry Flop," which revolutionized the high jump, was named for a man who knew the right way but did it his own way. The same could be said of Chris Evert's two-handed backhand, Olga Corbett's crowd-stunning back flip on the balance beam, and a multitude of other innovations by creative

143

The creative descent

Running downhill was no less monumental. We ran with reckless abandon. It was a dance of strides and jumps — over this log, around that bend, onto the flat rock through the trickle of water. Ever darting, weaving, ducking, floating, we were pulled on by gravity. With the ease of a gazelle we ran through the trees, down the mountainside. And then we saw it! About halfway down, past the bright orange mushroom and ahead of the smell of sweetgum stood the largest oak we had ever seen. We were convinced that tree had seen the founding of this nation. Beside its strong, massive, and towering trunk, our physical status seemed minuscule. We were exhausted and had reached an ecstasy only achieved by intense physical involvement. In our heightened state we named the oak Thor. We hugged that old tree while our lungs heaved for air, and we promised to return on another day to pay tribute again.

Down, down, forever down, until the splash of water at our feet told our boggled senses we were where we had begun. We dove in the stream which below us was being destroyed by progress. We drank the clear ambrosia which mercifully massaged our used-up limbs. We laughed. Then we said nothing. Silence. I was sitting in a pool of water on the edge of the stream when Mike first noticed the butterfly. She was black with deep royal-blue wings. She flew around my head, landed on my chest, and looked up at me. Hello. I told her she was beautiful. Mike said, "She knows what we did today. She understands the meaning." She then gently lifted from my chest and delicately placed a kiss on my nose. I fell in love . . . .

Terry Howell. A continuation of the introduction.

individuals in the sports world. It is exhilarating to progress toward the correct execution of a skill. At the same time, experimenting with body movements can lead you to a new and even more refined way of accomplishing tasks involved in sports.

Barriers to participation

Despite the significant extrinsic and intrinsic payoffs from vigorous physical activity, many adults do not practice it on a regular basis. Many believe that play is for children and that adulthood is the time to put away childish things. These people are so serious about everything that they lose their spontaneity and vigor. They tend to become quite dull and boring. It is not long after they become an "adult" that their day is filled with complaints, gripes, and cynical comments. They are the wet blankets of society and want everyone else to be as miserably "adult" as they

Participating in sports activity makes many achievement-oriented adults uneasy because it takes time from their work.

are. Do not expect these people to shoot the rapids in a white-water raft with you. They will laugh at you, call you childish, and go back to watching their favorite "adult" soap opera, "As the Stomach Turns."

Others view sports as the antithesis of fun and play. They are intimidated by the "work" that they see in physical activity. In recent years, most Americans have been exposed to extensive television coverage of athletic events, such as the Olympic Games, in which commentators describe the rigorous training procedures that athletes undergo. Thus, when some people contemplate physical conditioning, they envision themselves gasping for breath, regurgitating, writhing in physical pain, and experiencing muscular aches and spasms. Knowing that such is not to their taste, they get their exercise from raising their fork to their mouths at dinner and sliding their overweight bodies out of an easy chair in time for a midnight snack before going to bed. These people rarely stay with us long enough to give the eulogies for their more active friends.

Participating in sports activity makes many achievement-oriented adults uneasy because it takes time from their work. In dealing with this issue, we have come to think in terms of total living time. Other factors being equal, the individual who stays in good physical condition will live longer and more fully than the individual who does not. Taking an hour a day for vigorous physical activity will probably result in more total time for your career. In addition, time devoted to work is not the only variable that affects productivity. People obviously attack their work more energetically on some occasions than on others. Looking forward to sports activity following a segment of work can affect the zest with which you do that work. If you have tennis planned for a specific hour in the afternoon, you are far more likely to be productive up to that hour. Some people work better *after* a period of invigorating physical activity. Whatever your preference, you will often find that you can accomplish just as much by taking an hour a day for sports activity as by working an uninterrupted twelve-hour day.

Most inactive adults will admit that physical activity is a good thing. In fact, most of these people intend to become active very shortly — perhaps as early as next week. However, next week proves to be very elusive. They sincerely believe that they should exercise but continue to live in the future. They really think they will begin next week, but they fail to realize that the present is the only time to start anything. They don't have enough self-management skills to translate their intentions into reality.

The role of self-management

Whether you are bored, depressed, overweight, overworked, clumsy or graceful, lazy or energetic, athletic or nonathletic, married or single, young or middle-aged or a senior citizen, sports involvement can enrich your life. Sports participants represent a cross-section of age, economic status, and physical ability. They have learned that incorporating physical exercise into their daily experience can give them many moments of quality and an entire lifetime of pleasurable activity. Sports have become an integral part of their way of life. If you are not a member of the "involved" group, we hope our self-management approach to sports will allow you to join us, now!

Selecting a goal
A balanced exercise program will lead to increases in endurance, strength, and flexibility (Akchin, 1977). Of these three, endurance is the most indispensable to good health because it produces changes in the heart and lungs. Strength and flexibility are not so basic to survival as is physical endurance, but they often prevent the immobilizing injuries that plague the endurance seeker. Pulled muscles, strained backs, and sore knees and elbows are very likely to result from endurance activities unless you have adequate strength and flexibility.

As you recall from Chapter 2, a fundamental dimension of goal setting is the distinction between product and process. In this context, the most important product goals relate to changes in body structure and function, such as your weight, size of your waistline, circumference of your

146

biceps, your pulse rate after ten minutes of vigorous exercise, and your ability to assume a full lotus position. You should identify body-related goals that will encompass changes in endurance, strength, and flexibility. Other product goals relate to the performance of an activity, such as number of miles run, number of toe touches or sit-ups done, number of free throws made, and number of games won. Like your body-related goals, these performance goals should also encompass endurance, strength, and flexibility.

Product goals are essential, but in any exercise program you must initially emphasize process goals. Processes are the behaviors you exhibit to achieve a desired outcome, such as running on your toes, breathing rhythmically while running, getting in position to shoot the basketball, watching the goal while shooting, and following through after releasing the ball. These are the types of behaviors that will eventually enhance product. However, if you focus on product goals from the very beginning (on number of games won or the number of tennis serves in the court), you could seriously undermine your progress in a sport. You might be inclined to avoid difficult process behaviors that are necessary for improved play.

Defining your initial targets in terms of process behaviors could become a rather detailed undertaking. Many behaviors that are generally treated as discrete units are actually *chains* of smaller behaviors. Stroking a tennis ball may involve turning to run to the ball, getting your racket back, running to the ball, getting your feet set, bending your knees, watching the ball, keeping your front shoulder down, and swinging through the ball. Failure to hit a ball properly could result from a disruption of any link in this chain. Unless beginning players receive some preliminary instruction in a sport, they will have major problems in delineating appropriate behavioral chains. For example, if you've never played tennis, you will not know what specific behaviors constitute the chains that are called forehands, backhands, and serves.

Monitoring target behavior

Although a straight frequency count is probably the most usable type of self-recording in sports activity, a simple count of the number of times a response occurs can present a deceptive picture of how you're doing. The opportunities for a particular behavior may vary markedly from day to day. If this is the case, you should log occurrences of the behavior plus opportunities for that behavior. You can then calculate the percentage of times a specific behavior occurred when it should have occurred. This approach is equivalent to computing batting averages in baseball or shooting percentages in basketball.

In order to interpret your frequency data correctly, you should also record playing conditions. A windy day will affect your skills in tennis, a

What's your heart rate?

One response that you should monitor very closely in your exercise routine is heart rate — to insure that you're putting enough pressure on your body but not too much. You can use heart rate as a criterion for determining the appropriate intensity of a workout. The following procedure is one for computing your target heart rate during an exercise period.

1. Subtract your age from 220. The resulting number is your assumed maximum heart rate.
2. Measure your resting heart rate and subtract it from your assumed maximum heart rate. This will give you your range of heart rates.
3. Multiply the range by 60 percent.
4. Then add this figure to the resting heart rate to give you your target heart rate for exercise activity.

Example:
1. 220
   $\underline{-40}$ (years of age)
   180 (assumed maximum heart rate)

2. $\underline{-65}$ (resting heart rate)
   115 (heart rate range)

3. x   .60
   $\overline{69.00}$

4. $\underline{+65}$
   134 (target heart rate)

It is recommended that you not exceed your target heart rate during exercise periods. A good workout would involve a ten-minute warm-up period, fifteen to twenty minutes of continuous activity at target-rate level, and five minutes of tapering off to allow excessive blood to flow out of the muscles.

Adapted from Kuntzleman, C. T. 1977. Fitness considerations — The physiological. *The Journal of Physical Education 74*(4), 80–82.

muddy field will affect your skills in football, and choppy water will affect your skills in water skiing. Unless you record these conditions, you may incorrectly assume that your skills have regressed — when in reality you have performed better than the last time you encountered such conditions.

When self-monitoring your performance under game conditions, you must examine the contextual appropriateness of your behaviors. You must pose two questions about each situation: (1) Was the correct skill attempted? (2) Was the skill performed correctly? When your performance goes awry, it may be that the skill was well executed but inappropriate for that situation. On the other hand, you might have selected the right skill but executed it poorly. Unless you can answer these questions, you may try to change the wrong dimension of your behavior. You may be attempting to refine your waltzing while the band is playing a fox trot.

Changing setting events

Identifying sports activities   We say activit*ies* because it is unlikely that any one activity will lead to the changes in endurance, strength, and flexibility that you want. The major consideration in choosing sports activities is their effect upon body structure and functioning, but there are other important considerations, such as expense, accessibility, time involved, and number of participants required. Scaling Pike's Peak with a group of experienced mountain climbers may provide exhilaration and exercise, but it's hardly as accessible and inexpensive as playing badminton in the back yard. Table 7.1 should help you in choosing a range of activities that would be beneficial, attractive, and accessible to you. Two activities not described in this table that would be great for flexibility are yoga and ballet.

Identifying a playing period   If you have a specified number of hours per week to devote to physical activity, should you divide that time into several short periods, or a few extended periods? That depends, first of all, on the time you must invest in getting prepared to play (travel time, waiting). If preparation time is negligible, more frequent playing periods are preferable. Scheduling six one-hour blocks of physical activity is ordinarily wiser than scheduling two three-hour blocks. The shorter, more frequent activity periods are superior for both exercise value and skill acquisition. Furthermore, fatigue tends to undermine your effective use of time in lengthy practice sessions, and it can so completely undermine your skills that you leave the session feeling that you have regressed. As you will see in the next section, it is imperative that you leave a playing session feeling good about the experience. If your overall work schedule permits only longer periods of play, practice a variety of skills during each playing session. According to Rushall and Siedentop (1972), fatigue is less likely to be a debilitating factor if you intermittently practice different skills than if you single-mindedly focus on the same skill.

Choosing a playing partner   One important setting event is the person or persons with whom you play. You have undoubtedly heard that you should play with someone who is better than you in order to maximize your progress. Though that is partially correct, a person can be so much better than you that your skills are rendered nonfunctional. For example, a highly skilled tennis player may hit the ball so hard or place it so

Table 7.1
Exercise comparisons

Here are some of the benefits — and disadvantages — of eight of the more popular forms of physical activity.

Activity	Benefits	Disadvantages	Warnings
Jogging	Excellent conditioner for endurance, lung and heart capacity. Builds leg strength. Equipment inexpensive, requires no special facilities.	Requires preliminary start-up program. Does nothing for flexibility or strength (except legs). Tightens muscles in back of leg and calf, shortens Achilles' tendon.	Persons 30 and older should have a physical examination first. Wear good running shoes. Watch out for dogs.
Walking	Good beginning exercise, especially for people out of shape. When done briskly, maintains heart and lung capacity. No equipment or facilities needed.	Walking speed of 5–6 miles per hour necessary for conditioning effect on heart.	Don't expect fast results from walking alone.
Swimming	Excellent conditioner for endurance. Exercises virtually all muscles in body. Especially suitable for persons recovering from hip, knee, or ankle problems. Considered best all-around exercise.	Requires a body of water.	Do not swim alone.
Tennis	Excellent for body shaping, flexibility, and agility. May develop endurance if played vigorously. Strengthens arm muscles.	Requires a court and an opponent. Equipment and accessories moderately expensive. Activity is sporadic. Only improves endurance if players run for the balls; doubles play does not develop endurance.	May cause anxiety in players who worry about their game.
Cross-country skiing	Perhaps best sport for developing endurance. Develops arm and shoulder muscles. Injuries less common than in downhill skiing.	Requires preconditioning program to develop muscles. Requires snow and proper terrain. Moderate equipment costs.	Be prepared for cold and high altitude.

Table 7.1 *continued*

Activity	Benefits	Disadvantages	Warnings
Calisthenics	Good for flexibility and muscle tone. Good warm-up for other activities. No equipment necessary.	Boring. Does not develop endurance unless done very vigorously.	
Bicycling	Develops endurance if done vigorously. Develops leg and back muscles. Can see scenery while exercising.	Only builds endurance if done vigorously. Moderate equipment cost. Will not give maximum benefit to muscles in legs, ankles, and foot unless leg is fully extended when pedal is at bottom of circle.	Use a bicycle path if possible. Watch out for cars if not possible.
Weight training	Excellent for developing muscular strength. Can enhance performance in other athletic activities, including volleyball, basketball, and golf. Can be done at home with homemade or low-cost equipment.	Does not aid flexibility or endurance. Lifting heavy weights narrows blood vessels in muscles and reduces circulation. Advanced weight-lifting requires access to gymnasium.	Start light; start slowly; warm up first. May be hazardous to persons with tendency toward high blood pressure.

SOURCE: Reprinted with the publisher's permission from "I Was a 49-Pound Weakling" by Don Akchin which appeared in *Insider: Ford's Continuing Series of College Newspaper Supplements* © 1977 13-30 Corporation.

well that you cannot hit it at all. Such an arrangement would be reinforcing to neither party. It is best to seek a playing partner who is at approximately your level of skill and who shares your commitment to the sport. If you can find partners who not only want to improve their game but also want to help you improve your game, you have the optimal pairing for enjoyment and improvement. Surprisingly, feedback from inexperienced players may be as accurate as that from skilled performers (Osborne and Gordon, 1972). Therefore, it is important to find a playing partner who is willing to give you this kind of input.

Practicing alone   You do not need a playing partner to practice many sports skills. In fact, some skills can be practiced alone better than under game conditions. For such activities as shooting a basketball, stroking a tennis ball off a wall, and serving a tennis ball, independent practice gives you more opportunities to execute the skill than game conditions do. Independent practice also lets you keep playing conditions more consistent than you could under game conditions. This consistency is especially important when you first begin learning a skill. For example, it's very difficult to refine your tennis stroke when the ball is coming back to you in multitudinous ways. A wall will give you a more constant return than would an inexperienced playing partner. A ball machine would be even better than a wall, but most people cannot afford such luxuries.

Establishing effective consequences

Although much of the reinforcement for participating in athletics will evolve quite naturally from the activity itself, natural reinforcement is not inevitable. We all know about the man who eagerly goes out to play golf but ends up wrapping the clubs around a tree — or at least feels that his game has deteriorated. This sense of frustration can be overcome. The major objective of this section is to describe procedures for maximizing the reinforcement value of athletic participation while minimizing its frustration potential.

Winning as a payoff   Our initial recommendation is that you *not* make winning the principal payoff for playing. Although it's nice to win now and then, there are other, more fundamental payoffs for athletic participation. If you make winning the primary reason for playing, you achieve your reinforcement at another's expense. You feel good because you won, but the other person feels bad because of losing. Emphasis on winning can also impede your progress in a sport. It can keep you from practicing skills that would eventually lead to a higher level of play. Winning is also too much of a one-shot kind of reinforcement. Normally the winner is declared only at the conclusion of the game. A primary purpose of sports is to experience reinforcement while you play. So the question is: How do you approach a sport in order to experience reinforcement during play rather than at the conclusion of the game?

Exercise as a payoff   Participation in sports should involve two major objectives — exercise and execution of skills. As we previously indicated, the preferred sports are those that allow you to get lots of exercise quickly (see Table 7.1). We do not discount the therapeutic value of an afternoon on the golf course. The serenity of the setting undoubtedly enhances the reinforcement quality of this experience. However, you should not count on golf for keeping in good physical trim. In contrast, paddleball, although played in a much less picturesque setting than golf, can exhaust you in thirty minutes.[2] Many sports can be played as either singles or doubles. You will get more exercise and develop your skills more rapidly if you choose singles.

No matter how badly you play a game, vigorous exercise can still make that activity worthwhile. Unfortunately, when things go badly some people stop trying. They sulk, feel sorry for themselves, and curse the gods. These reactions will tend to accentuate their poor play. They give up trying the difficult movements in the sport and retreat into a half-hearted participation.

There will be days when your muscular coordination simply is not so sharp as it is on other days. You can't eliminate this problem, but you can control whether or not you try the difficult shots, and you can control the pace of your movements between shots. If you can control these behaviors, you can still get a great deal of exercise even when you're not playing well. There will be days when your primary satisfaction will come from being able to say, "I'm really playing hard," rather than, "I'm really playing well."

If you have some way to determine the amount of exercise you get, you can be more exact in reinforcing yourself for vigorous physical activity. A devise that may be useful in this respect is a pedometer, an instrument about the size of a stopwatch that clips onto your belt or pocket. While pedometers are generally used to measure mileage run, they can also be used to differentiate vigorous from mild activity.[3]

Skill execution as a payoff   The second major objective of participation in sports is skill execution. Most sports activity naturally provides some feedback as to how well you're doing. Rushall and Siedentop (1972) refer to this feedback as *intrinsic information feedback*. You can readily determine whether or not you hit the ball over the net, in the court, or in the hole. This kind of feedback affects your future attempts at that behavior. Skills that can be evaluated in terms of accuracy (whether you rounded all of the flags on a slalom course, whether the ball went through the hoop) usually give you enough intrinsic feedback to improve your skills on your own.

However, some sports activities such as gymnastics and dancing initially provide little intrinsic feedback, thereby making external feedback

---

[2]Kozar and Hunsicker (1963) have found that handball, paddleball, tennis, and badminton produce essentially the same mean and the same peak heart rates during thirty-minute workouts. Volleyball and bowling produce significantly lower heart rates.

[3]A pedometer can be purchased from several companies (for example, Amsterdam Company, Amsterdam, New York 12010 and Hoffritz Company, 20 Cooper Square, New York, New York 10003) for approximately ten dollars.

fundamental to improvement. Even in sports that give you a great deal of intrinsic feedback, external feedback is valuable. If you depend on intrinsic feedback alone, you may develop responses that will later severely limit your performance. As we have already suggested, improving your skills requires that you focus more on process behaviors than on behavioral products. Although you can make some on-the-spot judgments about process behaviors ("Did I lean too far forward on the ski?" "Did I decelerate at the proper time?"), external feedback will give you a more comprehensive evaluation of your performance.

One of the best ways to get external feedback is to use videotapes of your performance. A videotape can give you immediate and accurate feedback about your responses — feedback that can be very useful in adjusting those responses. Videotape feedback is most useful in sports that provide little intrinsic feedback, especially sports in which form is exceedingly important, such as gymnastics, horseback riding, archery, fencing, and slalom skiing. An important question with respect to videotaping is whether external visual feedback can be translated into *internal kinesthetic feedback*.* Robb (1966) found that concurrent visual feedback (feedback immediately after the behavior occurred) was the most effective kind of feedback in altering arm-movement patterns. She also found that once a skill was established by means of visual feedback, it could be accurately judged and regulated through internal cues. DeBacy (1970) has shown that golfers who have seen videotapes of their golf swings can more accurately self-assess their swings when videotape replays are no longer provided than they could before such were provided.

Consolidating your gains

There is probably no sphere of human activity that is more self-sustaining once you've securely established your involvement than is sports activity. You may need carefully programmed setting events and artificially arranged payoffs in the beginning, but eventually the inherent payoffs take over. We've had several inactive students who undertook exercise projects to satisfy requirements in our courses but who still engage in regular sports activity years after the courses have ended. Their involvement continued because of the aesthetic satisfaction of top physical conditioning and of flowing, coordinated movement in their chosen sport(s). For these students physical activity has become a regular and exhilarating part of each day's schedule.

Despite the unique beauty that sports add to your life, two hazards may undermine long-term sports participation. There may be a period of incapacitation (due to illness, accident, emotional problems, or work pressures) during which you lose the momentum built up over a period

*Terms set in italics and followed by an asterisk are defined in the Glossary.

Have you considered water jogging?

For approximately thirty years, Mike Castronis had jogged one to three miles and played basketball each day. However, several years ago he began developing osteoarthritis in both knees. Eventually he could neither straighten nor flex his left leg. He attempted to continue his exercise routine but the pain eventually became intolerable. He was left with continuous pain and a decided limp. He tried several special exercises, both to strengthen the knees and to maintain cardiovascular conditioning, but his condition continued to deteriorate.

While walking in the pool area one day, he was reflecting on the fact that exercising the thigh muscles is one of the most efficient ways to achieve cardiovascular conditioning; this is because of the many large blood vessels located in the thighs. If there was only some way to exercise his thighs without putting pressure on his knees! Then the insight came. While standing in waist-deep water, he tried to simulate running. As he vigorously pumped both legs and arms, he began to notice a lessening of the pain. Since the water was supporting a substantial portion of his body weight, much of the pressure was removed from his knees. After fifteen minutes of strenuous water jogging, he found that his heart rate came very close to what he would achieve by jogging two miles.

From that day on, water jogging became Mike's major daily exercise. He was able to participate in this activity without the slightest pain. Within a year and a half both his pain and his limp had completely disappeared. At the last accounting, he was once again running and playing basketball without discomfort but was continuing to water jog for ten minutes a day.

If an injury should prevent you from engaging in the sports activity of your choice, you can probably devise another activity that entails some of the movements of your favorite sport and allows you to regain a high level of cardiovascular conditioning. In such an eventuality, your creative potential would be at a premium.

Adapted from Castronis, M. 1976. Jog in the pool — no pain! *The Journal of Physical Education* 74(1), 8ff.

---

of years. If a sport has lots of aesthetic appeal, rather than simply being a rigorous way to get exercise, you will very likely return to it after a period of abstinence. However, if the inherent appeal is not sufficient to get you reinvolved, don't hesitate to go back to a basic analysis of setting events and external reinforcement contingencies to reactivate your sports participation.

Another hazard that can sidetrack your participation in a sport is a period of extremely poor play — what athletes call a slump. We suspect that everyone who has ever played anything has gone through some difficult periods when rhythm is greatly diminished and when the body will not do what it formerly did effortlessly. Some people respond to slumps by working even harder. If in the course of that hard work you carefully analyze the process behaviors you exhibit, you may be able to transcend the slump. However, hard work may generate additional muscular tension, thus adding further to your coordination problem. Other individuals assume that the slump represents a permanent diminution of their skills and consequently give up the sport.

We have found that the best way to deal with a slump is temporarily to focus our attention on physical activities in which we are less emotionally involved. If you participate in several sports activities, you can turn to other activities when you're performing very poorly in your major sport. Such a course will keep you in good physical shape, dissipate some of the muscular tension associated with your major sport, and help you achieve a healthier balance in your sporting outlook — that is, help you see that what is most important in sports activity is physical conditioning and enjoyment, not the precision with which you perform a particular set of skills.

Covert aides

There are few areas in which we have used covert verbalizations more extensively than in sports. In learning new skills or attempting to re-establish old skills, we spend a lot of time talking to ourselves. Just before we execute a behavior, we say to ourselves, "Do this and that." It is imperative that your self-verbalization focus on process rather than product. By focusing on the product ("Get it over the net"; "Hit it in the court") you anticipate the consequences of your actions, often diverting your attention from the immediate behavior you must execute. Self-verbalizations such as "Get in position," "Watch the ball," and "Swing through the ball" will focus your attention where it belongs. These verbalizations will also maximize your chances of getting the ball over the net and into the court. Self-verbalization provides an operational tool for achieving concentration during sports participation.

Though concentration is an elusive concept in sports, confidence is even more elusive. Whatever confidence is, it probably evolves primarily from success. We have described what we feel are the most appropriate norms for measuring progress, setting events that facilitate skill development, and procedures for reinforcing desired behaviors. Applying these strategies should help develop confidence, but the strategies do not represent the whole story. Confidence is a covert response that entails at least two dimensions, absence of extreme muscular tension and the belief that you can execute the required skills.

Unquestionably, extreme muscular tension adversely affects the performance of many sports skills. Muscular tension is most destructive to responses that require a high level of muscle coordination, such as diving, executing a 360° wake turn on trick skis, hitting a tennis ball, and shooting a basketball. (Tension would not be quite so catastrophic to interior line-blocking in football!) The muscular relaxation exercises described in Chapter 3 could increase your quality of play in sports activities that demand a high level of muscle coordination. You might engage in these exercises just before going to play. If you could put muscle relaxation under the control of a single stimulus (such as the word "relax"), you could periodically employ that stimulus during play. By using these relaxation procedures, one of our students has not only allayed muscular tension but has also calmed the sick stomach that had frequently plagued him just before important athletic events.

The second dimension of confidence, believing that you can execute the necessary skills, could be strengthened by Cautela's covert reinforcement procedure. By visualizing (1) the execution of a certain skill and (2) favorable consequences resulting from that skill, you may improve the skill. Modest support for this assertion is provided by Corbin (1967), who compared actual practice of skill with mental practice and with no practice. Not surprisingly, skill was more rapidly acquired with actual practice than under the other conditions. However, mental practice was superior to no practice. Corbin also found that mental practice was most effective when it was preceded by actual practice. To visualize yourself accurately performing a task, you must have had some experience in executing that skill. Therefore, covert reinforcement is most useful as an adjunct to actual performance of skills. Covert reinforcement appears to be a systematic way to develop a positive approach to the correct execution of skills.

Your overall perception of yourself as an athlete can be enhanced through positive self-references. In sports, as in most spheres of life, you can focus too extensively on your negative attributes. There are undoubtedly some positive aspects to your athletic participation (you are increasing the time that you can play without total exhaustion; you are executing new skills). By writing down these positive features and verbalizing them to yourself just before engaging in some pleasurable activity, you may enhance your perception of yourself as an athlete.

Concluding thoughts

This chapter has identified some principles of sports participation that will facilitate your skill development and enjoyment. Although we obviously have a strong bias toward tennis, our aim here is to prompt you to pursue regularly *some* type of physical activity, be it tennis or ballet or mountain climbing, in which you get vigorous exercise and enjoyment. Enjoyment is important because the reinforcement value of an activity will affect your willingness to engage in that activity and consequently the amount of exercise you get.

If sports activity is already an indispensable facet of your life, we encourage you to keep it that way. Vigorous physical activity should be a permanent aspect of living. However, if you are presently the paragon of inactivity, we hope this chapter will give you the impetus and technical expertise to get involved with sports. But watch out! It could lead to a lifelong love affair!

References

Akchin, D. 1977. I was a 49-pound weakling. *Insider,* 4–9.

Barger, B. 1968. Some relationships of physical education to mental health. *Journal of School Health 38,* 65–68.

Buber, M. 1958. *I and Thou,* 2nd ed. New York: Charles Scribner's Sons.

Castronis, M. 1976. Jog in the pool — no pain! *The Journal of Physical Education 74* (1), 8ff.

Corbin, C. B. 1967. Effects of mental practice on skill development after controlled practice. *Research Quarterly 38,* 534–538.

DeBacy, D. 1970. Effect of viewing videotapes of a sport skill performed by self and others on self-assessment. *Research Quarterly 41,* 27–31.

Furlong, W. B. 1976. The fun in fun. *Psychology Today 10,* 35–38.

Harris, D. V. 1972. Dimensions of physical activity. In D. V. Harris, (ed.), *Women and sport: A national research conference.* State College: Pennsylvania State University, College of Health, Physical Education and Recreation, pp. 3–15.

Ismail, A. H., Kane, J., and Kirkendall, D. R. 1969. Relationships among intellectual and nonintellectual variables. *Research Quarterly 40,* 83–92.

Ismail, A. H., and Trachtman, L. E. 1973. Jogging the imagination. *Psychology Today 6*(10) 78–82.

Kleinman, M. 1975. A central role for physical education in early childhood. *New York University Education Quarterly 6,* 23.

Kozar, A. J., and Hunsicker, P. 1963. A study of telemetered heart rate during sports participation of young adult men. *Journal of Sports Medicine and Physical Fitness 3*(1), 1–5.

Kuntzleman, C. T. 1977. Fitness considerations — the physiological. *The Journal of Physical Education* 74(4), 80–82.

Michener, J. A. 1976. *Sports in America.* New York: Random House.

Osborne, M. M., and Gordon, M. E. 1972. An investigation of the accuracy of ratings of a gross motor skill. *Research Quarterly 43* (1), 55–61.

Robb, M. 1966. Feedback. *Quest 6,* 38–43.

Rushall, B. S., and Siedentop, D. 1972. *The development and control of behavior in sport and physical education.* Philadelphia: Lea and Febiger.

Vincent, M. F. 1976. Comparison of self-concepts of college women: Athletes and physical education majors. *Research Quarterly* 47(2), 218–225.

Warren, W. E. 1970. Physical education and happiness. *Physical Educator* 27, 19–21.

Chapter 8
Panic in the stacks:

Managing study behavior

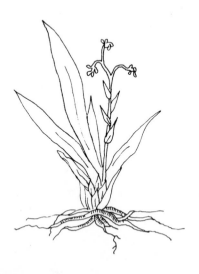

I will study and get ready and perhaps my
chance will come.

ABRAHAM LINCOLN.

Some rather important problems are directly or indirectly attributable to lack of study, ineffective study skills, or both. Consider the number of job aspirations that go unfulfilled because the aspiring persons never learned how to study. Think of the guilt feelings that accompany academic failure, a prospect that often undermines enjoyment of college life. The Saturday afternoon football game (better still, the party afterwards) just cannot be as exhilarating when you are faced with several Fs. The problems of study cut a broad swath across lives. People who are willing to devote themselves to academic pursuits and who develop effective study behavior can avoid many troubles. In addition, people who overcome study problems can develop new skills, explore exciting material, manage their time, and best of all control their own destiny.

Increasing study behavior

Some students are amazingly successful at study. They get all their work done on time and earn good grades. Then there are other students — those who have extreme difficulty in initiating and sustaining study activity. They have the best intentions, but everything seems to interfere with their acting on those intentions. Are such students less conscientious than their peers? It is not a question of integrity; their behaviors are merely under the control of different variables. The scholarly students have accidentally or purposely established conditions that facilitate study, while others have allowed certain conditions to produce nonstudy behavior. If you are concerned enough to try, you can increase study behavior by rearranging those environmental conditions. The self-management model described in Chapter 2 again provides a convenient format for identifying which environmental conditions should be altered.

Selecting a goal

If studying is presently a minuscule or nonexistent portion of your life, your initial goal should be to increase the amount of time you devote to study. Although quantity of time is perhaps less important than the quality of study, a minimal amount of time is obviously essential. If you are presently spending zero minutes per day studying, you will want to be very cautious in defining your initial goal. Perhaps studying ten minutes per day would be a good starting point. To expect more than gradual change is to set yourself up for disappointment. Many students fail because they expect too much too soon. You have probably known students who made a firm resolution to start studying a specified number of hours per day but who discarded the whole idea because it called for a

First things first

Bill, a student with above-average intelligence, was plodding along in his studies, maintaining grades just high enough to remain in school. Bill had studied our self-management model and was thinking of using it as a basis for improving his grades. However, when he started to establish his goal, he concluded that the model was not for him: "I don't really want to spend more time studying. I'm only in college because my parents want me here. If I had my way, I'd be doing something else."

We asked ourselves whether our self-management model could help Bill and students like him. If Bill were telling the truth, perhaps our model would be of little help, but he may never have faced the real issue. It's easy to say that you're doing something because others want you to. That's not always the truth, though. Sometimes you're reluctant to accept responsibility for your own actions. You may fear failure or be uncertain about how to succeed.

Whether you *really* want to achieve a particular goal is, of course, an issue that you must resolve before you can make much progress toward achieving that goal. If you think you're in college only because of the expectations of parents or friends, consider what alternative you would choose if those expectations were removed. What else could you be doing right now that would represent better use of your time? If you can't answer that question concretely, you're probably using parents and friends as an excuse for not assuming personal responsibility for your behavior. If you feel that you're dodging responsibility because you fear failure, stay with us. Application of the strategies in this chapter should substantially improve your chances for scholastic success.

---

too dramatic change in their present behaviors. "To hell with it," they say, thus ending their great expectations.

Monitoring target behavior

Record keeping is an especially significant step in altering the conditions affecting your study time. Those records should provide valuable information about why you are having difficulty. Your records may indicate that you have difficulty trying to study at one time but not at another, or that certain locations facilitate study while others hinder it. Once you are more aware of these conditions, you should be in a better position to implement a program of change. Your records may also reveal that you are spending less, or perhaps more, time studying than you realized. One of our students estimated that she was spending about fifteen hours a week studying. Her records, however, showed that only four hours weekly were devoted to studying outside of class. She was spending far more time thinking about studying than doing it. On the other hand, your records could indicate that you are devoting many hours to study

Do I need to monitor my study?

Obviously, not everyone gets the same benefits from self-monitoring study behavior. Some students keep a fairly accurate *mental* record of study time. Others are grossly inaccurate in keeping mental records. It is the students who are inaccurate or uninformed about their study who stand to gain the most from record keeping. At least that's what one group of researchers determined. C. S. Richards and his associates asked a group of undergraduate psychology students who were concerned about their study behaviors to estimate the amount of time they spent studying. The students were subsequently exposed to a variety of treatments including self-monitoring of studying.

The records revealed that although some students were accurate in estimating the time they actually spent studying, others were uninformed about their own study habits. Furthermore, it was the uninformed students who benefited most from self-monitoring. That is, their grades improved more, their study time increased more, and they felt more positive toward self-monitoring than students who were informed (accurate) about their study behaviors. The informed students, however, did improve their study behaviors more than control subjects not exposed to treatment conditions. How accurate are you in assessing your behaviors? A test run at record keeping could tell you.

Adapted from Richards, C. S., McReynolds, W. T., Holt, S., and Sexton, T. 1976. Effects of information feedback and self-administered consequences on self-monitoring study behavior. *Journal of Counseling Psychology 23,* 316–321.

with only poor grades to show for your efforts. This would suggest that a change in method of study is in order. Later in this chapter is a section about developing effective study methods.

To obtain data on your study behavior, you should record every instance that you initiate study, the time, the place, and exactly how long you remain at the task. You might also record your emotional state when you begin. For example, if you approach study with much anxiety, some type of covert control would be indicated. Also, you should keep a continuous record of your test scores and grades.

One week of baseline data should give you an adequate fix on your present study habits. After collecting baseline data, you should be ready to implement a self-management strategy. Of course, you will continue keeping records throughout your treatment program. These records should help you determine whether you are spending more time studying, whether you are less anxious, whether you are improving your test scores, and so on. The length of treatment will depend on the results you obtain and how long it takes for study to become a habitual part of your daily routine.

Changing setting events

Once you have established your record-keeping system and have pin-pointed the present level of your behavior, you are ready to begin a treatment program. The first thing to consider is ways of changing environmental events to increase the probability that you will indeed spend more time studying. Merely wanting to study may be insufficient; other events may negate your intentions. It is highly unlikely that you can overcome events in the environment that control behavior. There are ways, however, that you can control these events and thus increase the probability of study.

All of your behaviors, both study and nonstudy, occur in the presence of certain stimuli. Any of these stimuli can convey messages about what behaviors are likely to be or not to be immediately reinforced. For example, you might want to get in a few minutes of study at the student center. Before long a friend engages you in conversation or an attractive person catches your eye. These stimuli trigger socializing, not study. For the nonstudier, socializing is almost always more immediately reinforcing than studying. If you try to study at a time that you usually allot to tennis, you may find that you cannot get tennis off your mind. You relent and go to the court. If you try lying down to study, you may find that sleep or other more pleasant behavior occurs. You may unwittingly try to study while watching football on TV. Math probably cannot compete with professional sports. What happens is that the setting events (times and places) under which you attempt to study are associated with con-flicting interests. You want to study but cannot, so you end up doing something else. To remedy this situation, you first can control the time and place of your study behavior. This could very well be the most potent strategy you use. It certainly represents the principal way of changing setting events to facilitate study behavior.

A time for all things Part of the problem of getting control over study behavior is in developing a definite time for study so that study behavior will eventually be triggered during that time span. Behaviors become closely associated with the time when they occur. You might say that human beings are creatures of habit. More precisely, you might say that certain stimuli exert strong influences over behavior. That is why you get irresistible urges to do things at particular times. We are suggesting, therefore, that you designate times especially for study. Once you have decided to study at a particular time, you are in a position to resist extraneous temptations. It would be great to be able to say, "I'm sorry, but I have to study at three. Could we make it four-thirty?"

You may not be excited about the possibility of scheduling your study time. Many people are not. People tend to question any type of regimen-tation to which they are not accustomed. If you have never kept a time schedule, you may fear that it would take the fun out of living or transform you into a robot. Let us discuss these reservations before getting into the details of time management.

Will a time schedule take the fun out of living? Although some unplanned events turn out to be highly reinforcing, much unplanned time passes quite uneventfully. Have you ever caught yourself engaging in a terribly dull conversation? What about the time you spend just sitting around waiting for something to happen? In scheduling your time, you will probably uncover many nonproductive moments that could be put to better use. Students who schedule their study time report no lack of good times. The last thing we would suggest is that you divest your life of peak experiences.

Setting up a time schedule will not turn you into an automaton. *You* are the one who arranges the schedule. Consequently, you have the option of altering the schedule at your discretion. In essence, you are managing time to acquire more, not less, control. Who is master and who is servant when you have no plan of action?

If you have decided to schedule your study time, we have some suggestions to make. These suggestions have probably been used by many of your predecessors because C. G. Wrenn was advocating similar strategies as long ago as 1933. Human behavior is always subject to environmental controls; whether the suggestions worked then and whether they will work for you now depends on how they are used.

Begin by constructing a schedule covering your planned weekly activities. You could use a form similar to Figure 8.1. Your schedule first should include provisions for those fixed time intervals that cannot be changed. Sleeping, grooming, eating, class and laboratory time, and part-time jobs fall into this category. Be liberal when you allot time for essential behaviors. You may be surprised with the amount of time left for nonessentials. Next, allocate time for study.

There's no hard rule about how much time you should devote to study. That depends on how long you take to do assignments, the number of courses you are taking, length of assignments, and a host of other variables. Many college teachers feel that students should spend two hours in study for every hour of class time. We doubt that we have many students who consistently devote that much time to study. Our students report studying an average of only fifteen hours weekly. Other professors report even less study time for their students — about fifteen to thirty minutes a day. As a conservative rule of thumb, we recommend that you think in terms of devoting thirty to thirty-five hours weekly to academic pursuits (assuming you are taking a full load of courses). If you're in class for fifteen hours, allocate fifteen to twenty hours for study. (We can't resist asking for a little more than we're getting.) Such a schedule would be similar to holding a full-time job. You would still have ample time for recreation.

Time	Monday	Tuesday	Wednesday	Thursday	Friday	Saturday	Sunday
7:00							
8:00							
9:00							
10:00							
11:00							
12:00							
1:00							
2:00							
3:00							
4:00							
5:00							
6:00							
7:00							
8:00							
9:00							
10:00							
11:00							

Figure 8.1   Activity schedule.

We don't mean that you should go from zero to fifteen hours of study per week. Simply identify fifteen hours that you could devote to study. You might schedule for an hour of study after each class but begin by putting in only ten minutes. The logic of this strategy will be clarified in the next section. For the time being, allot sufficient time for study without expecting an overnight transformation in your behavior. Finally, in planning your study time, consider when you study most efficiently. Some people prefer to study difficult material early in the day when they are freshest, saving routine tasks for last. Some prefer to study late when it's quiet — and then sleep late or take naps. Take your pick.

After you've allowed for study time, fill in the rest of your schedule with activities you enjoy. If you finish your study early in the day, you can have your evenings free for recreation, exercise, transcendental meditation, or what have you. We also recommend that you allot most of your weekends to nonstudy activities. After all that conscientious study, you've earned it!

A place for all things   The second way to use setting events in controlling your study behavior is to restrict the number of places where you study. Suppose you ordinarily study in a room where you engage in all sorts of other behaviors as well. You may find yourself sitting down to study but then tuning in to other possibilities. The stimuli of that room

166

Accidental scheduling

Not all people are willing to schedule their own study behavior, but sometimes fate intervenes to reveal the benefits of scheduling. This is what happened to several of our skeptical students. They volunteered to do reading assignments with a blind student. He needed to have the reading done on a regularly scheduled basis. What happened? The volunteer students got their best grades in the classes in which they were reading to the blind student on a time schedule. These results attest to the efficacy of either time scheduling or oral reading — or maybe both.

Of course, others who have purposefully tried scheduling as a way of increasing productivity have also found that it really does help. Benjamin Franklin, Ralph Waldo Emerson, Plato, and William Shakespeare, to name a few, endorsed time management. Bill, Debra, Chuck, Jane, and Joyce (a few of our students) are sold on the idea too.

(such as lighting, sounds) may be more strongly associated with watching TV, drinking beer, or socializing than with studying. Those stimuli do not prohibit your studying. They merely increase the probability that other behaviors will occur. You have the option to behave differently, but who is strong enough to overcome all kinds of temptations? It seems more logical for you to arrange the place where you study so that it is supportive of study behavior.

By associating a particular setting exclusively with study behavior, you can dramatically increase the probability that you will study when you are in that setting. A number of researchers (Beneke and Harris, 1972; Briggs et al., 1971; Fox, 1962) have demonstrated the utility of this approach. The typical procedure is to leave your place of study whenever you begin to think of anything inconsistent with study, but before you leave, work one problem, read one page, or complete a small portion of your assignment. The next time you sit down to study, you might work two problems, read two pages, or complete a larger segment of your assignment after getting the impulse to stop studying. The strategy is to increase gradually the amount of studying by following *some* study with reinforcement (leaving the area to engage in another activity).

If you are going to use this tactic, you should keep your desk free of distracting materials (pictures of a girl friend or boy friend, *Playboy, Playgirl*); you should keep the room free of extraneous sights and sounds. Such stimuli frequently elicit behaviors that are incompatible with study activity. Fantasizing about your boy friend or girl friend, as pleasant as that may be, is incompatible with studying. Save those thoughts for your study breaks.

One event you don't want to overlook

One important strategy for sensitizing yourself to study behavior is to spend some time discussing your courses with others. Specifically, you could schedule time to talk with your professors about course-related matters. Such sessions should certainly help to keep studying on your mind. Unfortunately, some students have the idea that they should not "bother" their professors. They feel that professors would be inconvenienced if a student sought advice or made any kind of contact outside of class. This is generally not true. Most professors feel that it is their job to help students learn; they may even be encouraged or flattered that students care enough to seek their advice. What *is* irritating, though, is for students to wait until shortly before the term ends to ask, "What do I need to do to pass?" A better strategy is to make contact early and periodically. Another taboo is to miss class and then go by the professor's office to ask, "Did I miss anything?" Of course, you did! (At least from the professor's view.) Let professors know that you value what is going on in class and that you want to complete all assignments.

You may be thinking that contact with professors has little to do with actual success or failure. Perhaps you are correct, but consider these figures. At Appalachian State University, 415 freshmen and sophomores were academically ineligible to return to school at the end of spring semester in 1977, and of that number 350 had never sought advice from their faculty advisors. Of the 65 students who sought advice, the majority asked for help after — not before — getting into academic difficulty. Of course, many students perform well without getting help from their professors or without developing any personal relationships with faculty. However, we wager that many could benefit by talking with their advisors and professors. What's your opinion?

What produces incompatible behavior varies somewhat from student to student. For example, some students say they can study better with background music. The research evidence is divided on this point. Konz (1962) found that background music facilitates the performance of manual assembly tasks. Schlichting and Brown (1970) showed that background music during biology lectures leads to higher achievement in biology. In contrast, Freeburne and Fleischer (1952) reported that music had no effect on students' comprehension of Russian history. Kirkpatrick (1943) showed that music interferes with work that requires a high level of concentration, such as problem-solving activity. Apparently, the effect of music varies not only from person to person but also from task to task. If music makes your study environment more reinforcing and enhances your productivity, flood yourself with it. But be sure you're not fooling yourself. Empirically appraising the effects of background music on different types of study behavior might make an excellent addition to your self-management project.

Establishing effective consequences

Altering setting events is a good way to start changing study behavior, but you must not stop there. To encourage your efforts and to maintain any behavior changes, you need to establish effective consequences for your actions. You are unlikely to continue engaging in a behavior without a good reason for doing so. You may be thinking that getting a passing grade and remaining in college are awfully good reasons for studying; they are. The trouble is that many people do not consider these ultimate consequences until it is too late. However, if the thoughts of passing grades and remaining in school are meaningful enough to get you to study today, not just at the last minute, then perhaps you will want to develop a plan for systematically evoking such thoughts. You could include such a plan under covert processes.

Perhaps the most effective way to reinforce studying is to follow it with an immediate positive consequence. You may never have engaged in much study behavior because you never derived any immediate reinforcement from it. The events that have competed so successfully with study have probably had reinforcement naturally associated with them. What you will have to do is deliberately associate reinforcement with study. If an activity is associated with something pleasant, you are more likely to engage in that activity. This is undoubtedly a major way to develop an affinity for study. Enjoyment of study does not emerge magically. It is based on the number and types of reinforcers you receive from studying.

While study activities may never become the *most* reinforcing activities in your life, there are a number of ways that you can increase the probability of study. When you read one page and then leave a study area to engage in a more preferred activity, you have applied reinforcement for study. This sequence of events demonstrates the *Premack principle** (Premack, 1959). Simply stated, the principle suggests that a *high-probability behavior** (socializing) can be used to reinforce a less probable behavior (studying). The principle helps you to arrange the sequence of activities to obtain desired changes in behavior. In short, first work, then play. Part of your study problems in the past may have been due to the wrong sequence of events. You may have had fun first and then tried to study, which can be a letdown. By studying first you have something to look forward to. One of our groggy-eyed students found this principle particularly helpful. He reported that drinking wine and beer was interfering with his study. His solution was to reward study with drink. As a result of his project, he halved the time it usually took him to complete reading assignments. (*Our* next project is to cut his drinking in half.)

Don't assume that the Premack principle is the only way to reinforce studying. Once you have firmly established your study behavior, you

*Terms set in italics and followed by an asterisk are defined in the Glossary.

Perhaps the most effective way to reinforce studying is to follow it with an immediate positive consequence.

may wish to delay reinforcement for longer periods of time. You need not jump up immediately and engage in a more preferred activity. You could establish a point system to bridge the gap between study and subsequent reinforcement. If there's something you've been wanting to buy but have not felt that you quite deserved it, why not make this item contingent on a certain amount of study time? With a precise record-keeping system, you could reward yourself with a specified number of points for a specified amount of studying. Be sure to identify in advance how many points you'll need to make your purchases.

One last word about reinforcing study behaviors. Study behavior is not a one-dimensional concept. A later section will describe several different facets of effective study behaviors. A point system for reinforcing study behavior should entail credit for each of these components of effective study. There are also some prerequisite behaviors without which studying will not occur. These include getting into the appropriate setting (such as going to the library), taking the necessary materials, and getting out the necessary materials once you are in the appropriate setting. Each of these prerequisite behaviors should carry token credit toward the final payoff that makes the whole system functional. (One student at the University of Tennessee was thrown out of the library for bouncing his basketball. We thought he should have been given at least one token, since that was the first time he had ever been to the library!)

Consolidating your gains

If increased study time is to become a permanent part of your daily activities, some natural reinforcers must eventually assume control over

Once more with feeling

By now you have undoubtedly gotten the idea that reinforcement is an integral component of self-management. Nonetheless, we can't resist pointing out the merits of external rewards in modifying study behavior. Forty-seven university freshmen participated in a study skills program in which the students could earn back a ten-dollar deposit, one group through a combination of self-evaluation of their own progress and self-administered rewards and another group through a combination of a group leader's evaluation and externally administered rewards. The study habits and grades of both groups improved more than those of a no-reward group. A follow-up four months later indicated that the self-administered-reward subjects continued to improve their study habits more than the external-reward group. Would you have guessed otherwise?

Adapted from Jackson, B., and Zoost, B. V. 1972. Changing study habits through reinforcement contingencies. *Journal of Counseling Psychology 19*, 192–195.

study behavior. The natural payoff that seems most important to many students is high grades. We believe that the majority of students who are presently getting low grades could substantially improve their grades by increasing study time. We have known very few students to get failing grades despite expending vast amounts of time in study. Higher grades should sustain your increased study time as you phase out artificially arranged contingencies. However, if your grades do not improve with increased study time, the principal issue must be *how* you study and not *how much*. In that case, the remainder of the chapter should be especially helpful to you.

Don't overlook the intrinsic value of newly acquired knowledge as a source of natural reinforcement for study behavior. You will be more aware of that knowledge if you talk about what you're learning. Participating in class discussion and discussing newly acquired concepts with friends will surely heighten your interest in academia. For example, this text contains many discussable concepts. As other people mention the types of problems we've been treating, why not let them benefit from your new knowledge? However, we are not suggesting that you spend *all* of next Saturday night's date discussing setting events and reinforcement contingencies!

Covert alternatives

Probably no area of human behavior is more susceptible to mood swings than is study behavior. You may find that you can use positive thoughts and feelings to enhance study activities, but you may also find that you must reduce anxiety — over exams, your future in academe, or study in general — in order to engage effectively in academic pursuits. Consequently, you may want to consider including covert processes in your study program. Covert strategies such as relaxation will not replace thorough preparation, but they can help you make good use of thorough preparation.

A self-management survey

If you are still undecided about the need for establishing control over your study behavior, the following survey may help you reach a decision. The more statements you agree with, the greater the likelihood that a self-management project is in order.

____ I seldom set definite goals for how much studying I should do.

____ I have never tried to keep a time schedule for the purpose of regulating study.

____ I frequently put off studying until it is too late to get my assignments completed on time.

____ When I do try to study on a regular basis, something usually comes up to interfere with study.

____ I probably devote less than ten hours per week to study.

____ Ten or fifteen minutes is about as long as I can concentrate without getting restless.

____ My place of study sometimes gets cluttered with popular magazines and other material that could distract from study.

____ Bull sessions frequently occur in the locale where I study.

____ Daydreams keep interfering with my studies.

____ I have never consciously tried to reinforce any of my study behaviors.

____ Although I have good intentions, I periodically forget to do assignments.

____ I frequently feel anxious about a class, studying, or an exam.

____ I almost have to force myself to study.

Increasing reading comprehension

For some students the problem ends once they develop procedures for increasing study time. They know how to study once they actually begin. If you are such a student, perhaps you need read no further. For others, however, the problem is not one of study time but rather of how to study properly. Students who read for hours and cannot tell you what they have read, who memorize meaningless trivia, who cannot understand their notes, who end up underlining every other word in their books — these people are the victims of inefficient study habits. Efficient study means that you are utilizing the quickest and easiest methods of learning. Anything else is a waste of time.

To a great extent, success in any venture is a matter of determining what works for you and then systematically applying that procedure. To assist you, we offer *one* systematic approach for reading and studying books that follows an outlined, organized sequence. Since reading assignments constitute a major portion of your college work, becoming an effective reader is fundamental to success in college. Compare your present strategies with those on the following pages. Perhaps you'll pinpoint a weakness in those strategies or confirm their strengths.

The best known and probably the most widely tested strategy for improving reading study skills is Robinson's (1970) SQ3R method. Survey, question, read, recite, and review are abbreviated in the SQ3R title to make it easier to remember. Each step is briefly described below.[1]

S (Survey)

The first step in the SQ3R method is the survey. This step involves an examination of a chapter's headings and subheadings in order to get a general outline of the material to be studied. In this text primary headings, in boldface, represent the major ideas we wish to cover. The secondary headings, in light type, represent subordinate parts of the major idea. For example, our primary heading, *Increasing Study Behavior,* is a major idea. The secondary headings, *Selecting a Goal, Monitoring Target Behavior, Changing Setting Events, Establishing Effective Consequences, Consolidating Your Gains,* and *Covert Alternatives,* constitute subordinate parts. From the secondary headings, you immediately get a rough idea of what is involved in controlling study behavior. If you further examine the subheading of *Changing Setting Events,* you will determine that the concept involves the time and the place of study. Surveying can also include reading an occasional topic sentence. Topic sentences, as you know, contain major ideas and are usually found at the beginning or end of paragraphs. In addition, summary statements at the end of sections should be examined in your initial survey of material.

The primary value of the survey is to increase comprehension. By knowing in advance what you are to study, you can attend directly to the task of learning the material. You do not waste unnecessary time trying to figure out how material fits together. Surveying may also eliminate some of your reading. By looking at the headings, you may determine that you already know what is in a section. You don't have to read three or four paragraphs to determine that you need not study that section. Perhaps you already take note of headings. Quick check: What is the subheading of this section?

---

[1]"The SQ3R Method of Studying" in *Effective Study,* Fourth Edition by Francis P. Robinson. Copyright © 1970 by Francis P. Robinson. By permission of Harper & Row, Publishers, Inc.

Q (Question)

The second step calls for the creation of questions from section headings. You can begin the questioning process by turning the first heading into a question. In formulating questions you can use the familiar who, what, when, where, why, and how strategy of newspaper reporters. You might also check the end of the chapter to see whether the author has provided questions for you. You might decide to use the author's questions as a guide for structuring your own. You could also try posing the kind of questions that your professor typically asks in class.

Raising questions can provide you with an immediate purpose for your reading, can assist you in preparing for class discussions and exams, and might provide enough personal challenge to make study more interesting. When you raise questions to yourself, you become an active participant in the learning process; no longer are you a passive reader who trudges through an assignment. What are some questions you might pose regarding the next section on reading? One possible question would be, "How can I read for comprehension?"

R₁ (Read)

Having formulated a question on a section, you can begin looking for an answer. Some students feel that they have actually studied when they passively read every word in an assignment. However, everyone has had the experience of reading page after page without the slightest idea of what was just read. Words acquire meaning when you read them with a purpose, when you are no longer a caller of words or a reader of lines. Your purpose is to get an answer, and in pursuing that purpose you need not get bogged down with every *a, an,* and *the* on the page. Effective reading means that you are listening for an answer. When you hear that answer, you are prepared for the next step. This is what we mean by reading for comprehension. Robinson's strategy is obviously a much more active approach to reading than students typically take.

R₂ (Recite)

After you've read the first section, pause for a moment to recite the answer to your question. (What was the answer to our question on the preceding section?) You should close your book or at least look away from it while you formulate your answer. Being able to make your own response will insure that you comprehend the material. One useful means of conducting the recitation is to write down your answer from memory in very brief note form. Don't try to reproduce the text; that would undoubtedly make the process aversive. If you dislike taking notes, you could use underlining. To accomplish recitation through underlining, you first think of your response and then look for key phrases that correspond to your recitation. Don't underline until you have read the entire section and actually know what the important answers to your questions are. Even then, Robinson suggests that you use a coding system to indicate the order of importance of various points. For example, in our underlining system we divide material into three categories. Material of some importance merits an underline, that of greater importance brackets, and that of greatest importance brackets plus an asterisk in the margin. Just considering how to code a point will probably help you remember it.

After completing the recitation for the first section, continue with additional sections. Move to the next heading: question, read, and recite. Continue this procedure until you have completed the entire assignment. Although recitation may take as much time as reading, you will not regret that time. Spending time in recitation will probably make a far greater difference in your examination scores than spending the same amount of time in reading alone.

Self-recitation offers several important benefits, including increased retention of material. Recitation can also enhance the clarity of your expressions. Have you ever had an idea clearly in mind until you started to express yourself and wound up saying, "Oh, you know what I mean"? In casual conversation others may smile and nod understandingly to your "you see" and "you know" statements. Professors are a different breed, however. They neither see nor know, especially when it comes to exam answers! You must make yourself clear, and recitation will help. Students who do not use this method sometimes wear themselves out reading and rereading and still have trouble on exams, when they are reciting for the first time.

R₃ (Review)

When you complete your assignment, make a brief review of all the material. A review of most chapters shouldn't take more than a few minutes. You don't have to reread; you have your notes or your underlinings to go by. If you have made brief notes, look them over and then try to recall as many of the major points as possible. This procedure will help you establish the relationship between the parts of a chapter. Next, recite the details under each major point. If you used underlining, begin your review by looking over your underlinings and then proceed to recite answers to your questions.

There are some very good reasons for this early review. It can substantially reduce the rapid decline in retention of material that occurs immediately following study. Retention can further be aided by periodic follow-up reviews. You can determine whether you need a review by how well you recite answers. A fifteen-minute review for three consecutive days might be all that you need to remember large blocks of information for an entire term. In general, it is far better to have several short review sessions than a few lengthy sessions. It is a well-known fact of psychology that retention is greater with distributed practice than with massed (lengthy) practice.

Summary

Robinson's SQ3R is a well-established method for increasing reading and study skills. It can be adapted for all your reading, but the method described here is most applicable to texts that utilize an outlined, organized sequence. Texts in the social sciences, business, and applied arts, for example, usually follow such a pattern. Novels, poetry, and some of your other reading assignments may not. If you have a particular interest in adapting the SQ3R strategy for any or all of your reading, you are directed to Robinson's definitive text, *Effective Study* (1970). Before you decide on a method for dealing with your reading assignments, you may have to analyze the purpose for your reading (whether you are reading for a major idea, for details, for style), how the material differs from traditional assignments, and how you will be held accountable. In using a systematic approach such as SQ3R, be sure to reinforce yourself for the application of the various components of the approach. If you are using a point system, for example, allocate points (reinforce yourself) for "recitation" and "review" as well as for "time" and "pages read."

A self-management project

Now that you have explored procedures for controlling study time and have analyzed a systematic approach to reading, you might combine the two into a self-management project. You may need such a project if you have experienced difficulty in getting yourself to study and have had poor results (grades) when you did study. Putting in some time is essential, but how you use that time is also important. Let us run through the Williams-Long self-management model, reviewing briefly the procedures for increasing study time and examining how you might use Robinson's SQ3R method to enhance study efficiency. You might be interested in knowing that several researchers (for example, Beneke and Harris, 1972; Briggs et al., 1971; Greiner and Karoly, 1976) have successfully combined efforts to increase study time with the SQ3R method.

1. *Selecting a goal* How much time are you now spending on your studying? What would be a reasonable increase over your present level? Can you visualize how to utilize the SQ3R method while gradually increasing your study time? *Hint:* If you get the urge to stop studying after only ten minutes, try completing the SQ3R for one section. You already would have surveyed the material, so you would only need to question, read, recite, and review before leaving the study area.

2. *Monitoring target behavior* Are you recording the time, place, and mood of your study efforts? Could you also record how frequently you have used the SQ3R method? Are you actually surveying before you begin an assignment? Are you using the questioning technique? Are you using the SQ3R method to periodically review materials before exams? Do you plan to maintain graphs of your progress?

3. *Changing setting events* Do you see the need for changing your present time or place of study? Have you thought about recording assignments, posting assignments and record sheets, talking with professors, participating in class, and interacting with studious peers? Anything that reminds you of what you want to do (study) could be included under this section. Isn't changing your method of study (adopting the SQ3R method) essentially a change in setting events? For example, is your present system of underlining effective? If you have every other word underlined, it surely is not.

4. *Establishing effective consequences* Do you plan to use the Premack principle or a point system for reinforcing study behaviors? Remember that each component of study (such as preparing to study, getting out materials, keeping records, changing setting events, applying the steps in the SQ3R method) needs to be reinforced if you are to establish a smooth and enjoyable process. What eventually looks like one behavior (studying) is really a chain of many behaviors established through the controls you provide.

5. *Consolidating your gains* What evidence will you use to know that your self-management strategies are working? Comments from professors? Grades? A new attitude towards college or study? You should have some strategy for weaning yourself of unneeded prompts.

6. *Covert alternatives* Do you plan to use covert positive reinforcement, coverant pairs, desensitization, or other covert strategies to help you get down to the business of study and to help you function when you devote yourself to study?

Completing major projects

Some students have no problem with reading assignments or other work assigned on a regularly scheduled basis; they experience difficulty only when confronted with a major task, such as completing a term paper. They delay until the time is past for doing an adequate job. This problem gets to the heart of self-management. Students who can complete day-to-day assignments may be able to do so only because other people have laid out their work and are providing immediate consequences (class discussion, tests) to help control the study behavior. On the other hand, the student who is given an assignment to be completed by the end of a term does not have those immediate, externally imposed consequences. There is no sphere of academia that makes greater demands on your self-management capabilities than the infamous term project. If you procrastinate over term projects, this is the area of study in which a self-management approach might prove most helpful.

Pigeons show the way

B. F. Skinner's early work with pigeons illustrates how organisms learn to tackle major tasks. Skinner found that pigeons can be trained to peck a disc as many as 10,000 times for a food reinforcer. (That sounds almost as formidable as writing a term paper!) Skinner trained the pigeons by breaking the task into component parts and then gradually increasing the requirement for reinforcement. For example, he initially rewarded a pigeon for moving slightly in the direction of the disc, then for coming closer to the disc, and finally for pecking the disc. Eventually the number of pecks required for reward would be increased. Without such training, any pigeon would surely starve to death before delivering the required 10,000 pecks.

Pigeons aren't the only creatures whose productivity can be increased through an incremental approach. Greiner and Karoly (1976) have assessed the value of breaking down large or long-range goals into smaller subgoals. They found that training in planning strategies along with self-monitoring and self-reward were highly successful ways of increasing time spent studying, improving grades, and increasing the number of assignments completed. If you have been overwhelmed by term papers and other major projects, perhaps you too should consider programming your work. You can learn to do for yourself what your professors may have been arranging in short-term assignments — tasks in small parts and with immediate consequences.

Breaking down the task

The instructor announces that a thirty-page term paper is due in one month. You barely avert an anxiety attack, your hands get clammy, and finally you shake your head in self-pity. How can you possibly write a thirty-page term paper with the plethora of other tasks you have pending? As long as you think in terms of the *total* project, you probably will be immobilized. Only the severest of anxiety attacks (a day or two before the paper is due) will get you to the library. In absolute agony, foregoing sleep for forty-eight hours, you will frantically piece something together. Can there be any question that this is *not* the most reinforcing way to do a term project?

A first step in doing a term project is to break the task down into smaller parts. For example, writing a term paper might involve (1) se-

178

lecting a topic, (2) finding related materials, (3) taking notes on relevant materials, (4) formulating questions to be answered in the paper, (5) producing a tentative outline of the paper, (6) writing a rough draft for each section of the paper, (7) reorganizing the paper, and (8) preparing the finished draft for each section of the paper. Obviously, each of the subunits can be divided into smaller segments of work. Keep subdividing until you reach units of work that do not intimidate you. Some students might think in terms of what could be accomplished in a week; others may be discouraged by the prospect of any task that requires more than thirty minutes. Once you have divided your work into subunits, give your undivided attention to Subunit One. You will find this approach far more palatable than constantly reflecting on the total magnitude of the project, which would probably produce more brooding than working.

Formulating a time schedule

You know that the paper must be turned in by October 30, but what about those subunits of work? Formulate a tentative schedule outlining when each subunit is to be completed. The schedule should require early completion of the first subunit (to get you started on the project) and should specify a final completion date slightly before October 30 (to give you some breathing room at the end and to allow time for resolving unexpected problems). After defining your schedule, focus on one deadline at a time. Instead of saying, "I have a term paper due October 30," you now say, "I need to identify a topic by October 3."

In fact, most people do not work in such a highly organized fashion. Many students write term papers in the way we described initially. We have done a few like that ourselves. However, we have found that a more reinforcing and productive way to complete long-term projects is to define subunits of work, make out an overall time schedule, and then tackle one task at a time. In writing this text, for example, we thought first about the theme of the book, next about the kind of chapters we wanted to include, and then about the overall organization of the book. Then we made a commitment to our publisher about when we would submit each chapter of the book. Consequently, we were not faced with writing an entire book — we were faced with one chapter at a time. This strategy resulted in our writing the book during a six-month period, as we had originally planned. Nothing is more paralyzing than being bombarded by eighty-eight different tasks simultaneously. Manage Task One first, and the remaining eighty-seven will be just as manageable.

Reinforcing productive behavior

This impetus for attacking subsequent parts of a project is partially a function of completing earlier parts. Completing that first bit of work is

Please! Not the Klan!

In case you distrust your ability to administer self-imposed reinforcement contingencies, you might consider a strategy proposed by Nurnberger and Zimmerman (1970). They reported on a Ph.D. candidate who completed his doctoral thesis by committing himself to a series of small, attainable goals. He had successfully finished all his degree requirements except for a thesis. He took a teaching position and for two years did not write a single page of the thesis. He reported feelings of inadequacy, extreme sensitivity towards his colleagues, irritability, and insomnia. After undergoing fourteen, ninety-minute sessions of psychotherapy to help gain insight into his problem, he showed little behavior change with his multiple problems. He wrote nothing on his thesis. Finally, he and a therapist worked out a writing program with consequences to control the writing. The initial plan required that he submit three pages at the end of the first week. After completing a previously planned two-week vacation (not part of the program), he was to submit four additional pages after the fourth week. After the eighth, thirteenth, and seventeenth weeks, he was to submit twenty-six, fifty-five, and fifty-three pages, respectively. He had given his therapist five $100 postdated checks, one to be forfeited each time he failed to meet a deadline.

He met the first three deadlines but asked for a revised program before the fifty-five-page deadline was due. His writing had stopped. Consequently, the initial program was revised on the eleventh week to provide for daily and weekly deadlines. He wrote three $25 postdated checks to be forfeited one at a time for failure to meet deadlines. On the fourteenth week of the program, he moved back to a weekly schedule and this time made forfeitable checks payable to organizations that were highly aversive to him. The organizations were the Ku Klux Klan, the American Nazi party, and the John Birch Society. He wanted to be certain that the checks would not be forfeited.

Figure 8.2 shows this individual's writing progress. A follow-up indicated that he received his Ph.D. He accepted a highly responsible administrative position, relationships with his family improved, and his other problems subsided. To our knowledge he never had to give up a penalty check. You could utilize the strategies employed by Nurnberger and Zimmerman by enlisting the services of a friend who has the same problem you have. Why not agree to administer the contingencies to each other?

Adapted from Nurnberger, J. I., and Zimmerman, J. 1970. Applied analysis of human behaviors: An alternative to conventional motivational inferences and unconscious determination in therapeutic programming. *Behavior Therapy 1,* 59–69. Dr. Nurnberger is Professor of Psychiatry, The Institute of Psychiatric Research, Indiana University School of Medicine, Indianapolis, Indiana 46202.

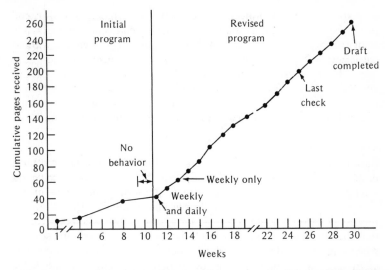

Figure 8.2 Cumulative pages of thesis copy successfully completed. (Nurnberger, J. I., and Zimmerman, J. 1970. Applied analysis of human behaviors: An alternative to conventional motivational inferences and unconscious determination in therapeutic programming. *Behavior Therapy 1*, 59–69. Dr. Nurnberger is Professor of Psychiatry, The Institute of Psychiatric Research, Indiana University School of Medicine, Indianapolis, Indiana 46202.)

especially reinforcing; it makes Part Two appear considerably less forbidding. The reinforcing effects of completing different segments of a project are probably cumulative in nature; that is, each subsequent part becomes easier to work on. You can see why it is important to divide a project into many subunits. That arrangement not only increases your frequency of positive reinforcement but also makes it easier to initiate and sustain work on a project.

Because of your reinforcement history, you may not find completing units of work intrinsically reinforcing. In that case you may wish to devise a system of external payoffs for productive behavior. Such rewards as getting a drink of water, reading the newspaper, and even changing work settings can serve as short-term reinforcers for completing a specified amount of work. We've found that simply moving to the other side of the library reinforces completion of work as well as provides a refreshing setting for additional work.

Beyond the natural reinforcers mentioned in the previous paragraph, you may want to establish a point system in which each of the subunits is worth a certain amount of credit toward tangible items or weekend privileges. A privilege or item that you have earned becomes doubly reinforcing. When you make purchases or partake of privileges without earning them, you sometimes experience ambivalence: "Should I have spent that much money on that item?" "Do I really need that?" "Can I spare the time?" However, when you have established your reinforcement contingencies, you seldom experience that ambivalence. In fact, you feel obligated to make good on your reinforcement commitments.

Choosing a topic

Because choosing a topic represents the first hurdle in doing a term project, we shall devote special attention to that task. Actually, selecting a topic may be the most confusing part of a term project. One of our students experienced near-panic in the library one day. He was in the process of trying to identify a topic for a term project when the realization that he was making absolutely no progress seemed almost overwhelming. We doubt that his experience is unique. Student anxiety is often exceedingly high during this period. You know you should be doing something, but you are not sure what. You go to the library, walk through the stacks, thumb through a few randomly selected books, and gain nothing for your efforts but bad feelings and a throbbing headache.

Trouble begins when students try to identify the most profound, far-reaching theme ever contemplated. Students often begin with aspirations of writing papers that will provide the ultimate cure for mental illness, revolutionize education, or whatever. As yet, no student has identified such a theme. The most profound human creations usually result from several years of relatively mundane and inauspicious work. You will save yourself a great deal of time and frustration by *not* looking for a topic that no other mortal has dared to think about.

Even though you probably will not be able to come up with a unique, infinitely erudite topic, you should search for a theme that interests you. Finding such a theme will make doing the project more reinforcing, and it will give you a place to begin searching for a topic. Here are starting points we have suggested to students trying to find topics in the field of psychology: (1) Population: Is there a particular group of persons (retarded, brain-damaged, gifted, infants) in which you are especially interested? (2) Behavior: Is there a specific kind of behavior (disruptive activity in the classroom, autistic responses, isolate behavior, covert activity) that you want to study? (3) Model: Is there a certain orientation (behavior therapy, psychoanalysis, nondirective therapy, gestalt therapy) that has excited you? (4) Technique or concept: Within your favorite system, is there a technique or concept that offers special intrigue? A student turned on to self-management (like you, for example) may find Cautela's concept of covert reinforcement unusually stimulating. (5)

Theoretical proposition: Is there some aspect of a given theoretical orientation that you think needs testing? If no aspect of your favorite theory can be reduced to a testable hypothesis, perhaps you should consider another theory. You can probably think of additional reference points for getting an initial focus on a topic. (If so, drop us a note and we'll include them in the next edition of this text, giving you proper credit, of course.)

If you can respond to only one of these considerations, at least you have a place to begin. If you can respond to a number of them, your topic will practically identify itself. For example, you may determine that your special population is the retarded, that you are particularly concerned about cooperative behavior, that you are interested in behavior modification, and that you are especially intrigued with the concept of token reinforcement. How does "The Effect of Token Reinforcement on the Cooperative Behavior of Mentally Retarded Children" sound to you? If you go to the library with this general topic in mind, you will undoubtedly accomplish far more than if you go expecting a topic to jump out of the stacks and seize you. Actually, this topic is probably too broad for most term projects. Of what age are the retarded children you want to study? What type of cooperative behavior do you plan to focus upon? What kind of token reinforcement do you have in mind? Answering these specific kinds of questions can sharpen dramatically the task of doing a literature review and/or defining an experimental design.

Self-management project

If you presently accomplish your work with impeccable efficiency, skip to the next section. However, if you are one of those last-minute students, consider the following suggestion. If this is a typical quarter or semester, you probably have more than one long-term project to do. Identify two projects that appear to be of equal magnitude and palatability. Do one project in the usual way. (Just stock up on your supply of coffee, ice water, and cigarettes for the last-minute rush.) Do the other project according to the Williams-Long format. See which project proves to be more reinforcing and/or yields the better grade.

Becoming more creative

Creativity is a concept that is extremely difficult to explain from a self-management perspective. The difficulty begins with defining exactly what creativity is. The principal criterion appears to be novelty or originality. Therefore, it is impossible to define in advance what a creative accomplishment will look like. As a result, then, it is very difficult to know what behaviors to monitor and how to arrange setting events and reinforcement contingencies to produce the unknown behaviors.

183

Another difficulty relates to the matter of external contingencies. Your social environment often supports the behaviors you attempt to produce by means of self-management. Turning in your work on time, losing twenty pounds of weight, and eliminating nervous tics would usually be reinforced by others. This pattern does not hold true for creative responses. Instead, society usually reinforces conforming behaviors. This reaction to creativity is unfortunate because external contingencies can be very facilitative of novel behavior (Goetz and Baer, 1971; Goetz and Salmonson, 1972). However, since external contingencies generally do not support creative responses, it is exceedingly difficult to achieve that mode of behavior through self-management.

In considering the relationship between self-management and creativity, you must recognize creativity. You may consider an accomplishment to be creative (and it truly may be for you), but someone else may see it as commonplace (and it truly may be for that person). Since we are examining creativity primarily in an academic context, we must consider your instructor's perception of originality. And that is a domain where we cannot offer much assurance. However, if you can produce a piece of work that you consider creative, it seems more likely that your instructor will also find some originality in that work.

Responses associated with creative accomplishments

It was previously recommended that you formulate questions about material that you are about to read. A similar strategy is suggested for writing. The originality of your work is related to the kinds of questions you are attempting to answer. A question that requires a direct factual response allows for a minimum of creativity, while a question that calls for a statement of opinion permits a high degree of originality. How original can you be in answering a question such as "What is the present population of the United States?" However, if you ask, "What effect will population control have on race relations in this society?" you have far greater potential for originality. Asking questions that do not have one correct answer or that require you to relate seemingly incongruous concepts (such as, "How can external incentives be used to foster self-direction?") will allow you to use more of your creative potential.

In formulating responses to your provocative questions, you may be inclined to go to the "authorities" for an answer. That could be a mistake. If you initially depend on what others have to say, you may have difficulty going beyond their thinking. The better strategy is to formulate your own responses to a question and then appeal to the authorities. In this way you prevent the enlightenment of others from blinding you to your own ideas.

In jotting down our initial responses to a question, we find it most helpful to do some brainstorming. We put down all ideas that come to mind and defer evaluating them until later. Nothing is more paralyzing than trying to formulate only *good* ideas. That is the kind of strategy that will keep you staring at a piece of paper for thirty minutes without recording a single word. Go the brainstorming route. Research (Meadow and Parnes, 1959) supports its value in generating more ideas and higher-quality ideas.

Setting events for creativity

While it is rather difficult to be creative on cue, certain times and settings may be correlated with original activity. This is a domain in which self-management is very idiosyncratic. No one can say what those times and settings should be for you, but you can keep a log noting when and where you do your most original work. We find a quiet setting early in the morning most conducive to new ideas. Your most auspicious setting events may be entirely different. In any case, you should monitor your behavior closely enough to be aware of relationships between times, places, and your creative accomplishments.

There may be instructional input that can enhance a person's ability to think creatively. Parnes (1967) has developed a set of *programmed materials** that present problem situations to which a number of different responses could be made. A key element in his approach is teaching people to define problem situations in more accurate terms. People are frequently unable to resolve problem situations because they misdefine the problem. In contrast to more conventional programmed materials, Parnes's program allows for a number of different responses to the same frame. Students are given feedback in terms of possible responses to that frame but are told that their response may be superior to any of the suggested responses.

Reinforcing creative behavior

Since others are frequently threatened by unusual responses (and therefore will not reinforce them), much of the reinforcement for these behaviors must come from you. Learning to respect your own ideas is a fundamental requisite to creativity. We take the view that every person's ideas are worthy of consideration. It is legitimate to pat yourself on the back any time you express your ideas. If those pats on the back are not sufficiently reinforcing, you will need to reward expression of ideas in a more systematic, tangible fashion. You might allow yourself an attractive privilege only after you have expressed a specified number of ideas.

Despite the pessimism of some of our earlier comments, support from others for creative accomplishments is not entirely out of the question. Chapter 10 suggests a correlation between approval given and approval received. If you approve others for expressing unusual ideas, they will be more inclined to support your unique responses. In other words, external support for novel behavior is to some degree a matter of reciprocal reinforcement.

Self-management projects

Why not put to test some of the ideas presented in our discussion of creativity? (On the other hand, you may have more original propositions to pursue.)

1. In defining a list of questions to be considered in a specified term project, make sure that at least 75 percent of those questions call for an opinion response. Formulate a way to evaluate the impact of this strategy, such as your grade on this project as opposed to grades on other projects, completion time for this project compared with completion time for other projects.

2. Each time you have what you consider to be a highly original thought, note the time and place. See if you can establish some kind of pattern in setting events for your creative behavior.

3. Identify a friend who tends to think very conventionally. Every time your friend expresses an idea that deviates even slightly from the norm, comment on the uniqueness of that idea and indicate that it is an idea worthy of much consideration. Systematically evaluate (you remember the baseline and treatment procedure) the effect of your strategy on the number of nonnormative ideas your friend expresses and the number of times that person approves your expressions of unusual ideas.

Concluding thoughts

The recommendations of this chapter can have an impact on your studying behavior and academic accomplishments. Of course, strategies to help you put in study time and enhance your study efficiency are effective only to the extent that you use them. Some students have told us that our tactics do not work. On close questioning we found that these students weren't really using our suggestions. However, we assume that you are still reading what we have to say because you care about your study behavior and are willing to try some new strategies for improving that behavior. On that optimistic note, we conclude our remarks on the topic and wish you well in your pursuit of scholarship. Remember — none of that last-minute stuff. There are better ways to spend the night before.

References

Beneke, W. M., and Harris, M. B. 1972. Teaching self-control of study behavior. *Behaviour Research and Therapy 10*, 35–41.

Briggs, R. D., Tosi, D. J., and Morley, R. M. 1971. Study habit modification and its effect on academic performance: A behavioral approach. *Journal of Educational Research 64*, 347–350.

Fox, L. 1962. Effecting the use of efficient study habits. *Journal of Mathetics 1* (1), 75–86.

Freeburne, C. M., and Fleischer, M. S. 1952. The effect of music distraction upon reading rate and comprehension. *Journal of Educational Psychology 43*, 101–109.

Goetz, E. M., and Baer, D. M. 1971. Descriptive social reinforcement of "creative" block building for young children. In E. A. Ramp and B. L. Hopkins (eds.), *A new direction for education: Behavior analysis*. Lawrence: University of Kansas, Support and Development Center for Follow Through, pp. 72–79.

Goetz, E. M., and Salmonson, M. M. 1972. The effect of general and descriptive reinforcement on "creativity" in easel painting. Lawrence, Kan. Paper presented at the 3rd Annual Kansas Conference on Behavioral Analysis in Education, May.

Greiner, J. M., and Karoly, P. 1976. Effects of self-control training on study activity and academic performance: An analysis of self-monitoring, self-reward, and systematic-planning components. *Journal of Counseling Psychology 23*, 495–502.

Jackson, B., and Zoost, B. V. 1972. Changing study habits through reinforcement contingencies. *Journal of Counseling Psychology 19*, 192–195.

Kirkpatrick, F. H. 1943. Music in industry. *Journal of Applied Psychology 27*, 268–274.

Konz, S. 1962. The effect of background music on productivity of two different monotonous tasks. Report to the Human Factors Society annual meeting.

Meadow, A., and Parnes, S. J. 1959. Evaluation of training in creative problem-solving. *Journal of Applied Psychology 43*, 189–194.

Nurnberger, J. I., and Zimmerman, J. 1970. Applied analysis of human behaviors: An alternative to conventional motivational inferences and unconscious determination in therapeutic programming. *Behavior Therapy 1*, 59–69.

Parnes, S. J. 1967. *Creative behavior guidebook*. New York: Charles Scribner's Sons.

Premack, D. 1959. Toward empirical behavior laws. 1. Positive reinforcement. *Psychological Review 66*, 219–233.

Richards, C. S., McReynolds, W. T., Holt, S., and Sexton, T. 1976. Effects of information feedback and self-administered consequences on self-monitoring study behavior. *Journal of Counseling Psychology 23*, 316–321.

Robinson, F. P. 1970. *Effective study*, 4th ed. New York: Harper and Row.

Schlichting, H. E., Jr., and Brown, R. V. 1970. Effect of background music on student performance. *American Biology Teacher 32*, 427–429.

Wrenn, C. G. 1933. *Practical study aids*. Stanford: Stanford University Press.

Chapter 9
Looking to the future:

Career planning

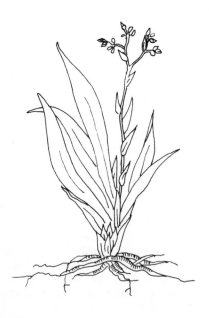

You can't plan for the future in the future —
you have to do it now.

ANONYMOUS QUOTE

In the first edition of this text, our career-planning chapter focused on helping readers choose careers that would bring the greatest personal fulfillment to their lives. We said little about the economic conditions of the times. We assumed that careful self-management would enable every individual to enter a vocation that would be personally fulfilling.

Certainly, college students of today should aspire to no less. However, we must admit that the demand for all types of college graduates is not what it once was — not even what it was as recently as 1975. An individual's choices are now markedly limited by the needs of society. Everyone who wants to be a teacher, for example, cannot get a teaching job. People should no longer think only in terms of one specific vocation they wish to pursue. They also need to think about what it is in the nature of work (all types of work) that can bring them happiness. We're not asking that people lower their ambitions and accept any job they can get. We *are* suggesting that career planning be enlarged so that individuals understand the full range of their interests in order to take advantage of the opportunities that cut across many vocational categories. People who believe there is only one job that can bring happiness may be in for bitter disappointment when someone else lands that job. On the other hand, people whose planning takes into consideration society's needs as well as their own are far more likely to find employment in personally reinforcing vocations.

To our dismay, as we look about us, we see few people who get maximum satisfaction from their work. Yes, you probably know of those who invest long hours in their labors; if you look closely, however, you may discover that it is the economic payoff, not the work itself, to which these people are attracted. Others literally detest their work and stay on the job only to avoid financial difficulties. Both of these circumstances are an affront to the dignity of the individual and an unnecessary compromise of the potential fulfillment of work. We believe that work should satisfy three kinds of goals: economic comfort, contribution to humanity, and self-fulfillment. Whether your labors will lead to these goals is intimately related to the career planning you do in your college years.

Although we recognize that career planning is essential for reaching the goals we describe, we also realize that any number of obstacles can interfere with making appropriate educational-vocational decisions. These obstacles include lack of self-understanding, inadequate information about educational and vocational opportunities, and reactions of others. In this chapter we shall explore how to cope with each of these factors as you plan a college major. We shall emphasize the selection of a major because a college major is ordinarily chosen with a vocational goal in mind. However, almost as important as a choice of a major is the selection of a minor and of elective courses; these can appreciably increase your career flexibility. As you work through the chapter, consider

One helpful way of getting occupational information is to interview people who have the kind of jobs that interest you.

career options and the preparations needed to pursue those options. We shall conclude the chapter by summarizing how the self-management approach can be used within the entire scope of career planning.

Self-understanding

Surprisingly, one of the principal obstacles in making satisfying vocational-educational decisions is lack of self-understanding. Students frequently sign up for psychology courses hoping to learn more about themselves. Unfortunately, the study of psychology does not always yield self-information. Many psychology courses, for example, stress general principles and theoretical positions rather than individual behavior. A better way to learn about *yourself* is to conduct a self-examination. You undoubtedly already know a great deal about yourself — more than anyone else — but you may still have some blind spots. Perhaps you have been reluctant to confront your abilities and interests. A multitude of social pressures and expectations can keep you from evaluating yourself candidly. Our aim here is to determine what an objective self-examination involves. You cannot decide wisely on a career without a candid self-examination.

Tech's for me too

When Charles was a senior in high school, he was uncertain about the type of career he really wanted. All of his friends seemed to have already made up their minds; they wanted to become engineers. Charles had taken a college preparatory program that included courses in math and science, but he had only vague notions about what engineers really do. Despite his lack of knowledge and the absence of any established interest in the field, Charles decided to enter the state's major engineering school along with his friends. He even got as excited as the others whenever they talked about leaving for Tech. Unfortunately, Charles and several of his friends discovered more than a year later that they had no enduring interest in engineering. They had gotten too caught up in their own verbalizing and in Tech's reputation to make fundamental discoveries about themselves.

Interests

Assessing the range of your interests can be a valuable starting place in making academic and career decisions. Surprisingly, few individuals ever take the time for a systematic assessment of their interests. Often people will even make major commitments based on someone else's interests. They will overlook long-standing interests in favor of passing attractions, become diverted by the "glamour" of certain fields, or pursue careers that are best suited to the interests of others. We don't want this to happen to you. Therefore, we suggest that you begin making a list of *your* interests. You might find it helpful to group your interests according to their primary emphasis — association with people, with things, or with ideas — since the amount of time devoted to these areas will vary among different career fields. To assist you in assessing your interests, we ask that you give attention to the following topics.

Course work Determining which college courses you enjoy is indispensable to career decisions. It is also vitally important to determine why you enjoy a course before launching a major in that area. Was it the teacher's charisma, the grading system, the attractive student who sat next to you, or the subject matter? Enjoying the subject matter obviously provides a much stronger foundation for long-term decisions than do the other reasons. If you enjoyed a course mostly because of the subject matter, you should then analyze what was most emphasized: interpersonal relations, ideas, or things (such as manipulations of data, objects). On the other hand, if you dislike a course, don't shut yourself off forever from that area. Self-examination may reveal that you were turned off by something other than the subject matter. The fact that the class met at 6:55 A.M. probably didn't contribute to positive attitudes about the course.

Extracurricular and leisure-time activities   When you have finished examining your courses, take a look at your extracurricular involvements and leisure activities. How do you spend your out-of-class time? (You can't be studying all the time.) These outside activities undoubtedly indicate strong interests and should be considered when exploring possible majors. Maybe you work as a writer or photographer on the college newspaper, perform in plays, participate in athletic activities, broadcast on the college radio station, or serve on the debating team; perhaps you jog, golf, or play tennis. What is it about these activities that attracts you? Is it coordinating, supervising, being on a team, competing, or being alone? These dimensions suggest academic and career possibilities. Just think of earning a living by doing what you enjoy! We were lucky enough to find such a profession. In fact, we've often said that if we were independently wealthy, we would work as college professors without pay!

Work experience   Your previous work experience may provide useful clues for making educational-vocational decisions. Any work, whether volunteer or paid, can tell you something about what is and is not reinforcing to you. A job in a hospital, even as an attendant, could give you an idea of what it's like to work in a hospital setting. Work as a counselor in a summer camp could indicate whether you would enjoy supervising young people. Similarly, sales work, production work, or work in a social agency might reveal that one of these activities holds reinforcement potential for you.

As with courses, you should try to identify what it was about an occupational experience that proved reinforcing. Perhaps the earnings, place of employment, freedom to be creative, opportunity for advancement, social status of the profession, or opportunity for public service were attractive to you. If you had an unsatisfactory work experience, don't automatically rule out that vocation without considering why the experience was distasteful. Maybe one aspect of the work was undesirable, but other features might offer clues about what you'd really like to do. Even if you disliked the entire job, don't give up. The work you did as a part-time or summer employee may be vastly different from what you would do as a full-time employee. We know one student who did not exactly relish his summer job of preparing hamburgers, but he now thoroughly enjoys his supervisory role for a chain of fast-food franchises.

Interest tests   Taking a test to find out where your interests lie might seem silly, but standardized interest tests often reveal vocational possibilities that do not emerge from your previous courses and work experiences. Such tests are called *interest inventories*, since there are no right or wrong answers, no good or bad scores; you simply express your preferences among a wide variety of activities. Your preferences may be compared to those of individuals engaged in a variety of occupations or career programs. The basic assumption underlying this approach is that if your interests are similar to those of people successfully engaged in a given occupation, you are likely to find satisfaction in that occupation. Two of the most widely used interest inventories are the Strong-Campbell Interest Inventory (1974) and the Kuder Occupational Interest Survey (1966). Either of these inventories can help you identify general occupational groupings that you may wish to investigate further.

You should remember that interest inventories are not measures of ability. Interests may influence whether you enter a field, but you will need ability in that field if you are to succeed. However, even when you lack certain abilities, a knowledge of your interests can prove exceedingly useful. You may not display ability in theoretical engineering, but you may decide on a technical field that is part of the engineering family. Similarly, although you may have interests in becoming a physician, the requirements for that occupation may be higher than your past achievements. You could nevertheless enter a related health field. You surely increase your chances for success and happiness when you identify areas in which your abilities and your interests correspond. Incidentally, if you took an interest test in high school, you probably should take another one now. Research has shown that interest patterns may change considerably between the ages of fifteen and twenty-five.

Development of interests   You may have been thinking as you read the preceding paragraphs that you don't have any interest strong enough to suggest what you should do with your life. Or you may have been thinking that you would like to broaden your current interests. It is not uncommon to have underdeveloped or limited interests. Any number of strategies exist for developing interests. Getting to know more about a subject, becoming actively involved in an activity, looking for the positive qualities in a course or job rather than pinpointing the negative, and seeking associations with people who are enthusiastic as well as talented in a particular field can do much to cultivate your interests. Perhaps the best way to approach interests is to realize that they are changeable. If you have a number of well-established interests, they may provide clues about career possibilities. If they don't, you can develop other interests.

Abilities and potential

Before making a career choice, you should assess both your current abilities and your potential abilities. This appraisal will demand a high degree of honesty. Your past performance may suggest certain alternatives, but it may also indicate weaknesses that you must remedy before you can consider other alternatives. Knowing your limitations can be just as helpful as knowing your strengths. Your past accomplishments may have fallen short of your potential; if so, you are faced with the challenge of accurately appraising your potential to perform better in the future.

Here, again, you may want to list your abilities according to whether they are primarily oriented toward people, things, or ideas. An ability to work with people may be reflected in how easily you can carry on a conversation, whether you can present your ideas in a convincing manner, or in how well you can coordinate or supervise an activity. These skills could easily be put to use in psychology, teaching, selling, or managerial positions. Your ability to work with things may be revealed in how comfortable you are working with numerical data, solving problems, and understanding machinery and tools. These skills could easily be associated with jobs related to mathematics, computer programming, and engineering. Ability to work with ideas may appear in how well you are able to handle abstract concepts, whether you can create new ways of doing things, and in how well you can combine information into a meaningful whole. Work in the arts or in writing might emerge from such skills. Investigation of the following topics will suggest additional ways in which your skills are related to people, things, and ideas and to possible careers.

Course grades The first area to examine is your course grades. Although grades are not a precise index of ability, they may suggest potential abilities and limitations. For example, if you are majoring in psychology and getting good grades in your first few natural science courses, you might consider a minor in that area. A natural science minor would probably enhance your study of psychology; in addition, many graduate schools in psychology prefer students with a good background in the biological and physical sciences. We're not suggesting that you major or minor only in fields in which you earn the highest marks; average grades in some fields might open more occupational doors than superior grades in an overcrowded field. However, when all other things are equal, high grades are certainly one reason for selecting a course of study.

In addition to considering areas in which your grades are good, don't overlook the impact of poor performances on your career choices. You cannot realistically choose a program in drafting, accounting, math, or forestry if you are failing courses required for entering that field — not

194

I think I'll transfer

Mike was a second-semester sophomore majoring in psychology. He had performed well in all his studies except foreign languages. He had enrolled in a foreign-language class during the first semester but dropped the class after performing poorly on the first test. His objective now was to avoid foreign languages altogether. He asked the help of his faculty advisor in exploring alternatives to the language requirement. Mike's advisor explained that an A.B. degree in psychology required two intermediate courses in a foreign language, preferably French or German. Mike inquired whether a tentatively planned program in applied psychology without the language requirement would be operative before he was to be graduated. Receiving a negative response, Mike then asked whether he could get a B.S. degree from another department without the language requirement. This option was available, but Mike rejected the idea because the other major held less interest for him. Finally, Mike decided he would transfer to an institution that did not have the language requirement. We don't know what happened to Mike at his new school. Perhaps he successfully completed his program of study. We venture to guess, however, that his fear of a difficult assignment (or his aversion to particular topics) may emerge again in the future.

unless you can find a way to improve your performance in that area. Current poor performance does not automatically mean that you can never do well. It does mean, however, that you must analyze the reasons for your poor performance and take steps to correct them. Your difficulty might be due to your study habits or your lack of prerequisite skills. Maybe you did not take certain subjects in high school, or perhaps your instruction was less than adequate. You may have been sidetracked by emotional involvements when you took the prerequisite courses. It may be helpful to withdraw from a course, get tutoring, take an incomplete, or begin a remedial or developmental program to correct your deficiencies. These steps could lead to career options that would be otherwise unattainable.

Perhaps you're not doing poorly in any of your present courses but are about to rule out a certain option because you fear one or two courses. For example, people who are interested in nursing sometimes eliminate that career option because it requires some basic courses in chemistry. People also often avoid majors that require physics, statistics, or mathematics. Frequently, however, there is nothing to fear except your own imagination. A good student sometimes avoids taking courses that are not likely to result in As and Bs. Ironically, courses with bad reputations often are not closely related to activities within a career. You might be willing to tolerate an average grade in a few of these subjects in order to

195

reach a career goal that you really want. A program of self-relaxation aimed at reducing unnecessary anxiety about these courses might prove helpful. The need to always make As can be a terrible burden — a burden that can preclude some worthwhile career alternatives.

In additon to assessing your grades in individual courses, you might also consider your overall grade point average (GPA). If you don't know your GPA, your registrar can supply that information. By keeping a record of your cumulative GPA and your GPA for each grading period, you can determine whether you are making any improvement. A trend in your GPA can sometimes be as important as your overall GPA. For example, people who are thinking about careers that require graduate training (for example, counseling) or professional school (for example, law) might be encouraged by upward trends in GPAs.

Aptitude test scores   In assessing your abilities and potential, you may want to examine standardized tests you have taken or to arrange for additional testing at your counseling center. A word of caution is in order, however: Tests cannot make decisions for you. The test is yet to be devised that can tell you what you should or should not do. However, tests can identify areas in which you might benefit from remedial or developmental programs; they can also point out abilities you never knew you had.

When you applied to college, you probably took some tests that purported to assess your ability or potential to achieve in college. A test required for entrance into many colleges is the Scholastic Aptitude Test (SAT), which yields scores on your verbal and mathematical potential. Another commonly used entrance examination is the American College Test (ACT), which yields scores on English, math, social science, and natural science. If you have taken a standardized test to gain college admission, examine your scores on that test. (Your counseling center may have a copy, or you can probably get a copy from the admissions office.) These and other aptitude tests may help you to identify areas in which you can expect to do well and areas in which you will need remedial training.

Nonacademic abilities   We have primarily stressed academic abilities, but you may have other skills that could suggest occupational choices. Perhaps you have sports skills, artistic skills, or musical talents. There are many fields of endeavor that capitalize on these abilities. You might become a recreation director, a physical education instructor, a coach, or a dancer. It has often been said that college athletics provide useful preparation for the responsibilities of adulthood. Something can be said for team effort, rigorous training, and the ability to perform under stress. These experiences provide benefits that also apply to many nonathletic vocations.

I have a yearning

When John graduated from college, he thought that making money was the way to happiness. John was unusually blessed. He was persuasive, articulate, and handsome, and he had a special gift with people. In brief, John was the kind of person who could sell refrigerators in Antarctica. He got a job as a sales representative for a well-known company, and as you would suspect, he immediately started making money — lots of it. But John wasn't happy. He felt that he was often stretching the truth, persuading people to buy what they really didn't need. The commissions he made didn't seem to bring satisfaction; neither did all the things he could buy. John told us that he hurt inside. He yearned to be of service, to contribute, to feel a part of something more. John did not depreciate the value of money or of his job. He was simply seeking something that could give greater substance and meaning to his life. At the time of this writing, John is still searching. However, he has changed his sales tactics, and he now strives for greater honesty in his sales promotions. He has also involved himself in a number of community-service projects. These projects seem to be helping John make sense out of *his* life.

Values

Besides assessing your interests and abilities, you may also want to clarify your *values*. Although values are closely related to interests, they more often represent what you seek in life on a long-term basis rather than what you find immediately reinforcing. You may find money reinforcing, but you may not consider it the basic reason for working. Values reflect that for which you strive to bring fulfillment to living. Some people strive mainly for economic security; others want to upgrade the educational opportunities of disadvantaged persons; still others value restoring the natural environment, promoting equality among the races, or enhancing the lives of the aged. What do you most want to achieve with your major? Your career? Your life? Since you will spend a significant portion of your life at work, it is imperative that you choose a career that has expectations consistent with your values. Otherwise you substantially undermine your potential for living a meaningful life.

Perhaps you still are uncertain about what you really want to accomplish in a career. If so, the following exercise may help you determine what's most important to you in a career. Since it's unlikely that any career will provide all the opportunities that you value, you must have a sense of priority about which opportunities are most indispensable.

In the following exercise, instead of assuming that you're beginning a career, assume that you are ending one. As you reflect upon your career accomplishments, which of the following would give you the greatest

197

personal satisfaction? Rank the five accomplishments that would be most important to you. If we have failed to mention accomplishments that would be significant to you, add them to the list.

Rank		*Career accomplishment*
___	1.	You traveled widely.
___	2.	You made a tremendous amount of money.
___	3.	You influenced others to adopt an ideology (religious, philosophical, political) of personal relevance to you.
___	4.	You produced ideas and/or products that were viewed as original and useful.
___	5.	You met many different people.
___	6.	You helped numerous individuals with their personal problems.
___	7.	Your work allowed you to live in communities that you really enjoyed.
___	8.	You were your own boss.
___	9.	You supervised many other people.
___	10.	You were able to work alone most of the time.
___	11.	You produced many changes in the agency or firm for which you worked.
___	12.	You were recognized as a leader in the agency or firm for which you worked.
___	13.	You scheduled your work so you could spend considerable time with your family.
___	14.	You never had to worry about losing your job.
___	15.	You never had to compromise your personal ethics to do your job.
___	16.	Your income was large enough to contribute your share toward the basic needs of your family.
___	17.	Your work contributed to a change in society.

Summary of self-understanding

Deciding on a college major and a possible career requires that you know a great deal about yourself. Since you will probably be working four or five days a week for the next thirty to forty years, it will be to your advantage to examine thoroughly and honestly your interests, abilities, and values. To determine what academic and career activities would be reinforcing to you, you should identify the courses, extracurricular activities, leisure-time experiences, and work responsibilities you have found enjoyable. In addition, examine your scores on interest tests and think about ways in which new interests can be developed. To appraise your academic and career potentials, consider your grades in various courses, trends in your GPA, your scores on such standardized tests as the ACT, and your skills in such areas as music, art, and athletics.

Self-management checklist

Before we discuss other obstacles related to career choices, let us determine where you stand relative to the behaviors recommended in this first section. At the conclusion of the chapter, we shall describe how to use self-management to achieve the desired behaviors. Those items you do not check could become goals of a self-management project.

_____ I have identified in rank order the five courses I have enjoyed most in college and have isolated the specific factors that account for my enjoyment of each.

_____ I have identified three facets of my extracurricular and leisure-time involvements that I find especially rewarding.

_____ I have taken at least one standardized interest inventory and know my score profile on that inventory.

_____ I have considered how my interests have developed and have identified at least three areas where my interests could be expanded.

_____ I know the kinds of courses in which I do well and have identified the factors responsible for my success in those courses.

_____ I know my overall GPA and any consistent changes that are occurring in that GPA.

_____ I know my score profile on at least one standardized aptitude test such as SAT or ACT.

_____ I have identified at least three of my nonacademic skills that should be considered in making a career decision.

Knowledge of educational-occupational opportunities

A second major obstacle to effective career planning is lack of knowledge of educational-occupational opportunities. Few students can identify all the majors open to them at their own college, much less identify the myriad of jobs that exist for the college educated. Too frequently students select a major or career by relying on what a friend has told them rather than by determining facts for themselves. They let rumors and hearsay dictate important choices. Many other students try to get all their information from a single (usually friendly) faculty member. Students often ask us what they can do with a major in _____. The truth is that we often have limited knowledge of the possibilities. Wise choices require more than just asking someone else what you might do and where the jobs might be.

We are not suggesting that you discount professors as important sources of information about careers. They can be of immense help. Professors can often identify a variety of jobs related to their specialties and collateral areas of study, as well as elaborate on how they made their own career decisions. They can also be helpful in identifying schools that offer specialized training, in offering suggestions on appropriate reading material related to their fields, and in providing feedback on your efforts.

Information about possible majors is undoubtedly also available at your college library, counseling center, or placement office. You can probably also get facts on what you might do with every conceivable major. You can get ideas about the future of a field; the abilities, skills, and other personal traits required; the duties performed; lines of promotion; and how your interests, abilities, and values fit into that occupation. You can also locate up-to-date information on economic conditions and the overall job outlook for college graduates. You need not rely on rumors. To get you started in developing knowledge about your educational-occupational opportunities, we shall explore the general occupational outlook for the 1980s. Then we'll indicate some specific sources of information about occupational families and about the kinds of jobs entered by people with different college majors.

General outlook

Occupational growth   You may be apprehensive about the vocational outlook for college graduates. You have probably heard talk about unemployed college graduates pounding the streets looking for work. Perhaps you have even thought, "Why stay in college if I can't get a job when I finish?" The boom period of the 1960s, when employers came to colleges in large numbers looking for graduates, is past. Data from the Bureau of Labor Statistics indicate that the potential supply of college graduates over the next few years is greater than the demand for college graduates in jobs traditionally held by the college educated. Some 13.1 million new college graduates are expected to enter the labor market between 1974 and 1985, to fill an estimated 12.1 million jobs. These figures mean that your prospective employers can be much more selective in their hiring, but it does not mean that you should deemphasize the importance of a college degree. All projections indicate that college graduates will face the brightest prospects, although some areas will offer more promise than others. Unfortunately, many college graduates may have to accept *entry-level* jobs that do not fully utilize their skills.

Figure 9.1 shows how professional and technical occupations will grow in comparison with other occupations. It also provides an indication of the growth expected for various professional groups. Notice that the need for registered nurses, one of the largest occupational groups, will grow by more than 50 percent. In all, about 400,000 new nurses will be needed. Notice also the tremendous growth in the computer field. The demand for programmers and systems analysts will exceed the supply. The same is true of the engineering field. That should be good news for computer specialists and engineers. In many other areas as well, the supply of college graduates will fall short of the demand.

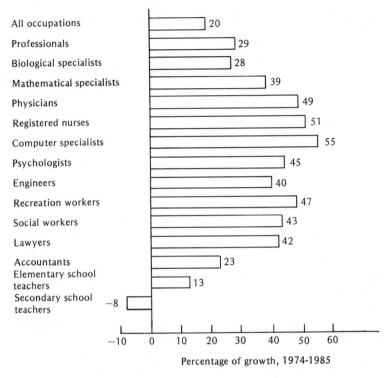

Figure 9.1 Job outlook for future graduates. (Department of Labor)

Growth, however, is not the only indicator of employment demands in an occupation. Death, retirement, and movement of workers to other fields create many vacancies each year. Note that elementary teaching will experience only minimal growth in the years ahead and that the number of secondary school teachers will decline. However, the fact that more than two million people now work as elementary and secondary teachers means that many replacements will be needed each year. Unfortunately, the supply may exceed the demand, thus creating keener competition for employment in teaching. Opportunities for teachers in math, physical science, special education, and reading are expected to be very favorable.

In thinking about projected opportunities within a field, you should also consider how many people are preparing to enter that profession. Psychology, for example, is expected to enjoy substantial growth by 1985, but currently there are more persons in graduate schools preparing to be psychologists than there are members in the American

Psychological Association (Woods, 1976). Here again, keen competition can be expected for traditional jobs held by psychologists (such as college teaching), but opportunities in other areas (such as private practice, industry, and the judicial system) may hold promise for new psychologists.

At this point in career planning, it is important that you not be shaken by unfounded rumors and skepticism about the future. Although no one can predict the future, current trends make the future occupational outlook appear optimistic for well-trained people. Government, education, service agencies, trade, finance, and practically every sector of the economy needs college-educated and highly trained workers. No one is demanding less educated workers. You may have to plan more carefully, be better prepared academically, and be more flexible than your college predecessors, but the overall job market is far from dismal.

Women   We are not discriminating against men by giving additional information to women, but there are certain areas in the job market to which women should give special attention. Shortages of well-trained workers in selected areas plus legislation barring discrimination in employment should enhance the employment outlook for qualified women. However, there are potential problems. Labor statistics show that most professional female workers are concentrated in a limited number of professions. Teaching, for example, employs about 40 percent of all women engaged in professional work. Library science, social work, and nursing also have a high percentage of women. Although these professions can expect growth in the future, they alone cannot accommodate the increasing numbers of women who are going to college. In addition, women can expect increasing competition from men in what were once "female" occupations. If most women continue to train for a restricted number of professional occupations, they can expect keen competition for employment.

To enhance their employment prospects, women should consider occupations in which shortages are apt to exist and in which women are underrepresented. More women are needed as chemists, engineers, physicians, optometrists, dentists, and technical writers, and in business and management. Women are also underrepresented in law, but the supply of lawyers is at least equal to demand. Women should also consider fields in which new technology is developing; computer programming and related work, for example, hold considerable promise. Finally, women who are going into teaching should definitely explore fields in which teacher shortages may exist and/or in which women are underrepresented. School administration, math, physical sciences, and industrial arts are prime examples. New possibilities are emerging every day; occupations are sexist only to the extent that you allow them to be so.

Published information

An abundance of published material is available to help people learn about the thousands of occupations that exist. Your library probably has most of this occupational information. Your reference librarian can tell you about government documents, pamphlets, indexes, tapes, and occupational files that you never knew existed. You should make a tentative list of the occupations that you would like to explore. You may be interested in training requirements, worker traits, duties, salaries, discrimination practices against women and minorities, or lines of promotion for these occupations. If you have some idea of what you are seeking, your librarian can help you locate the appropriate materials.

Occupational Outlook Handbook One of the most accurate and useful sources of occupational information is the *Occupational Outlook Handbook*, published biennially by the Bureau of Labor Statistics. The *Handbook* provides monographs on more than eight hundred occupations. For each occupation there is a concise and readable description of the nature of the work, training and other qualifications, advancement, employment outlook, earnings and working conditions, and sources of additional information. You will find the information up-to-date since the *Handbook* is revised every two years. The boxed information from the *Handbook* on page 204 will give you an idea of the nature of the work of psychologists.

A supplement to the *Occupational Outlook Handbook* is the *Occupational Outlook Quarterly*, which is published between editions of the *Handbook* and provides more current occupational information. The *Quarterly* contains timely articles on practically every aspect of career planning. Recent *Quarterly* articles have included: "The College Graduate — 1989 Job Prospects," "Why Junior College?" "Putting a Bachelor of Arts Degree to Work," "Toward Matching Personal and Job Characteristics," and "Women College Graduates — Will They Find Jobs?"

Materials related to your major Many colleges publish brochures and books that tell what students can do with different majors. This information is often based on follow-up surveys of the college's graduates. One excellent example of such a book is *What Can I Do with a Major in ___ ?* (1975), prepared by Lawrence Malnig and Sandra L. Morrow of Saint Peter's College. This text offers information on the jobs that graduates of specific departments entered upon leaving college and that they held in later years. Maybe your college placement office or counseling center has prepared similar materials.

Another book that can be of help in identifying the type of jobs that persons with various majors can enter is *The Occupational Thesaurus*,

Psychologists — What do they do?

Areas of specialization in psychology include *experimental psychology* — in which behavior processes are studied in the laboratory; *developmental psychology* — the study of the causes of behavioral changes as people progress through life; *personality* — the study of the processes by which a person becomes a unique individual; *social psychology* — in which people's interactions with others and with the social environment are examined; *educational and school psychology* — which are concerned with the psychological factors related to the process of education; *comparative psychology* — in which the behavior of different animals, including man, is compared; *physiological psychology* — the study of the relationship of behavior to the biological functions of the body; and *psychometrics* — the development and application of procedures for measuring psychological variables.

Psychologists often combine several areas of psychology in their specialty. *Clinical psychologists* are the largest group of specialists. They generally work in mental hospitals or clinics, and are involved mainly with problems of mentally or emotionally disturbed people. Clinical psychologists may also deal with the emotional impact of injury or disease, helping the client to readjust to life with altered physical capabilities. They interview patients, give diagnostic tests, provide individual, family, and group psychotherapy, and design and carry through behavior modification programs. *Counseling psychologists* help people with important problems of everyday living. In their work, they may use any of a number of counseling techniques. Other combined fields are *industrial and organizational psychology,* where problems of motivation and morale in work situations are studied; *engineering psychology,* the development and improvement of human-machine systems; *consumer psychology,* the study of the psychological factors that determine an individual's behavior as a consumer of goods and services; and *environmental psychology*, the relationships between individuals and their environment.

Adapted from Bureau of Labor Statistics. Psychologists. *Occupational Outlook Handbook*, 1976–77, pp. 505–506.

by E. A. Teal (two volumes, 1973). The first volume of the *Thesaurus* covers majors in anthropology, economics, history, languages, mathematics, political science, psychology, and sociology. The second volume covers majors in accounting, biology, chemistry, finance, geology, management, marketing, physics, and transportation. While the *Thesaurus* is somewhat dated, you can still use it to get an idea of a broad range of entry-level positions that might otherwise be overlooked. For instance, major areas of employment for graduates with an undergraduate degree in psychology include: advertising, banking and finance, communications, education, insurance, manufacturing, marketing, medical services, merchandising, personnel and industrial relations, publishing, social services and government, and transportation. Each major area listed in the *Thesaurus* is further broken down into more specific job opportunities. For example, opportunities for psychology majors in the area of banking and finance include: community relations, job analysis, personnel, placement, public relations, publicity, sales, statistics, and many more.

There are some texts that deal in detail with the opportunities of a single major. *Career Opportunities for Psychologists: Expanding and Emerging Areas* (Woods, 1976) is an example of such a book; it contains information on a number of options not ordinarily considered by new graduates of psychology. Every psychology major should examine this text. If you don't happen to be a psychology major, we imagine you can find a similar text related to your major.

Other published materials   After you examine the *Handbook*, the *Quarterly*, and texts related to your major, you may want to look for additional information. Your librarian can help you locate the materials you need. Women should inquire about materials especially relevant to women. Your library probably has publications from the Women's Bureau of the Department of Labor. For example, there is a series of pamphlets entitled *Why Not Be _____* (an Engineer, an Optometrist, a Pharmacist, and so forth). Whatever the source, evaluate carefully who has prepared the material and for what purpose. For example, don't take too literally glamorized information disseminated by organizations (such as the French Foreign Legion) trying to recruit workers. Finally, be exhaustive in getting all the current facts on the few occupations for which you seek information.

Interviewing professionals

One helpful way of getting occupational information is to interview people who have the kind of jobs that interest you. These individuals can give you first-hand information about the kind of training they received, how they got their first position, local supply and demand for their services, and the nuances of their work. Of course, one individual can't have all the answers, but that individual can probably give you some answers you couldn't get from published sources.

We advise you to prepare thoroughly for this kind of interview. Read what you can about the occupation and know what information you are seeking. You will probably want to prepare a list of specific questions, in order to get details without taking an undue portion of the person's time.

Rather than asking, "Would you tell me about the field of accounting?" you might ask, "What opportunities exist for accountants in this town?" "What college courses did you find most useful?" "How is your work similar or different from that of other accountants?" You should avoid putting the individual on the spot. For example, "What do you find unpleasant about your work?" would be more diplomatic than "Do you dislike your work?"

Behavioral checklist

At first glance, becoming knowledgeable about educational-vocational opportunities may seem like a massive undertaking. To reduce an overwhelming task, we suggest that you use the following checklist, which tells you the specific things you must do to increase your knowledge of occupations. If you are willing to do these things one by one, you will not find the task overwhelming.

_____ I know where the *Occupational Outlook Handbook* and *Quarterly* are located in the college library.

_____ I have looked at these documents.

_____ I have examined at least one text that identifies what students can do with various majors (*The Occupational Thesaurus, What Can I Do with a Major in____?*).

_____ I have identified at least three vocational areas (consistent with my interests, abilities, and values) for which employment opportunities look good in the 1980s.

_____ I have interviewed workers in all three of these vocational areas.

Reactions from others

A third major obstacle to making satisfying career choices involves the reactions of others. Sometimes these reactions are openly critical and demeaning. We have known several people who were chided so much by friends that they gave up their initial career choices. However, the reactions of friends more often take the form of aloofness or social ostracism. You discover that your peers are not quite so friendly as they used to be and that they are less likely to seek out your company. These reactions hurt, and they shake the strongest resolves.

Though social and vocational norms are changing, unrecognized stereotyping still exists even in the most unlikely places. Many teachers, parents, and counselors hold to notions that certain jobs are intended for males and certain others for females. You must be particularly careful to recognize when you are being talked out of or talked into an occupation solely on the basis of your sex. You must also be careful not to let others influence you because *they* think a program is too difficult, too easy, too

Too many jokes?

For some time Ralph had held a secret interest in medicine. Specifically, he was interested in becoming a nurse. Ralph finally got the nerve to express his ambitions to his guidance counselor. The counselor responded enthusiastically, and eventually Ralph felt quite comfortable in discussing his nursing interests with the counselor. Unfortunately, Ralph quickly became the butt of jokes. Many of the jokes were not intended to be malicious, but they hurt just the same; a few of them were harmful. Ralph learned that several people thought it was "unnatural" for him to have an interest in nursing.

Despite the abuse, Ralph enrolled at a regional university to pursue a nursing career. When he returned home on weekend visits, he was faced with the inevitable question: "What are you majoring in?" The fear of ridicule made Ralph reluctant rather than proud of telling others his major. He was slowly losing his own enthusiasm for nursing. After experiencing academic difficulties in one of his more rigorous courses, Ralph withdrew from the nursing program. Possibly the negative reactions of others took away the initiative that Ralph needed in order to achieve success. No one knows for sure.

demeaning, and so on. At times others may criticize your choice because it represents a direction that they would like to pursue but for various reasons feel they can't. What you must do is to develop whatever support you need to follow through with what you want for *your* own life.

To support you in overcoming negative reactions from others, you might try one or more of the following suggestions. First, talk with others who have successfully overcome personal obstacles to enter their professions. Both women and men who hold nontraditional jobs could be a source of support. Second, you could associate with people who have career interests similar to yours. Third, learn the facts about your career choice, such as the demand for new workers and the rewards and shortcomings within the field, in order to help counteract unsubstantiated arguments from well-intentioned parents and friends. Finally, remember that career counselors may be a source of support. Research (such as Thoresen and Krumboltz, 1967) has shown that students who receive counselor approval for seeking information will seek information more frequently. Professionals may also help you to recognize and prepare for the influences you face from others.

Self-managed planning

The major goal of career planning is not really to find that *one* career for which you are best suited, but rather to expand your career options.

Many people grow up hearing others say, "Oh, you'd make a great law-yer," "You're a born teacher," "You'll never be happy unless you become a doctor." Too many then believe that happiness is a matter of finding the one job for which they are suited. The truth is that there are more than 46,000 different kinds of jobs and that any person can probably find happiness in hundreds of different jobs. The skills that make for a suc-cessful teacher can undoubtedly be employed to make, say, a successful administrator, recreation director, restaurant manager, or TV an-nouncer. Thus, the major quest of self-management is to expand the directions you can go in the choice of a career.

You can expand your options by pursuing the following suggestions. First, you can achieve this flexibility with most majors by merely includ-ing basic courses that cut across all types of careers: English, math, psychology, public speaking. At a time when many students are opting to take a large number of vocationally oriented courses, you should consider general courses as well. Stop and ask yourself what employers really want in an employee; they want the ability to reason, to cope with change. They want people with specific skills, but they also want workers with basic knowledge of math and English, with interpersonal skills and ability to communicate. These kinds of workers can easily be retrained if their specialty is no longer needed.

The second way you can achieve flexibility is by the judicious selec-tion of a major and a minor. Students who choose psychology as a major and sociology as a minor, for example, add minimal diversity to their studies. However, a psychology major who minors in computer science, statistics, math, or business will have employment opportunities in a wider range of occupations.

The obstacles discussed in this chapter can substantially limit the career options available to you at the conclusion of your college program. Thus, we have suggested strategies for increasing your self-under-standing, for increasing your knowledge of educational-occupational op-portunities, and for coping with negative reactions from others. Now it is up to you to move from *thinking* about career planning to *doing* some-thing about it. This is where self-management is important.

Like all areas discussed in this text, career planning involves certain specifiable behaviors. We shall now identify self-management strategies that can be used to produce such behaviors.

1. *Selecting a goal* Your overall goal is to increase your knowledge of occupational opportunities consistent with your interests, abilities, and values. In responding to the earlier checklists, you may have discovered that you first need a systematic assessment of your abilities and inter-ests. You may then want to match your interests and abilities against tentative job choices. (An excellent article, "Toward Matching Personal

208

and Job Characteristics," by D. Dillion, in the Spring 1975 issue of *Occupational Outlook Quarterly* can help you match your personal traits with those deemed useful on many jobs.)

2. *Monitoring target behavior* Next, you might keep a record of all the people you have consulted or wish to consult about your career plans (such as professors, department heads, counselors, librarians). You might also record the time you spend exploring your interests and abilities. In a word, record any behavior directed toward any activity on our two checklists.

3. *Changing setting events* You may find that establishing a time schedule for such behaviors as visiting the library, interviewing, and taking interest tests would help to produce those behaviors. Another good step would be to begin your project in the setting that you find most supportive. Would the counseling center, the library, or an industrial site be the best starting place for you? Remember that you want to arrange conditions (time and place) to facilitate career planning.

4. *Establishing effective consequences* There are many procedures that you could use to establish consequences for your information-seeking and decision-making behaviors. You might try setting up a token economy and reinforce yourself after each action you take, regardless of how small the action. You might contract with a friend who is also attempting to make career decisions to provide reinforcement for each other. One of your major problems may be finding sources of approval that will counteract parental pressure. Dad may want you to be a physician and be disappointed if you consider other career possibilities. Can you identify some significant other people — fellow students, counselors, teachers — whose approval would soften the impact of parental disapproval? If so, how can you marshal that approval for your career choices?

5. *Applying covert control* You could use covert processes to facilitate information seeking or to help deal with related problems that occur in your career planning. For example, you might use covert positive reinforcement to facilitate information-seeking behavior. Or you may find yourself anxious over a course that you must take to meet certain career objectives. In this case relaxation exercises might be helpful.

6. *Consolidating your gains* Since career planning is increasingly viewed as a lifelong process, every bit of information that you gather about your interests, abilities, values, and career opportunities represents tangible progress. The major challenge will be organizing that information in such a way that it points to a college major and minor and supporting courses. If you begin to feel real dissatisfaction with a series of courses in your major or minor or if you become aware of a change in economic conditions that drastically affects career opportunities in your chosen field, you may need to engage in more information seeking.

Concluding thoughts

The purposes of this chapter were to specify the major obstacles to effective career planning, and to suggest procedures that you could apply to overcome those obstacles. If you follow some of our suggestions, you will come into contact with librarians, counselors, teachers, and workers in the field, but don't expect any of these people to make decisions for you. If you go to these people with specific requests, they will probably help you decide judiciously. The career planning you are doing today can fundamentally affect the quality of your life tomorrow. Joy, excitement, and fulfillment can be found in many careers. Please accept no less.

References

American college testing program — technical report. 1965. Iowa City, Iowa: American College Testing Program.

Angoff, W. H. (ed.). 1971. *The college board admissions testing program: A technical report on research and development activities relating to the scholastic aptitude test and achievement tests.* New York: College Entrance Examination Board.

Kuder, G. F. 1966. *Kuder occupational interest survey, general manual.* Chicago: Science Research Associates.

Malnig, L. R., and Morrow, S. L. 1975. *What can I do with a major in ___?* Jersey City, N.J.:Saint Peter's College Press.

Occupational outlook handbook, 1976–1977. Washington, D.C.: Bureau of Labor Statistics.

Occupational outlook quarterly. Washington, D.C.: Bureau of Labor Statistics.

Strong-Campbell interest inventory. 1974. Stanford: Stanford University Press.

Teal, E. A. 1973. *The occupational thesaurus,* Vol. I and II. Bethlehem, Pa.: Lehigh University.

Thoresen, C. E., and Krumboltz, J. D. 1967. Relationship of counselor reinforcement of selected responses to external behavior. *Journal of Counseling Psychology* 14(2), 140–144.

Why not be ___. Washington, D.C.: Women's Bureau, U.S. Department of Labor.

Woods, P. J. (ed.). 1976. *Career opportunities for psychologists: Expanding and emerging areas.* Washington, D.C.: American Psychological Association.

Chapter 10
Wealthier than kings:

Enhancing interpersonal attractions

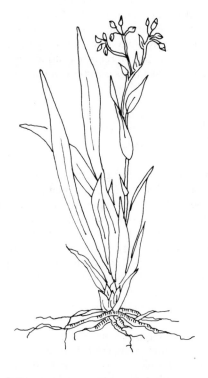

For thy sweet love rememb'red such wealth brings
That then I scorn to change my state with kings.

WILLIAM SHAKESPEARE

The couplet from Shakespeare graphically illustrates the importance of our present topic. Interpersonal attractions contribute fundamentally to the quality of life. A life devoid of friendship and love is rarely considered fulfilling. Fortunately, human beings can do something to increase the likelihood of love and friendship in their lives. Being liked, loved, disliked, or hated is not a chance happening. You can influence how others act and feel toward you.

This chapter will consider only those verbal and nonverbal behaviors that directly affect a person's interpersonal attractiveness. Obviously this is not the whole story. Practically every area of behavior discussed in this text has implications for personal attractiveness. For example, your eating and exercise behaviors will certainly affect physical attractiveness. Keeping yourself in good physical trim also conveys a pride in yourself that is often very appealing to others. Outside the physical domain, consider how behavior in areas such as smoking, drinking, study, time, money, and household management could affect your attractiveness. People who are viewed as competent, as having an array of skills, as taking care of themselves physically, and as managing their domestic affairs well have a strong base for interpersonal attractiveness. However, the behaviors we shall discuss in this chapter can markedly enhance or detract from that base.

Becoming reinforcing to others

Many psychologists believe that the principle of *reciprocal reinforcement* affects all interpersonal relations. In nontechnical terms, this principle asserts that others will like (or value) you to the extent that your behavior is reinforcing to them. In other words, people reciprocate according to what they perceive themselves as receiving. The validity of this principle is well documented in Byrne's (1971) comprehensive study of interpersonal attraction. Thus, the first task in enhancing your interpersonal relationships is to identify ways in which your behavior can become more reinforcing to others.

Listening to others
The way to begin being reinforcing to others is to listen to them. Unfortunately, many people become so eager for their turn to speak that they miss much of what other people are expressing, both verbally and nonverbally. Four factors possibly account for the added personal attractiveness that results from listening: (1) you clearly demonstrate to others that you value them and what they have to say; (2) you improve the accuracy of your comments by knowing what others have said to you;

(3) you increase the probability that others will listen to you when it's your turn to speak; and (4) you accentuate your uniqueness by exhibiting a rare behavior (good listening).

Amount of listening To improve your listening ability, you might start by recording the times that you listen and the times that you speak. One of our students undertook such a project to improve family communications. Family members recorded the occasions that they talked and that they listened. Our student found that initially she was doing most of the talking. By increasing her listening, she produced a greater balance in conversation, which proved highly reinforcing to the whole family. Rather than recording the number of times that you listen, you may want to use a stopwatch to record the amount of time you listen, especially if your episodes of talking and listening tend to be quite extended. To help increase your listening time in group conversations, you could ask a friend who is a good listener unobtrusively to cue you when it's your time to listen.

Perhaps you are beginning to wonder just how much listening and how much talking you should actually do. We have two suggestions: 1. Restrict your talking to an equitable portion of the time; that is, if you are talking to one other person, talk no more than 50 percent of the time; if you are talking to two other persons, talk no more than one third of the time. 2. Avoid long-winded comments. A point usually can be made in a minute or less. Effective interpersonal relations depend on two-way communication. If the sheer quantity of your verbalizations prevents others from talking, you can be assured that your reinforcement value will not be embellished.

Active listening Active listening requires more than just letting the other person talk. Paraphrasing and commenting directly on what another has just said are basic ways of demonstrating that you are tuning in to what is being said. Paraphrasing has two major benefits. It lets other people know that you are listening to them, and it permits them to correct any error in comprehension on your part. A good way to begin a paraphrase is to comment, "You're saying that . . . ," "So you want . . . ," "Your feelings are . . ." Counselors have used this technique for years to let clients know that they are being heard. By paraphrasing or commenting directly on what other people say, you indicate that their comments are worthy of further discussion. In contrast, what kind of message do you convey when you respond to another person's comment by abruptly changing the subject?

When you listen actively, you listen for more than words. Hardly anything is more fundamental to a relationship than tuning in to the other person's feelings. We have found that "caring about my feelings" is

So you had a bad day?

The following conversations might help clarify what we mean by active listening. Susan does an equal amount of listening in each of the following episodes, but she listens more actively in one than in the other. We think you'll be able to tell the difference.

Episode One

Jim: This has not been one of my red-letter days. First thing this morning, the boss . . .

Susan: Oh, do you know who called me today? Steve Turner. I haven't seen Steve in five years. Boy, did he look great!

Jim: As I was saying, the boss came in and blasted me for not having completed the Dobbins Report. He doesn't seem to understand . . .

Susan: Well, did you get the report finished?

Jim: Yeah, but John and I had a terrible time agreeing on it. Every time I rejected one of his recommendations, he seemed to take it personally.

Susan: How can grown men act so infantile?

Jim: Well, in trying to appease the boss, I asked him to go to lunch with me. Thought I'd take him to that little place down on the wharf, since he likes seafood so much.

Susan: Steve and I went to Marty's Steakpit for lunch. I never realized that place was so intimate.

Jim: On the way to lunch, I had a flat tire, which wouldn't have been so bad except that the spare was also flat. By the time I had walked to a service station and gotten the tires fixed, we wound up taking an hour and a half just to get to the restaurant.

Susan: How much did it cost to get the tires fixed?

---

the principal criterion used by college students in judging the humanistic qualities of another. When people interact with you, try to identify the feelings they express. When you sense that someone feels angry, sad, frustrated, elated, or in love, comment to that effect. Nonverbal cues (body posture, facial expression), tone of voice, and rhythm of voice often convey a different message from that expressed verbally. You might ask whether the other person agrees with a particular view and receive an affirmative but hesitant reply. Instead of saying, "Okay, you agree that . . . ," you should respond, "You feel very ambivalent about . . . ," or "You're uncertain as to whether . . ."

In sum, we suggest that an indispensable first step in becoming reinforcing to others is to listen carefully to what they have to say. Putting aside other activities when they are speaking to you, looking at them

---

Episode Two

Jim: This has not been one of my red-letter days. First thing this morning, the boss came in and chewed me out for not having completed the Dobbins Report. He didn't seem to understand that I had to get some information from John before I could complete it.

Susan: So you feel he was really criticizing you very unfairly.

Jim: Yeah, plus John kept getting upset when I would reject one of his recommendations about what should go in the report.

Susan: That must have been very frustrating to you.

Jim: You bet, but to top it off, I took the boss to lunch — trying to appease his feelings, you know. On the way I had a flat tire and discovered that my spare was also flat. By the time I had located a service station and gotten the tires fixed, we had spent an hour and a half getting to lunch. Can you believe it — an hour and a half?

Susan: Bet you were feeling almost paranoid by then.

Jim: Right! But that's enough about my glorious day. What happened with yours?

Susan: You remember Steve Turner from college. Well, he was passing through on his way to the Coast. He called and we got together for lunch. It was great reminiscing and talking about where people are now.

---

when they speak, being careful not to interrupt their comments, and commenting directly on what they have just expressed — these behaviors communicate to other people that you care about and understand what they are saying. Incidentally, you might apply the same criteria in determining whether other people are interested in what you have to say.

Conversing with others

Talking can be as important as listening in determining your reinforcement value for others. For example, many individuals become quite uncomfortable when trying to talk with an extremely reticent person. People who have little to say provide minimal stimulation for others and may be perceived as uptight or aloof. Other individuals have no trouble talking but are still viewed as boring, egotistical, or offensive. Thus, we shall direct our discussion more toward changing the quality of talking than toward the sheer quantity. However, having a clearer perception of what to talk about should help reticent people increase the quantity of their talking.

Asking questions   The effective conversationalist typically asks lots of questions, with many of these questions focusing on the other person's views, feelings, and interests. Most individuals are delighted to talk about their lives but seldom receive the direct invitation to do so. Asking questions helps you identify similarities between you and others, and perceived similarity contributes greatly to interpersonal attraction (Berscheid and Walster, 1969). Thus, after identifying areas of similarity, you can comment, "I agree with you on that," or "I'm also interested in . . ." Asking questions also helps you to become aware of subtle aspects of others' lives and thus to identify additional events that would be reinforcing to them. You may discover, for example, that an individual has an interest in an exotic form of art. This could be valuable information in selecting a gift for that person on a special occasion.

Your questions will be far more provocative if they are *open ended,* that is, if they can be answered in several different ways. Open-ended questions typically ask for a person's views and feelings whereas *closed questions* ask for specific facts. Closed questions seldom stimulate comments beyond the mere answering of the questions. Examples of closed questions would be: "How long did it take you to get here?" "What did you have for dinner last night?" "Do you practice yoga?" There is obviously a time for acquiring factual information about another person, but the conversation will be more mutually reinforcing if you ask a lot of open-ended questions, such as "What did you enjoy most about your trip?" "How did you like the meal last night compared to . . .?" "What led you to decide to take up yoga?" Such questions are more interesting both to ask and to answer.

However, if you initially ask too many questions dealing with another person's views and feelings, you may be viewed as prematurely personal. Thus, you might begin a conversation with a combination of factual and opinion questions about areas of assumed mutual interest, such as university life, sports activity, or recreational experiences. The kinds of questions that you could safely ask a new acquaintance at a university social function would be: "How long have you been at the University?" "What's your major?" "What have you liked best about the University?" "Where is your home originally?" "Do you know other people from that area here at the University?" "Are you currently involved in any sports?" "Have you visited . . . yet?" "Has the University measured up to your expectations thus far?"

We must admit that the most innocent question can sometimes touch a sensitive area in another's life. A colleague told us about an incident when he was conducting his first master's thesis exam. Wanting to put the candidate at ease, he asked how she had developed an interest in her thesis topic. She immediately broke into tears, and the meeting was quickly adjourned. Our colleague later found that the major reason the student had chosen this particular topic in child development was its relationship to abuses she had suffered as a child. Thus, we can't guarantee that any particular question will be both safe and stimulating. However, we can guarantee that other people will generally feel more appreciated and more important if you ask questions that allow them to relate important aspects of their lives.

Discussing your own experiences   Isn't there a time for talking about your own experiences, views, feelings, and priorities? Absolutely, but the conversation of many begins and ends at this level. In trying to impress others with their accomplishments, they are often perceived as self-centered and insecure. The best time to talk about *you* is when the other person asks about you; these questions suggest a readiness to learn about your views, feelings, and experiences.

You may determine that there are aspects of your experience about which the other person might like to know. When others mention experiences similar to yours, you can point out that similarity: "I know exactly what you mean because I was once involved in . . ." You need not say, "I once achieved . . ." Others will ask about your achievements if they care to know about them. For example, you might mention that you can appreciate the other person's interest in cross-country track since you also participate in this activity. You needn't mention that you've been the conference champion twice, unless the other person questions you to that extent. Frequently others will probe to the degree that you probe. If you ask about other people's achievements in cross-country, they are more likely to ask about yours.

If the other person fails to bring up topics relating to your interests and achievements, you can legitimately take the initiative. You can mention that the track coach is exceptionally competent, that your psychology instructor has high expectations in her course, that you've enjoyed music since childhood, that the University has an Olympic-size pool, and that tennis is wonderful exercise. These comments may lead to questions regarding the nature of your interests and accomplishments in each area.

Giving approval

Verbal approval is unquestionably the most widely used (and abused) of all would-be reinforcers. Seldom do others accept verbal accolades without examining closely what is proffered. People are interested in determining whether you mean what you say or whether you are acting from ulterior motives. If your approval is judged to be sincere, it can be tremendously reinforcing, but if your approval appears even slightly artificial, others will be repulsed by it. We reject the idea that conveying sincerity involves nothing more than being sincere. Being sincere helps, but it is quite possible for sincere people to seem artificial. For that reason we shall provide specific guidelines for giving approval in an authentic and reinforcing way. Specifically, we shall examine what you approve, how you approve, redundancy of approval, consistency of approval, frequency of approval, and pairing approval with other reinforcers.[1] These factors can greatly enhance your efforts to foster interpersonal attractions.

What you approve   One of the easiest ways to judge the sincerity of people's approval (praise) is to consider *what* they approve. Most individuals enjoy being praised, but they prefer being praised for bona fide accomplishments. Thus, before giving verbal approval, determine what others consider to be significant accomplishments. To do this requires careful observation and listening. People usually engage in or talk about activities that they deem important. You can use these high-priority activities and conversations as a basis for legitimate compliments. For example, when your friend Marsha gives a speech, about which she has talked for days, you could congratulate her on having completed a difficult assignment. In addition, there may be facets of Marsha's speech worthy of commendation. If you observe and listen closely, you will have little difficulty identifying things worth complimenting.

Generally speaking, the more specific you make your approval, the more reinforcing the approval will be. It doesn't take much effort or insight to say, "Great job," "I enjoyed your presentation," "Inspiring performance," or "You did beautifully." You could make these statements after sleeping through a performance. However, if you want to enumerate features of a performance that were especially impressive, you will have to pay attention. The more specific you make your compliments, the more intently you have to listen and/or watch a person's performance. For example, we would be pleased if you wrote us saying that you had given our book to several of your friends because you thought our ideas were worthwhile. However, we would be especially delighted if your letter detailed *which* suggestions you had found particularly useful.

How you approve   People judge the sincerity of approval not only by what you say but by how you say it. Some people are so lavish in their compliments that you tend to minimize what they have to say. Insincere flatterers often elicit a host of side glances when they deliver their lofty words of commendation. They may note that your behavior is the

---

[1] For a discussion of the effects of verbal approval on student-teacher relationships, see R. L. Williams and Kamala Anandam. *Cooperative Classroom Management* (Columbus, Ohio, Charles E. Merrill, 1973).

"greatest," "the most fantastic," "the best ever," or even "beyond comparison." Since many people tend to dislike ostentatious, flamboyant approval, we suggest that you reserve superlatives for very special accomplishments.

The authenticity of your approval may also be questioned on the basis of your nonverbal behavior. The individual who offers congratulations in a halfhearted tone, the person who says, "That's really a funny story," but fails to laugh, the individual who is "so happy for you" but doesn't smile, and the person who thinks you look "just great" but hardly notices you — these people illustrate our point. In summarizing the research on nonverbal communication, Mehrabian (1969) noted that people turn more toward, stand nearer to, and make more frequent eye contact with those they like than with those they dislike. Such simple acts as a touch, a smile, or a nod of the head can be profoundly important in conveying the sincerity of your approval.

Redundancy of approval Another factor that affects the reinforcement value of your approval is its redundancy. An initially reinforcing phrase such as "keep up the good work," "very good," or "you look nice" may lose much of its reinforcement value with repeated usage. Most people assume that the individual who repeatedly makes the same pronouncement regarding their behavior really is not paying attention to them. Because this is an important issue, you should develop a list of different approval comments and then practice verbalizing them. Otherwise you run the risk of being perceived as insincere simply because of your limited verbal repertoire.

There are two major ways to word a compliment. First, you can highlight your personal reaction to another's behavior: "I enjoyed . . . ," "I especially liked . . . ," or "I was inspired by . . ." Second, you can make blanket statements about the quality of another's behavior: "What you said about . . . was inspiring," "Your emphasis on . . . was great," or "Your analysis of . . . was very creative." To minimize redundancy, you should periodically use both types of compliments. Admittedly, personal-reaction statements are more consistent with reality than are blanket statements. In complimenting another person, you ordinarily can speak only for yourself. Personal-reaction statements reflect that limitation while blanket statements may imply a more pervasive judgment. However, we suspect that most people who are being complimented realize that when you say, "That was a great job," you are speaking only for yourself. Therefore, the blanket statement generally is considered acceptable. Our point on redundancy is inextricably tied to our earlier emphasis on specificity. The more specific your approval, the less you are likely to be redundant — regardless of which category you use.

Consistency of approval Anticipated reinforcement can generate a great deal of pleasureful excitement. Recall looking forward to attending a party, going on a date, or participating in an athletic event. We believe that your approval can generate similar anticipation; that is, others will look forward to seeing you because of your expected approval. To create such an effect, you must consistently give approval for particular behaviors. Following significant accomplishments, people often seek out a particular individual who will appreciate and compliment their achievements. This is because past experiences have taught them that this individual approves of such accomplishments. Friendships usually evolve with people who become reliable sources of reinforcement. In fact, some psychologists define love as the anticipation of reinforcing events.

People need to know what they can expect when they are with you, but they are equally interested in how you respond to them in their absence. Criticizing others in their absence epitomizes the kind of behavior that erodes relationships. Obviously, people will not relish your approval if you criticize them when their backs are turned. They will judge what you say in their absence by listening to what you say about others who are not present — that is, they assume you talk about them in their absence in the same way you discuss others who are not present. Because the approval of two-faced or backstabbing individuals is so open to question, the approval of individuals who are consistent in both public and private situations is especially meaningful.

Frequency of approval We suggest that you increase the frequency of your approval at a very gradual pace. An abrupt increase could make you appear awkward and insincere. "Coming on too strong" is a well-known blunder in interpersonal relations. Therefore, we suggest a practice similar to that in changing your hair color — change slowly enough to let others adjust to the new you.

Pairing approval with other reinforcers A final way to add potency to your approval is to pair it with events you know to be reinforcing to the other person. Approval that initially lacks value may acquire some of the reinforcing properties of the other event. Praise could be delivered during or after a meal, on a coffee break, while playing tennis, or at any other reinforcing time or place. In other words, the pairing and timing of approval are important elements in making your approval maximally reinforcing. There is modest evidence that your mere presence during reinforcing activities will cause others to like you better (Griffitt, 1968; Lott and Lott, 1960).

Having praise over lunch

Linda was a twenty-two-year-old graduate student in English who wanted to increase the frequency of her compliments to others. She initially focused on a friendly lunch-time gathering with three or four fellow students. She tried to increase personal compliments, noting admirable characteristics ("You keep yourself so trim.") and compliments based on others' remarks ("You seem to really understand that.").

Linda used a pencil and paper to record the frequency of her compliments. She made this procedure unobtrusive by pretending to be doodling on a piece of paper. During her baseline of ten lunch sessions, the highest number of compliments she gave was three. To increase that number, Linda first tried to find a quiet setting for the lunch rendezvous, such as a room away from the general dining area or out-of-doors. She also gave herself immediate and back-up reinforcers for her approval comments. If she made ten or more compliments during lunch, she immediately indulged in a fudge brownie. In addition, she gave herself one point for each set of ten compliments. For every five points, her husband agreed to buy her a stereo album. She kept a record of these points on a chart at home.

While the reinforcement contingencies were in effect, Linda made a total of ten or more praising remarks each day. However, even after phasing out the external contingencies, she continued to give compliments at a rate much above the baseline level. She assumed that the approval she was receiving from her reinforced friends and husband was serving to maintain the target behavior.

Adapted from Bingham, L. 1976. Self-management of praise. Unpublished class project, University of Tennessee.

Summation of approval Giving approval is a major means of reinforcing others and, consequently, of being reinforced by others. However, not all approval is reinforcing to others. Approval sometimes can seem manipulative and artificial. To increase the reinforcement value of your approval, you should (1) approve specific achievements and behaviors that the other person considers worthwhile; (2) avoid ostentatious approval and make your nonverbal behaviors consistent with your verbal approval; (3) use different ways of expressing approval rather than depending on a few stock phrases; (4) make your approval consistent over time and consistent across public and private situations; (5) gradually increase the frequency of your approval; and (6) pair your approval with events known to be reinforcing to the other person.

Unless you are a very atypical individual, you exhibit some behaviors that are aversive to those with whom you have daily contact.

Minimizing aversive features

Unless you are a very atypical individual, you exhibit some behaviors that are aversive to those with whom you have daily contact. These behaviors may be so irritating that others may fail to see your many reinforcing qualities. Though different people respond to the same behavior in a variety of different ways, some behaviors appear to be generally aversive to others.

Verbal habits   Periodically you might find it useful to make tape recordings of your interaction in different situations, such as conversing in an informal group setting or giving a report in class (see Figure 10.1). Listen first for redundancies and clichés. You can be pretty certain that others find repeated use of "you know," "well," and "okay" unattractive. Platitudes such as "in one ear and out the other," "should have stayed in bed," "raining cats and dogs," "beat around the bush," "dog eat dog," "swept off his feet," "hang in there," "right on," "chip off the old block," and "signed, sealed, and delivered," will also diminish the reinforcement value of your conversation.

While you have your tapes available, also listen for the directness of your speech. When you're asked questions, do you give direct answers, or do you ramble? When you're relating experiences, do you include so many parenthetical sidelights that it's difficult to keep the principal focus in mind? Parenthetical commenters want to supply all the details

Figure 10.1
Analysis of conversation

You should tape your conversations in a number of different settings. For each setting, indicate the number of people involved and the kinds of topics being discussed. Since your conversational behaviors may vary considerably in different settings, you should do a separate analysis for each setting.

I. *Quantity of conversation*
   A. Percentage of total time you were talking. Compute from a time-duration assessment.
   B. Number of your responses that were 1 to 15 seconds, 16 to 30 seconds, 31 to 60 seconds, and more than one minute in duration. Compute from a frequency-count assessment.

II. *Type of conversation*
   A. Active listening. Record the number of instances in which you paraphrased or otherwise commented directly on what another person had just said.
   B. Questions
      1. Closed. Record the number of questions that called for a factual response.
      2. Open-ended. Record the number of questions that asked for an opinion or judgment from another person.
   C. Approval comments. Frequency-count assessment.
   D. Redundant expressions. Frequency count of verbalizations such as "uh," "you know," "well," "okay."
   E. Clichés. Frequency count of phrases such as "you're kidding," "don't spend it all in one place," "scared to death," "heaven help us."
   F. Complaints. Frequency count of negative comments about how you feel and how you're being treated.
   G. Cynical comments. Frequency count of critical comments about others' motives, ideas, and behavior.
   H. Defensive responses. Frequency count of times you responded to others' criticism by defending your own behavior and/or launching a counterattack on the other person.
   I. Sweeping generalizations. Frequency count of statements that affirmed that all people in a particular category behave in the same fashion, for example, "high school students just . . . ," "psychology students act as if . . . ," "women don't really . . ."
   J. Circuitous responses. Frequency count of times you didn't answer others' questions immediately and directly.
   K. False starts. Frequency count of times you stopped in mid-sentence to begin a new sentence.
   L. Interruptions. Frequency count of times you broke in while another person was speaking.
   M. Garbled words. Frequency count of words not spoken audibly and clearly.

in whatever experience they relate. Thus, if they happen to mention person X, they will then go into great detail in describing this person. In the course of describing person X, they may mention person Y — necessitating another detailed personal history. The parentheticist's accounts are obviously given to much proliferation. It is not unusual for this person to seek help from the audience in re-identifying the initial focus of the conversation.

Many individuals have difficulty in closing conversations. They find it necessary to repeat their point several times. Their initial good-bys are followed by thirty minutes of additional conversation — including several more good-bys. You can count on extended conversations any time you encounter these persons. Such anticipation may cause you to avoid them or to respond cooly in their presence in order to discourage further conversation. However, such individuals seem to be somewhat impervious to these nonverbal cues. They mistake others' silence for rapt listening. So bear in mind: Unless others are continuing to talk, they probably don't want to continue conversation with you at that time.

You must also gear the emotional tone of your conversation to the nonverbal cues of others. Some individuals always insist on joking or being deadly serious irrespective of others' moods. On the one hand, these individuals may come at you with a backslapping, "How are you doing, pal?" approach, regardless of how subdued you feel at the moment. On the other hand, they may persist in work-related conversation despite the informality and lightheartedness of the occasion. Eventually these individuals are left off of others' party lists. How responsive are you to cues from others? Do you habitually engage in one type of conversational behavior, or do you carefully notice cues from others before setting the tone of the conversation?

In an effort to set themselves forth as authorities, some individuals make very strong statements about practically any issue being discussed. These statements often take the form of overgeneralization, for example, "all adolescents are . . . ," "Northerners just don't . . . ," ". . . is a lousy president," "people are just . . ." Such statements typically elicit an antagonistic response from someone in the group and nonresponses from most others. Individuals who consistently overgeneralize are typically perceived as uninformed and attention seeking. Whatever the interpretation of such behavior, the overgeneralizer is not likely to enhance the joy of conversation.

Some types of humor can be extremely aversive. If your joke puts the other person in a bad light, the fun will be one-sided. A tennis-playing acquaintance who had had chronic service problems related the hurt he experienced in receiving a "serve" as a Christmas gift from his buddies. Humor that disparages women, certain ethnic groups, or alumni of particular colleges is very risky. Though no members of the target group may be present, someone in the immediate group may have strong

A mouth-cleaning project

Vera had developed the habit of using such epithets as S.O.B. when she became angry with another person. As you might expect, this habit was not enhancing her attractiveness among her coworkers. In fact, it was precipitating withdrawal or counteraggression. So her self-management goal was to reduce the frequency of profane references to others.

She devised a small card on which to record the frequency of the target behavior and the times and settings in which it was occurring. For example, if she made a profane reference while talking on the telephone, she put a T in the appropriate time slot; if she made the comment in face-to-face conversation, she used an F. Her baseline assessment revealed that most of her profane references occurred in face-to-face encounters. She also found that in most of these instances she would point her finger at the person when she made the profane remark. Inasmuch as she was not sure which behavior was precipitating which, she decided to eliminate both the remarks and the finger pointing.

Since Vera's baseline data indicated that she was exhibiting inappropriate behaviors (profane comments and finger pointing) about seven times a day, she decided for the first week of treatment to shoot slightly below that mark. Specifically, she decided that if she emitted inappropriate behaviors seven or more times a day, she would throw away a quarter by tossing it out her car window. If she exhibited the behavior fewer than seven times daily, she would put a quarter in her jewelry box; the money would later be used to buy a pair of earrings. However, if at the end of the week she had 75 cents or less in the jewelry box, she would give it to her mother and start over the next week. For each subsequent week of treatment, she would require herself to exhibit one less inappropriate behavior to earn the reward. Thus, by the end of seven weeks, she could exhibit no inappropriate behaviors if she was to get the daily payoff.

When Vera submitted her class project, she was five weeks into treatment. She had not thrown away one quarter and was well on her way to accumulating enough money to buy the earrings. Even more reinforcing was her coworkers' increased attraction to her. They spent more time talking to her and were giving her considerably more positive cues. Interpersonal problems that she had previously attributed to the bad behavior of others had begun disappearing.

Adapted from Tuggle, V. 1977. Self-modification of profane references to others. Unpublished class project, University of Tennessee.

---

ethical convictions about the impropriety of such humor. The safest kind of humor is that which pokes fun at yourself.

Some individuals use conversation as an occasion for airing grievances. Often the listener neither is responsible for the problems nor can do anything to resolve them. You may experience mild relief in letting others know about your problems, but if you habitually discuss your problems, you can be sure that others will not enjoy your company. They will attempt to terminate conversation with you, will seek you out less, or will actively avoid you.

Closely related to focusing on your problems is habitually making pessimistic, cynical, and disagreeable comments. If your comments tend to focus on the bleak side of whatever is being discussed, or if they emphasize the deficiencies of whatever view is being expressed, you can be sure that you will not be a popular dinner guest. Certainly there is a time for these behaviors, but a steady diet of them is very likely to produce social malnutrition.

Nonverbal habits   A basic reinforcer for conversational behavior is eye contact. If your eyes shift hither and yon while others talk to you, be assured that they will talk to you less frequently. Shifting of eye contact is often interpreted as a sign of disinterest in what the other person is saying. There is a host of other potentially aversive nonverbal habits such as gum chewing, eating with your mouth open, breathing through your mouth, tugging at your clothing, stroking your beard, fiddling with your hair, slouching in your chair, putting your feet on others' furniture, invading others' personal space (standing extremely close to others), slapping others on the back, touching others without a clear invitation to do such, smoking in others' presence, shaking your head sidewise while others are talking, and looking very grim during conversation. A great many of these nonverbal behaviors are unconscious behaviors. It is not unusual for individuals to view themselves as the paragon of warmth, and yet be exhibiting a multiplicity of nonverbal behaviors that make it difficult for others to interact with them. Thus, these individuals may need feedback from others to identify their nonverbal behaviors that are aversive to others.

Self-management exercises

You might already have been aware of much that was presented in this section, but have made little headway in improving interpersonal relations. You can be knowledgeable about many matters and not apply what you know. If you are to learn new behaviors, you must *practice* those behaviors. You can no more become a skillful social reinforcer by reading about social reinforcement than you can become a skillful golfer by reading about golf. We now offer a few exercises to help you begin implementing what you know about reinforcing others.

1. If you know someone who is also interested in developing listening skills, take turns listening to each other. You could earn your turn to talk by correctly paraphrasing what the other person has said. The other person could then rule on the adequacy of your listening.

2. Identify someone to whom you should listen — a child, an elderly person, a friend, or a spouse. Provide provocative (leading) questions and discuss solutions to that person's problems. You have probably noticed that when three or four people start talking, someone always seems to get left out. You may wish to direct questions to that person.

3. Scan the school newspaper or interoffice newsletter for praiseworthy items about your peers. Try to use these items to increase the frequency of compliments passed on to others.

4. Make tapes of your conversations in several situations. Then use the rating system in Figure 10.1 to analyze the tapes. Your analysis should reveal a target behavior that you want to change and the baseline level of that behavior. Finally, develop some self-management strategies for changing that behavior.

Developing romantic relationships

The principles that govern liking generally apply to loving. People learn to like and they also learn to love. Although we hear claims of instantaneous love — love at first sight — we suspect that this phenomenon involves the generalization of learned responses to the new person. You may feel drawn toward the new acquaintance because that person reminds you of a pleasant old acquaintance. In spite of the learned quality of love, it is always possible to love someone who does not love you, or the reverse. However, the prospect of unrequited love can be minimized by the suggestions in this section.

What can you do to win the affections of another person? At first you might think, "She (or he) will have to take me or leave me as I am." On reflection, however, you should realize that since love is learned, you can do something to affect its course. The concept of reinforcement is the essence of love. The development of reciprocal love is essentially a matter of making yourself more reinforcing to the desired individual.

Becoming a generalized reinforcer

The best reinforcer is a stimulus, person, or thing that has been associated with a variety of satisfying events. Such a stimulus is called a generalized reinforcer; praise and money are examples. Some psychologists have concluded that "when a person becomes a generalized secondary reinforcer for someone (s)he is loved by that person" (Miller and Siegel, 1972). To achieve this status, you need to provide reinforcement to the other person in many different ways and in many different settings. Praise, willingness to listen, thoughtful gifts, outings with mutual friends, movies, parties, and serene settings offer broad opportunities for reinforcement. In other words, love must have a chance to grow through a wide range of pleasant interactions. Limited reinforcement in one setting or of one kind can lead to the declaration, "I'm very fond of you, but we can never be more than friends."

Playing hard to get   When that special person begins to tune in to your generalized reinforcement potential, should you, in turn, play hard to get? Yes and no. Researchers (Walster et al., 1973) who have extensively investigated this phenomenon among females say that playing hard to get increases a woman's desirability but may also scare away would-be pursuers. Walster and his colleagues concluded that a woman can intensify her desirability by developing a reputation for being hard to get but then conveying her attraction to the target person. Playing hard to get for everyone, including the desired person, is a highly efficient way of deactivating your love life.

Exclusivity in romantic relationships   As you develop a romantic relationship, you will probably have to confront the issue of exclusivity in that relationship. Strong arguments can be made on both sides of the exclusivity issue. Some individuals feel that having intimate experiences with several people diminishes the reinforcement value of such intimacies. Others contend that human beings are naturally attracted to different people and that it is emotionally healthy to act upon those attractions. Whatever arrangement you and your lover work out should be voluntary, that is, the arrangement should not be based on prohibitions. For example, voluntary monogamy is a relationship in which two individuals find so much emotional and sexual satisfaction from the other that they simply don't desire to pursue other relationships. Forced monogamy, on the other hand, is a relationship in which the exclusivity is maintained through societal, religious, or personal prohibitions. Forced monogamy may produce so much resentment toward a partner that it eventually erodes the positive attraction to that person.

A major hazard in romantic relationships is spending too much time together. When you're in the process of discovering that rare individual, you will have so many things to talk about that you will be tempted to spend all of your time with that person. If you do spend most of your time together for a period of several weeks or months, the hour may come when you begin to lose your sense of exhilaration in being together. Some writers ("Six Styles of Loving," 1977) view this as an inevitable, natural change. One thing that happens in this process is that you simply run out of things to discuss. If you spend most of your time interacting with each other, you don't allow yourself to grow outside the relationship. Eventually you have little new to contribute to the relationship. Lovers should preserve time for cultivating interests apart from their primary relationship. By pursuing outside activities and friendships, they're more likely to enhance than to detract from the relationship. Thus, you may choose to be exclusive in your sexual activity, but don't be exclusive in the myriad nonsexual aspects of life.

Altering sex-role behaviors

You may wonder what a discussion of sex roles is doing in a section on romance. Sex-role stereotyping relates to such issues as job discrimination, domestic responsibilities, and the social status of men and women, but it also affects the more personal aspects of human interactions. Rigid sex roles certainly prevent many male-female romances from reaching their maximum potential. We feel that overcoming rigid sex-role behaviors can make a person more loving and more lovable. Our concern at this point is how to use self-management procedures in changing sex-role behaviors.

Commitment to change　　There is probably no area in which commitment to change is more indispensable than in the realm of sex-role behaviors. You may have received enough negative input already to make you eager to change. If not, consider some concrete examples of how sex-role stereotypes can adversely affect male-female relationships. Take the common example of the husband and wife who both work outside the home while the wife still assumes most of the domestic duties in the home. Even if the husband is not chastised for this arrangement, he pays a price for it. His wife may be covertly or overtly negative in her responses to him, and this in turn may adversely affect many dimensions of their relationship, including the sexual dimension. By assuming an equitable share of the domestic responsibilities, the husband not only develops a respect for domestic work but also is more likely to evoke positive reactions from his wife.

In spite of intellectual commitment to change, most people find it easier not to change. Taking a nap, reading the evening newspaper, and watching television probably have higher intrinsic reinforcement value for the husband than washing dishes, vacuuming the house, and doing the laundry. If the wife tolerates her husband's behavior, he may make no effort to change. From a woman's point of view, asking for dates, picking up her share of the tab, and initiating sexual play may represent behaviors to which she is intellectually committed but which she still finds intimidating. For both males and females, setting events and reinforcement contingencies often favor stereotypic behaviors.

Behaviors to change　　As we have repeatedly recommended, begin modestly in defining your goals. For a woman, inviting a man to have lunch or to take an afternoon coffee break with you might be a starting point.

For men, a behavior that many should consider is the open expression of emotions. Perhaps you can learn to express emotions directly by first talking about emotions. To be able to say "I feel like crying" may be a prerequisite to actual crying. Thus, an appropriate first goal for a man might be to increase the number of instances in which he verbalizes his feelings.

Another behavior with which many men have difficulty is the admission of fault. To say "I was wrong in saying that," "I made a terrible mistake," "You're right about that," and "I'm sorry for what I did," is not easy for most men. To back down, to admit errors, or to walk away from the bully are commonly considered unmasculine. Men think that standing firm increases their manliness. What it actually does is to make them appear nervous, insecure, and insensitive. There are few things that would be more therapeutic for male-female relationships (or for male-male relationships, for that matter) than for men to be able to admit fault. The simple admission of error often can avert days of resentment and conflict. The Williams-Long dictum is that it is better to switch than fight!

Strategies for change We have found two procedures especially useful in altering stereotypic responses. Both depend on assistance from others who share your commitment. The first, role reversal, can best be practiced in a relaxed small-group setting. In this procedure individuals emit behaviors normally exhibited by members of the opposite sex. We have found that these role reversals not only produce a good deal of hilarity, but they also sensitize individuals to problems created by the conventional sex-role behaviors. Furthermore, they give people a chance to exhibit behaviors (notwithstanding their initial awkwardness) that they eventually want to emit naturally and comfortably.

The more long-range strategy for changing sex-role behaviors is to seek out the company of people on whom you can count to reinforce nonconventional behaviors. You will find that their very presence provides some potent cues for nonstereotypic responses. Since you have nothing to lose by exhibiting nontraditional behaviors around these people, you will have an opportunity to learn new behaviors without jeopardizing previous sources of reinforcement. For example, the man who wants to be able to express his emotions openly should initially work on that behavior among individuals who are sympathetic to human liberation.

Enhancing sexual interaction

Although we strongly favor the elimination of sex-role behaviors that produce difficulties for one sex or the other, we do not favor deemphasizing human sexuality. When sexual interaction involves exploitation, it is destructive; but when it produces mutual pleasure and fulfillment, it is

One check or two?

What do males and females expect from each other? College students of today may have more difficulty answering that question than did their predecessors. Men appear to us to be more ambivalent than women in their expectations about the opposite sex. Should they open doors for women? Should they pay the bill when they have an evening out together? Should they habitually initiate social and sexual contact?

To get a clearer perception of what women expect of men, we developed a short inventory that described a variety of male-female situations and alternative male responses within those situations. A sample of women students taking educational psychology courses at the University of Tennessee were asked to rank the attractiveness of the various male responses to each situation.

In the domestic domain, women ranked an equal sharing of domestic responsibilities by the man as the most attractive response. However, in the area of social amenities (such as paying for nights out, opening doors, helping put on coats, carrying loads), the majority of women indicated that they wanted men to assume either most of the responsibility or all the responsibility. Women also indicated that they were more attracted to men who usually initiate their social contacts (such as calling and arranging dates). However, they found relationships most reinforcing where the initiation and control of sexual interactions were equally shared by men and women. The subjects indicated that they preferred men who engage in extended periods of touching and caressing during lovemaking rather than those who indulge in brief sexual encounters. Most women preferred that intimate sexual relationships with a man be sexually exclusive for both parties.

The picture emerging from this study is a mixture of the old and the new. The women students prefer equality of responsibility in the domestic and sexual areas but still see the social amenities and initiation of social contacts as a male responsibility. You should interpret these results with great caution. The preferences of female students in your college may differ markedly from those of women at the University of Tennessee. Besides, you're probably more concerned about the preferences of a few select individuals than with those of women and men in general. One way to clarify the preferences of these special people is through a combination of open-ended questions and active listening.

Adapted from White, K., Travers, G., and Williams, R. L. 1977. Perceptions of masculinity. An unpublished manuscript, University of Tennessee.

fantastic! Although some phases of that interaction may defy behavioral explanation, the principles we have previously discussed for enhancing interpersonal attractions do have something to contribute. You cannot separate your impact as a lover from your general reinforcement value as a person. Some people who are physically quite attractive behave in such a nonreinforcing or aversive fashion that their sex life is nil.

Other people have difficulty when they get to the actual sexual activity. We are sure that you are familiar with how-to-do-it books on this subject, so we shall not attempt to delineate methodology. However, if reinforcing the other person is your paramount consideration, it is very likely that you will become much more stimulated yourself. Identifying the facets of sexual activity that are most reinforcing to your partner and then freely exhibiting those during sexual play is a good way to heighten the reinforcement for both persons. There are some basically nongenital modes of tactile stimulation (such as giving a lotion rubdown) that can also be used to enhance the reinforcement value of the sexual experience.

Meaningful sexual interaction obviously involves a great deal more than physical stimulation. The quality of sexual interaction cannot be divorced from the quality of other interactions. If other interactions with that special person are reinforcing, it is probable that sexual interaction will also be reinforcing. Similarly, many abrasive conflicts during the day rarely can be negated by sexual interaction in the evening.

A self-management project

A painful experience that most people have to endure a few times in their lives is failing to gain the affection or losing the affection of someone very attractive to them. It's as important to know how to get over a lost affection as to know how to win an affection. We propose, therefore, that you devise a plan for dealing with your hour of disappointment. How do you get an old love off your mind? If love is learned, how can it be unlearned?

1. *Selecting your goal* In this case, your goal might be twofold. You may want to reduce the amount of time you spend brooding over the lost romance and at the same time increase your contacts with members of the opposite sex.

2. *Monitoring target behavior* You might try recording the names of the people and places that trigger the unwanted memories.

3. *Changing setting events* Use the recorded information to alter (or avoid) setting events that produce brooding. Identify other setting events that will lead to added exposure to members of the opposite sex.

4. *Establishing effective consequences* You know your reinforcement priorities better than we do!

5. *Consolidating your gains* The very best cure for rejection by one person is acceptance by another. There are probably many members of the opposite sex who would appreciate the qualities you possess. Regularly participating in social outings (especially with informal, small-group interaction) is an excellent way to find some of those individuals and to recover from the hurt of a lost love.

6. *Covert alternatives* Try thought stopping for the old memories and covert reinforcement for visualizing new kinds of interaction.

Concluding thoughts

We have no question that you can enhance your interpersonal attractiveness. There are so many dimensions that affect a person's attractiveness that you should have no difficulty identifying target behaviors. Though we're convinced that you already have some attractive qualities and can develop still more, we're not saying that everyone will appreciate those qualities. The values of some people may be extremely different from yours, and these people may actually be turned off by qualities that are attractive to most others. Neither are we contending that you can always establish a friendship or mutual love with a special person. However, if you're willing to develop other acquaintances, other special people will emerge — some of whom can appreciate just what you have to offer. You need not live without special loves and friendships.

References

Berscheid, E., and Walster, E. H. 1969. *Interpersonal attraction*. Reading, Mass.: Addison-Wesley.

Bingham, L. 1976. Self-management of praise. Unpublished class project, University of Tennessee.

Byrne, D. 1971. *The attraction paradigm*. New York: Academic Press.

Griffitt, W. 1968. Attraction toward a stranger as a function of direct and associated reinforcement. *Psychonomic Science 11*(4), 147–148.

Lott, B. E., and Lott, A. J. 1960. The formation of positive attitudes toward group members. *Journal of Abnormal and Social Psychology 61*, 297–300.

Mehrabian, A. 1969. Significance of posture and position in the communication of attitude and status relationships. *Psychological Bulletin 71*(5), 359–372.

Miller, H. L., and Siegel, P. S. 1972. *Loving: A psychological approach*. New York: John Wiley and Sons.

Six styles of loving. 1977. *Intellect 105*, 294–295.

Tuggle, V. 1977. Self-modification of profane references to others. Unpublished class project, University of Tennessee.

Walster, E., Walster, G. W., Piliavin, J., and Schmidt, L. 1973. "Playing hard to get": Understanding an elusive phenomenon. *Journal of Personality and Social Psychology 26*, 113–121.

White, K., Travers, G., and Williams, R. L. 1977. Perceptions of masculinity. Unpublished manuscript, University of Tennessee.

Williams, R. L., and Anandam, K. 1973. *Cooperative classroom management*. Columbus, Ohio: Charles E. Merrill.

Chapter 11
"If not now, when?":

Developing assertive behaviors

If I am not for myself, who will be for me? If I am not for others, who am I for? And if not now, when?

THE TALMUD

Ralph had promised to cook a special dinner for Susan, but a delay at work left him without the time or the energy to make good on his promise.[1] When Susan got home, expecting a dinner on the table, Ralph announced they would get a quick bite to eat elsewhere.

There are three basic ways that Susan might have responded to this turn of events. She might have reacted nonassertively by denying to Ralph how much she had looked forward to a home-cooked meal and a quiet evening by the fire. Later on, at the noisy pizza parlor, she would have been complaining about the service, the noise, and the cramped quarters. Neither Ralph nor Susan would have enjoyed the evening. A second reaction for Susan would have been to respond aggressively by telling Ralph that he never plans ahead and that his work is not all that important anyway! A fight would very likely have ensued, and both would have got their wishes — Susan would have a home-cooked dinner and a romantic evening (a TV dinner and a melodramatic 1942 movie on TV) and Ralph would have gone out to dinner (by himself at a local hamburger stand). A third, and more appropriate, reaction for Susan would have been to respond assertively by expressing her disappointment about not having that quiet evening at home, but also acknowledging Ralph's reluctance to cook under the circumstances. This would have allowed Ralph and Susan to come to a compromise in which they might go out to eat at an intimate restaurant, come home for the remainder of the evening, and work out another time for Ralph to cook that special dinner.

Nonassertive, aggressive, and assertive behaviors tell us a great deal about how people view themselves and others. The nonassertive person is self-denying. A nonassertive response by Susan would have conveyed respect for Ralph's feelings and desires but little for her own. In contrast, the aggressive person is self-enhancing but other-denying. An aggressive response by Susan would have involved much consideration for her feelings and desires (too much, in fact) but little respect for those of Ralph. The assertive individual strives for self-enhancement *and* other-enhancement. Susan's assertive response showed a respect for the feelings and desires of both Ralph and herself. Assertive behavior conveys a message of mutual dignity.

There are specific verbal behaviors that differentiate assertive, nonassertive, and aggressive persons. Some researchers (Eisler et al., 1973) have found that assertive people make more requests of others and speak louder than do nonassertive individuals. Assertive people also take less time to respond (Eisler et al., 1973) and use fewer words to give

[1]Paul Carson, a doctoral student in educational psychology at the University of Tennessee, served as editorial consultant for this chapter. Paul has a master's degree in clinical psychology and is emphasizing assertive training and biofeedback in his doctoral study.

their message (Galassi et al., 1975). A request such as "Please go to the grocery store for me" is more effective than the statement with an "umm" stuck between every word. It is also more direct than "I'm sure you don't have the time, but how far away will you be from the grocery store this afternoon?" Assertive individuals are likely to use "I" language when discussing their feelings. Compare the assertive statement, "I would like for you to stop making jokes about my new hair style because it embarrasses me," with the aggressive statement, "You should be more considerate when you comment on other people's features." The first statement lets the other person know exactly what the problem is and what the speaker wishes to be done to correct the situation. The latter statement is vague and communicates an attitude of condemnation.

Assertive, nonassertive, and aggressive people also reveal characteristic nonverbal behaviors, of which eye contact is perhaps the most revealing. A nonassertive person will often look in every direction but where the other person is standing, whereas an aggressive person might attempt to "stare down" the other person. An assertive individual will generally maintain eye contact during conversation but will also break eye contact from time to time. Body posture, gestures, and facial expressions are likewise indicative of assertiveness. People who stand erect with their heads up are usually assertive individuals. People whose smiles and grimaces match what they are saying are also likely to be assertive. In contrast, people who contend that they are not angry but whose teeth and fists are clenched are not behaving assertively.

Benefits of assertive behavior

A principal payoff for assertive behavior is reduced anxiety. This is true because assertiveness and anxiety are inversely related (Orenstein et al., 1975). In other words, the more anxious you become, the less you are likely to behave assertively, and the more assertive you become, the less you are likely to be anxious. For this reason, assertiveness training has been an effective means of reducing anxiety (Percell et al., 1974), particularly anxiety that is related to *specific* situations as opposed to general anxiety (Orenstein et al., 1975). By behaving assertively, you may remove many environmental factors that contribute to your anxiety.

Being more assertive seems to be related to other positive subjective states. People who rated themselves high in assertiveness also reported fewer neurotic tendencies (Orenstein et al., 1975) and fewer fears (Morgan, 1974). Assertiveness training has helped college students to become more self-accepting and to develop more positive self-concepts (Ball, 1976). In a somewhat different vein, Rimm et al. (1974) found that

236

assertiveness training was especially helpful to people who had trouble controlling their anger. In addition to becoming less angry, these individuals reduced their uptightness and became more comfortable in situations that they previously found frustrating. Thus, becoming more assertive should generally make you a happier individual.

Becoming more assertive may even reduce physical problems. Assertiveness training used in conjunction with other forms of treatment has been successful in reducing the frequency, duration, and intensity of migraine headaches (Lambley, 1976; Mitchell, 1971). Verbal tics associated with *Gilles de la Tourette's Syndrome** have been successfully treated by combining assertiveness training with other forms of treatment (Tophoff, 1973). When combined with sex therapy, assertiveness training was useful in treating premature ejaculation (Yulis, 1976).

Gibbs (1965) used assertiveness training to treat a man who had a problem with excessive blushing when dealing with others. The subject was first to practice being assertive in a situation that was least likely to produce aversive consequences. Surprisingly, he chose his mother-in-law as an initial target person. (His relationship with her was so bad that he figured he had nothing to lose.) He practiced responding assertively (politely disagreeing) whenever she made dogmatic statements. His success surprised the mother-in-law, the subject, and his wife; his mother-in-law even began to respect his opinion! In later counseling sessions he learned how to express his opinions and feelings more in all types of settings. Six months after the termination of counseling he still had a 70 percent reduction in blushing when dealing with people.

Assertive behavior certainly has some important social payoffs. If you become more assertive with your spouse or friend, the behaviors of that other person may in turn become more positive. One distressed couple dealt with their marriage problems by engaging in assertiveness training that focused on direct expression of feelings, understandable communication, and making requests to each other (Fensterheim, 1972). One year after this training they no longer considered dissolving their marriage, their sexual relationship had improved greatly, they felt they were growing closer to each other, and the husband's relationships outside the marriage had improved. In a study of professional women, assertive women reported greater sexual satisfaction than nonassertive women (Whitly and Poulsen, 1975).

Whole families may be affected by the assertiveness of one of the parents. Bugental and Love (1975) contrasted the interactions of mothers and children in disturbed families with those of mothers and children having no notable problems. The authors found that mothers in the disturbed families actually used a less assertive tone of voice when

---

*Terms set in italics and followed by an asterisk are defined in the Glossary.

The assertive route to marital happiness

Three nonassertive husbands were trying to improve their marital relationships. A baseline of their nonassertive behaviors was established via videotapes of discussions with their wives. The husbands were then given four, forty-five-minute assertiveness training sessions in which they had to do some role playing. One husband was given role-playing scenes that dealt with nonmarital situations such as having someone cut in front of him while he was standing in line. The other two husbands role-played scenes that related directly to interactions with their wives (being criticized by their wives, being falsely accused by their wives).

After their assertiveness training, the three husbands were again videotaped talking with their wives. The husbands who role-played marital scenes during training now looked at their wives more than in the first videotapes; they gave more positive responses, gave fewer negative responses, smiled more, talked longer when they did speak, spoke louder, and were rated by observers as being more assertive overall. A more important finding, however, was the effect of the husbands' changed behaviors on their wives. In the earlier videotaped discussions the wives had generally "dominated" the discussions by making more requests than their husbands, speaking louder, and speaking longer. But in the videotape after assertiveness training, the wives were less domineering, gave more positive responses, exhibited fewer negative behaviors, and smiled more. Although the husband who had role-played the nonmarital scenes behaved slightly more assertively toward his wife in the second videotape, his wife's behavior was generally unchanged from the baseline tape.

Adapted from Eisler, R. M., Miller, P. M., Hersen, M., and Alford, H. 1974. Effects of assertive training on marital interaction. *Archives of General Psychiatry 30*, 643– 649.

expressing approval or disapproval to their children than when making neutral statements. In contrast, the other mothers were much more verbally expressive when showing approval or disapproval than when making neutral statements. Thus, assertiveness may be a part of "healthy" families while the lack of it may contribute to family problems.

Assertiveness may also contribute to good leadership. Shelton and Mathis (1976) gave assertiveness questionnaires to residence-hall assistants (RAs) at a university. They then asked the residents of the dormitories to evaluate the RAs. The RAs who scored high on assertiveness were rated by the residents as more honest and open, less likely to avoid conflicts, better able to handle discipline, better communicators, and generally more effective in their work. Although being assertive does not automatically mean that you will be a good leader (or even want to be a leader), many of the characteristics of good leadership go hand in hand with assertiveness.

Barriers to behaving assertively

There are some very attractive excuses for not behaving assertively. Some people think that nonassertiveness is equivalent to politeness, that being assertive would just upset others, and that it's more admirable to help others than to respond assertively to them (Lange and Jakubowski, 1976). With respect to politeness, some people are reluctant to indicate that the behavior of another (such as puffing on a cigar, cutting off their conversation) is unpleasant to them lest they be viewed as impolite. Is remaining silent under such circumstances really an act of politeness, or just a reflection of nonassertiveness? You can distinguish politeness from nonassertiveness by paying attention to how much tension you feel. If your muscles are tight, if you are getting a headache, or if your stomach feels queasy, chances are that you are behaving nonassertively rather than politely.

You may also fear that if you tell others that you dislike certain of their behaviors (such as arriving late for appointments, impugning your motives), they will get upset and make life difficult for you. The possibility of negative consequences for assertive behavior is a legitimate concern. However, you can minimize that possibility by applying the self-management strategies to be described shortly. Furthermore, the positive consequences for behaving assertively usually far outweigh the negative.

Many individuals have the most trouble behaving assertively when someone asks for their assistance. Such individuals may feel compelled to help no matter what they have planned for the moment. Helping other people is certainly commendable, but some people may help others so much that they neglect to help themselves. Also, overwilling helpers can easily be manipulated by individuals who are shirking their own responsibilities. One way to determine whether you are being genuinely helpful or just nonassertive is to ask yourself whether your helpfulness is adequately reciprocated. If you are the one who does most of the giving, chances are that you are being nonassertive.

Some people don't want to be assertive for quite a different reason. These people, who are usually aggressive, prefer to dominate others. Although life may be more convenient when you can pressure others into doing what you want, at what cost do you achieve that convenience? When people are coerced or manipulated, they tend to build resentment and as a result avoid the person who is doing the manipulating. People who demand that friends always do what they want to do on Saturday nights will get their way for a while but will soon spend Saturday nights alone. Even though the short-term consequences of aggressive behavior may be positive, the long-term consequences are usually very negative.

Application of the self-management model

Let's turn now to developing assertive behaviors via self-management strategies. There is hardly any behavior that is more compatible with the goals and methods of self-management than assertive responding. Appelbaum et al. (1975) contrasted subjects who attempted to control their environment (internals) with subjects who simply took things as they came (externals). The internals scored significantly higher on a test of assertiveness than did the externals. Thus, there seems to be a high degree of compatibility between assertiveness and the control of one's environment.

Selecting a goal

Nobody is assertive all the time, just as no one is perpetually aggressive or nonassertive. Though you may think of yourself as a totally nonassertive person, surely there are some situations in which you behave assertively. Maybe you usually don't compliment a teacher, but you do compliment your best friend. Perhaps you cannot bring yourself to ask a good friend not to smoke in your presence, but you have no trouble making this request of a stranger. Maybe you choke up when you try to give others negative feedback, but you have no difficulty complimenting them. Thus, we contend that you already exhibit *some* assertive behaviors in *some* situations.

Since assertiveness is situation specific, any attempt at developing more assertiveness should focus on specific behaviors within specific situations. We suggest that you begin with behaviors and situations in which you're most likely to be successful. Several nonverbal behaviors, such as erect posture, eye contact during conversation, and smiling, would be relatively easy to exhibit, applicable in many situations, and generally supported by others. Safe initial targets among the verbal behaviors might include using "I" language, complimenting others, and thanking others for compliments. Whatever the target response, specify some situations in which that behavior will be easy to exhibit and likely to produce good results.

Some assertive goals are hard to achieve and involve social risk. A task that's difficult for many college students is to ask for a first date. You may have passed up more than one opportunity to ask out someone who

A time and a place

Eisler et al. (1975) investigated the assertiveness of male psychiatric patients in various situations. These individuals were asked to role-play a variety of scenes dealing with either positive or negative events, with either familiar or unfamiliar people (for example accepting praise from a boss, being asked by the boss to work late for the third time in a week, having a stranger cut in line in front of them). Their behaviors in these scenes were videotaped and then rated for assertiveness.

Several assertive behaviors were more common in the negative scenes than in the positive. The negative scenes produced longer replies, more eye contact, and more expression of emotions. On the other hand, the subjects smiled more in the positive scenes and were rated as generally more assertive. The tape analysis also revealed that unfamiliar persons evoked more overall assertiveness from the subjects than did familiar ones. In the positive scenes the subjects gave more praise to unfamiliar persons but smiled more at familiar individuals. In the negative situations the unfamiliar persons received more smiles.

Does all this sound confusing to you? It may help you to know that a few behaviors (such as compliance, requests for new behavior, and the ratio of speech disturbances to the duration of speech) did not change substantially in different situations. However, the authors concluded that assertiveness does not consist of a set of behaviors that remain consistent in all situations, but rather that these individual behaviors change with each situation.

Adapted from Eisler, R. M., Hersen, M., Miller, P. M., and Blanchard, E. B. 1975. Situational determinants of assertive behaviors. *Journal of Consulting and Clinical Psychology 43*, 330–340.

---

is superattractive to you. If you get nervous at the mere thought of approaching that person, a goal of immediately asking for a date would be unrealistic. Your initial goal might be little more than saying hello. You could then gradually increase the amount of time that you talk to that person until asking for a date would seem like a natural step. You might want to consider a snack in the student center rather than a meal at your place for the first rendezvous.

Many people have difficulty expressing views with which others may disagree. You may, for example, sit by silently while the group decides to do things you really don't want to do, or you may fail to disagree when others express views that are actually offensive to you. This kind of nonassertive response shortchanges everyone. For example, saying "It doesn't matter" when you have a definite preference may cause you to feel resentful and to relate poorly to others because of those bad feelings.

A task that's difficult for many college students is initially arranging a date with someone who is highly attractive to them.

A good initial target for group situations is honestly expressing your preference when it's requested. You can move from there to volunteering your preferences and views.

Numerous individuals find it hard to initiate conversation with a person they've just met. If this is your problem, you can try to increase the frequency of four different skills suggested by Phelps and Austin (1975). First, you can ask more open-ended questions, that is, questions to which the other person can give a long response rather than a simple yes or no answer. Open-ended questions often begin with the words *what, when, where, who, why,* or *how.* Second, you can listen for free information (extra information that you had not requested in your question) and comment on it. Third, you can give free information about yourself. Fourth, you can give compliments.

Monitoring target behavior

Generally you will need to keep track of your own assertive behaviors; it would be difficult for someone else to monitor them in all situations. Let's assume that you have a difficult time making requests of other people. These requests could range from asking someone to open the door for you to asking a friend to take care of your pet cobra while you're away on vacation. You should keep track of opportunities to make requests as well as the requests you actually make. At the end of one week you might group all these requests into various categories. For example, you could include "requests that require a short time investment from the other person," "requests that focus on others' social behaviors," "requests that involve money," and so on. These categories will help you determine where to focus most of your attention. For each day, take the number of opportunities to make requests and divide it into the number of requests actually made. This is your "request ratio," something you want to increase during your self-management program.

Suppose you want to increase the fluency of your speech. A good starting point would be to reduce the "uhs" that you interject into most sentences. You could tape-record your speech at various times and places in your day. A word of caution: Make sure the other people in these situations know that you are recording and why you're recording. You want to avoid any suspicion of CIA involvement! You could play back the tape at the end of the day and compute the frequency of your "uhs." You could also note the number of "uhs" in each situation so that you can determine where the problem is greatest. We suspect that you'll find that you use far more "uhs" in some situations than in others. For example, they may increase dramatically when you express views that run counter to the prevailing sentiments in a group.

If your goal is to increase the amount of time you spend conversing with someone you have just met, you can unobtrusively carry a stopwatch and then record the length of each conversation once it is finished (which may be quickly). You might also record the number of new people whom you meet each day. Think of the opportunities to exhibit this behavior — in your classes, over lunch, and while waiting in the overnight line to get tickets to the championship game!

There may be some behaviors that will be impossible for you to self-record. In that case you will need some external monitoring by another person. External monitoring is necessary for behaviors of which you are unaware; using the interjection "uh" could be one of those. If you can't carry a recorder, a friend could join you at a certain time during the day and record each "uh." However, that friend wouldn't be able to participate in the conversation while doing the monitoring. Sometimes you may be unaware of the emotional tone of your statements. Your comments may convey tension, hostility, or ambivalence to which you are oblivious. A candid observer can help you identify and monitor such responses.

Changing setting events

Rehearsing a desired assertive behavior sets the stage for exhibiting that behavior in the actual situation (Friedman, 1972). McFall and Twentyman (1974) conducted four different experiments and concluded that assertiveness training with rehearsal was much more effective in producing assertive behavior than assertiveness training without rehearsal. Although you can rehearse some assertive behaviors (such as talking louder) by yourself, other rehearsals will require the aid of a friend not directly involved in the target situation. Have this friend play the role of the person with whom you will be dealing in the actual situation. This rehearsal will give you some indication of how the other person might respond to your new assertive behavior. After you have completed the scene, your friend can comment on the verbal and nonverbal assertive behaviors you exhibited. You can keep role-playing the scene until you reach the desired level of refinement.

There are two variations of this basic role-playing format that might also prove helpful. Try to round up another friend to observe the two of you during role-play. This friend will be able to give you more comprehensive feedback than could a person who is participating in the role-play. Another variation would be to switch roles with your first friend; that is, after the initial try the friend would play you and you the other person. Your friend might be able to exhibit assertive behaviors that you hadn't thought of or that you were unable to execute. Thus, the other person could demonstrate another way of being assertive. Playing the role of the other person may make you more sensitive to how that person will respond to your new-found assertiveness.

A good subject matter for role-play might be returning a defective product to a store. First you would make a list of the specific points you want to mention: when you bought the article, what part is broken, and the possibility of getting an exchange. Then you would role-play the scene with a friend acting as a sales clerk. Your friend can be cooperative in the first rehearsal, but nasty in the second. This second scene will give you a chance to be prepared in case the sales clerk resists your request. You might also want to change roles with your friend so that you can observe another way of approaching the sales clerk. (It may also give you a chance to find out the concerns of the sales clerk.) Once you are satisfied with your performance, you're ready to head to the store. (No crossing your fingers behind your back!)

Sometimes your verbal assertiveness is negated by nonverbal messages. For example, failure to look the other person in the eye while asking for a date may result in your eating by yourself. Serber (1972) has described a "silent movie" method for dealing with this disparity between verbal and nonverbal behaviors. You first role-play the scene without using words; you have to convey your message through your hands and face. If a friend is not immediately available to assist you, the mirror can certainly provide indispensable feedback regarding your nonverbal expressiveness.

Another way to use setting events to increase assertiveness is to leave yourself reminders. If you want to speak more slowly when you comment in class, leave a written message to that effect in your notebook. If you want to increase eye contact, post pictures featuring eyes all over your apartment. (However, watch out for those feelings of paranoia!) If your goal is to give more compliments, you can first make a list of the positive characteristics of your friends. When you are going to meet various friends, you can refer to the list so you will be attuned to their virtues.

Many people have the problem of not speaking loudly enough to be heard. For example, our colleague Paul Carson had a tendency to speak very softly while conducting counseling sessions. Because his voice was practically inaudible, he found it difficult to review tape recordings of these sessions. The tape recorder soon became a reminder to speak louder. You might learn to speak louder by running your tape recorder some distance from where you are speaking.

You can learn a great deal about assertiveness simply by observing others who are effective in interpersonal situations. If a person's comments are consistently followed by positive reactions from others, what is it about those comments that made them effective? For practically any assertive behavior that you want to exhibit, you can find someone who successfully employs that behavior. By observing this person over time, you can more fully understand what the response involves and can increase your motivation to acquire the response (by seeing all the nice things that happen to that person as a result of exhibiting the behavior).

Establishing effective consequences

Since spontaneous social responses may not at first provide the needed support for your assertive behaviors, you may initially want to arrange for other sources of reinforcement. For example, you could start by granting yourself a special privilege for behaving assertively in a particular situation. Assertive responses are not always easy to learn, so you may not execute the target behavior perfectly on your first attempt. Consequently you may want to reward yourself for simply making an attempt at the assertive response. After a few tries you can raise the criterion of acceptability. If you are attempting a high-frequency assertive behavior, such as establishing eye contact, you could use a counter and reward yourself for a particular number of responses. If you are role-playing your assertive responses with a friend, you could ask your friend to give you some verbal support when you behave assertively.

Consolidating your gains

You will probably find that assertive behaviors learned in one situation will tend to affect responses in other situations. This is called generalization. Hersen et al. (1974) demonstrated that generalization is most likely when the novel situation is similar to the situation in which the response is acquired. In order to increase your chances of generalizing an asser-

Joey emerges from his shell

Joey was a twenty-year-old college junior who had acquired the reputation of being a very quiet person. He wasn't quite sure how this quietness began, but as far back as he could remember he had been labeled "the quiet one." Unless called upon, he never said a word in his classes, and he spoke infrequently in social settings. As he perceived it, he was pretty much ignored in group situations. Inasmuch as his acquaintances had become accustomed to his not talking, they seldom directed remarks his way or asked his opinion about issues under discussion.

To say that his reticence had become a source of pain would be to state the case mildly. He longed to be able to talk freely in social situations, to state his views, and to tell jokes like he saw others doing. After reading the self-management model described in Chapter 2, he decided that his problem could best be solved gradually. He could not expect to become the life of the party overnight.

Joey first identified some simple target behaviors (such as agreeing with others, asking noncontroversial questions, complimenting others) that he might exhibit in social settings. To increase the likelihood of actually emitting these behaviors, Joey turned to a self-managed token economy. He decided to use as back-up reinforcers some activities that he thoroughly enjoyed but for which he seldom took time: a walk in the park, a quality movie, a concert, an art show, a hike in the mountains. He required a certain number of points, which he could earn by exhibiting the target behaviors, for each of these payoffs. Thus, while the interactive behaviors were still too awkward to be intrinsically satisfying or to elicit much social response, they could produce some satisfying prearranged consequences, such as seeing a movie or relaxing in the park.

---

tive behavior, you should choose a behavior that could be applied in a variety of similar situations. With each new assertive response that you acquire, you will probably find it easier to acquire additional assertive behaviors. You may get to the point where assertiveness has become your life style!

One of the nicest things about assertiveness is that it naturally elicits many positive reactions from others. When you maintain good eye contact, when you speak loudly enough to be heard, when you use "I" language, when you smile at others, when you compliment others, and when you clearly express your preferences to others, you're going to be an easier, more pleasant person with whom to associate. Although some assertive behaviors may initially ruffle an individual who has dominated you, you can expect supporting reactions in most situations. These are the payoffs that will be most crucial in sustaining assertive behaviors.

The library letdown

Sometimes the most innocent assertive behavior can lead to involved and hurtful consequences. In the University library one day, Jim Long ran into a student whom he'd taught a year ago in an off-campus course. Jim began the conversation by asking, "Didn't we have a class together last year?" Because of the disparity in Jim's clothing (he wore a suit and tie when he taught the class but had on jeans and a casual shirt this particular day), the student remembered his face but not that he was the instructor in the class. She responded, "Yes, I think that was Long's class," and then described everything that was wrong with the course. Jim had never received such ultra-candid feedback about his teaching. When she concluded her treatise by asking, "By the way, what's your name? Where did you sit in the class?" Jim's reply could not have been deciphered by the most sensitive hearing device. He walked away, questioning his adequacy as a teacher and the wisdom of talking to former students!

One threat to the maintenance of assertiveness is having an assertive behavior elicit a negative reaction. When you insist that your rights *not* be ignored, someone may accuse you of being selfish, immature, uncooperative, or egotistical. When you finally ask that certain person out for a date, that person may respond as if you had just committed an act of indecent exposure. These experiences can cause you to question your basic worth and to retreat into a nonassertive shell. When we have such deflating encounters, we respond by seeking support from those who view us positively. We may share our hurtful experience with an empathic friend or simply put ourselves in the company of those who like us. Calling a dear friend with whom you haven't spoken recently might quickly reverse the tide of negative feelings. After you've been rebuffed, you may be inclined to feel sorry for yourself, but don't allow a few distressing experiences to permanently disrupt your quest for assertiveness.

Thus far, we've described only the most essential strategies for acquiring assertive behaviors. A person who is committed to lifelong assertiveness could certainly benefit from continued reading in this area. Although several contemporary texts are available on this topic, there are three that you might find especially useful: (1) Alberti, R. E., and Emmons, M. L. 1975. *Stand Up, Speak Out, Talk Back*. New York: Pocket Books; (2) Fensterheim, H., and Baer, J. 1975. *Don't Say Yes When You Want to Say No*. New York: David McKay Co., Inc.; (3) Osborn, S., and Harris, G. 1975. *Assertive Training for Women*. Springfield, Ill.: Charles C. Thomas. The first two books describe how to behave assertively in domains such as vocational, academic, consumer, sexual, and marital situations. *Assertive Training for Women* explains how sex-role stereotyping in this society has produced passive and dependent women; it then makes use of many concepts presented in this text to teach women how to overcome that passivity and dependence.

Covert alternatives

Chapter 3 indicated that the two major covert techniques that can be used to increase assertive behavior are covert modeling and covert positive reinforcement. Covert modeling consists of imagining an appropriate situation for a particular assertive behavior and then imagining a model engaging in that behavior. It would be helpful to use a variety of models and to imagine positive consequences for the models' assertive behavior. If you use covert positive reinforcement you should imagine yourself in a situation in which assertive behavior is appropriate, imagine yourself emitting the target behavior, and then imagine positive consequences or simply a pleasing scene. (See Chapter 3, pages 67–68, for a detailed description of these covert procedures.)

If you become anxious over behaving assertively in a particular situation, the relaxation strategy described in Chapter 3 might also be applied. Using this strategy would be especially helpful when you know ahead of time that you're going to be in a particular situation. You would engage in the muscular relaxation exercises just prior to the experience and use learned relaxation cues while in the situation. You could use this approach in situations such as asking someone out on a date, bringing a defective product back to the store, or asking your professor to re-explain a concept covered at the beginning of the course.

Since people often talk themselves out of behaving assertively ("It wouldn't do any good," "I don't want to hurt his feelings," "She wouldn't listen"), perhaps they can also talk themselves into behaving assertively. Some of the self-verbalizations that would be consistent with assertive behavior are: "I have a right to express my needs to others," "Others will appreciate knowing how I feel," "It's not necessary that everyone respond positively to me all the time," "An assertive person doesn't have to be smooth to be effective," and "Instead of blaming others or feeling sorry for myself, I will tell others what upsets me." If you write down these and similar statements, you can read them to yourself just before taking on an assertive task or just prior to engaging in a reinforcing activity.

Concluding thoughts

This self-management text is based on a belief in the ultimate worth of the individual. Assertiveness affirms that worth. Though assertiveness is a means of expressing your rights, it is also a means of recognizing the rights of others. You neither place your rights above someone else's (as in aggression), nor do you place your rights below someone else's (as in nonassertion); your rights are equal. In expressing your wants and needs, you are not *telling* other people what to do; you're letting those people know what's important to you, and you're giving them an opportunity to assist you. You're also giving them a chance to reciprocate by letting you know their wants and needs.

You may wonder how our society would function if everyone were aggressive or nonassertive or assertive. Obviously if everyone behaved aggressively society would crumble in a short period or would be controlled coercively by the person who emerged as most powerful in that society. If everyone behaved nonassertively, there would be minimal progress. Nonassertion would result in little exchange of ideas and little cooperative activity — for who would assume the initiative for getting people together? There would also be very little dignity or self-worth. On the other hand, if society were founded on assertive principles, it would emphasize both individual growth and social responsibility. There would be time for individuals to help themselves and to help others.

References

Alberti, R. E., and Emmons, M. L. 1975. *Stand up, speak out, talk back*. New York: Pocket Books.

Appelbaum, A. S., Tuma, J. M., and Johnson, J. H. 1975. Internal-external control and assertiveness of subjects high and low in social desirability. *Psychological Reports 37*, 319– 322.

Ball, P. G. 1976. The effect of group assertiveness training on selected measures of self-concept for college women. Unpublished doctoral dissertation at the University of Tennessee, Knoxville.

Bugental, D. B., and Love, L. 1975. Nonassertive expression of parental approval and disapproval and its relationship to child disturbance. *Child Development 46*, 747– 752.

Eisler, R. M., Miller, P. M., and Hersen, M. 1973. Components of assertive behavior. *Journal of Clinical Psychology 29*, 295– 299.

Eisler, R. M., Miller, P. M., Hersen, M., and Alford, H. 1974. Effects of assertive training on marital interaction. *Archives of General Psychiatry 30*, 643– 649.

Eisler, R. M., Hersen, M., Miller, P. M., and Blanchard, E. B. 1975. Situational determinants of assertive behaviors. *Journal of Consulting and Clinical Psychology 43*, 330– 340.

Fensterheim, H. 1972. Assertive methods and marital problems. In R. D. Rubin,

H. Fensterheim, J. D. Henderson, and L. P. Ullman (eds.), *Advances in behavior therapy* (IV). New York: Academic Press, 13– 18.

Fensterheim, H., and Baer, J. 1975. *Don't say yes when you want to say no.* New York: David McKay Co., Inc.

Friedman, P. H. 1972. Effects of modeling, roleplaying, and participation on behavior change. In B. A. Maher (ed.), *Progress in Experimental Personality Research* (Vol. 6). New York: Academic Press.

Galassi, J. P., Kostka, M. P., and Galassi, M. D. 1975. Assertive training: A one year follow-up. *Journal of Counseling Psychology 22,* 451– 452.

Gibbs, D. N. 1965. Reciprocal inhibition therapy of a case of symptomatic erythema. *Behaviour Research and Therapy 2,* 261– 266.

Hersen, M., Eisler, R. M., and Miller, P. M. 1974. An experimental analysis of generalization in assertive training. *Behaviour Research and Therapy 12,* 295– 310.

Lambley, P. 1976. The use of assertive training and psychodynamic insight in the treatment of migraine headache: A case study. *Journal of Nervous and Mental Diseases 167,* 61– 64.

Lange, A. J., and Jakubowski, P. 1976. *Responsible assertive behavior.* Champaign, Ill.: Research Press.

McFall, R. M., and Twentyman, C. T. 1974. Four experiments on the relative contributions of rehearsal, modeling, and coaching to assertion training. In C. M. Franks and G. T. Wilson (eds.), *Behavior therapy: Theory and practice.* New York: Brunner/Mazel 127– 163.

Mitchell, K. R. 1971. A psychological approach to the treatment of migraine. *British Journal of Psychiatry 119,* 533– 534.

Morgan, W. G. 1974. The relationship between expressed social fears and assertiveness and its treatment implications. *Behaviour Research and Therapy 12,* 255– 257.

Orenstein, H., Orenstein, E., and Carr, J. E. 1975. Assertiveness and anxiety: A correlational study. *Journal of Behavior Therapy and Experimental Psychiatry 6,* 203– 207.

Osborn, S., and Harris, G. 1975. *Assertive training for women.* Springfield, Ill.: Charles C. Thomas.

Percell, L. P., Berwick, P. T., and Beigel, A. 1974. The effects of assertive training on self-concept and anxiety. *Archives of General Psychiatry 31,* 502– 504.

Phelps, S., and Austin, N. 1975. *The assertive woman.* San Luis Obispo: Impact.

Rimm, D. C., Hill, G. A., Brown, N. N., and Stuart, J. E. 1974. Group-assertive training in the treatment of expression of inappropriate anger. *Psychological Reports 34,* 791– 798.

Serber, M. 1972. Teaching the nonverbal components of assertive training. *Journal of Behavior Therapy and Experimental Psychiatry 3,* 179– 183.

Shelton, J. L., and Mathis, H. V. 1976. Assertiveness as a predictor of resident assistant effectiveness. *Journal of College Student Personnel 17,* 368– 370.

Tophoff, M. 1973. Massed practice, relaxation, and assertion training in the treatment of Gilles de la Tourette's syndrome. *Journal of Behavior Therapy and Experimental Psychiatry 4,* 71– 73.

Whitly, M. P., and Poulsen, S. B. 1975. Assertiveness and sexual satisfaction in employed professional women. *Journal of Marriage and the Family 37,* 573– 581.

Yulis, S. 1976. Generalization of therapeutic gain in the treatment of premature ejaculation. *Behavior Therapy 7,* 355– 358.

Chapter 12
Adjusting the automatic pilot:

Domestic self-management

Doest thou love life? Then do not squander
Time, for that's the stuff life is made of.

BENJAMIN FRANKLIN

Life is more likely to become a hassle because of inefficient control over little things than because of poor control over major events.[1] Examine the frustrations and anxieties you may feel at this moment. Did they result from one major mistake, or from gradually letting certain areas of your life get out of control? You may not even be aware of inadequate control over minor events until a major hassle develops (for example, losing your job, flunking out of school, having a relationship terminated).

The cumulative effect of poor control over day-to-day events is illustrated by a graduate student who was devoting more and more time to his job and girl friend but less and less time to his academic work (Whitman and Dussault, 1976). Not only was his academic work suffering, he was also tense and restless, had trouble sleeping, and had a poor appetite. He often did not feel like going to class, and he studied only occasionally. He got very little sleep, skipped numerous meals, and was perpetually tired. He had lost much of his resistance to colds and infections, and over the course of six months had lost about twenty pounds. He often neglected shaving, bathing, and washing his clothes. He felt guilty, but his guilt seemed only to worsen the situation. His plight illustrates the vicious cycle surrounding domestic mismanagement: Mismanagement leads to negative feelings about yourself and those negative feelings accentuate mismanagement.

Just as lack of control in seemingly minor areas can cause major problems, achieving a few modest goals in these areas can make life more efficient, pleasurable, and successful. These areas include time management, household management, and money management. Since they generally relate to the home-based aspects of your life, we shall refer to them cumulatively as domestic self-management. This chapter will identify typical kinds of mismanagement, appropriate goals, and self-management strategies for reaching your goals in these domestic areas.

Time management

The most common example of poor time management among our students is failure to get up on time. Many students have come from home situations in which they've been awakened by parents, and they're quite unprepared to take personal responsibility for this task. For most people, there is something inherently unpleasant about getting out of bed in the

---

[1]Opal Fraker, a doctoral student in educational psychology and guidance at the University of Tennessee, Knoxville, served as editorial consultant for this chapter. Opal is emphasizing educational research strategies in her doctoral study.

The most common example of poor time management among our students is failure to get up on time.

early morning. Without specially arranged setting events and reinforcement contingencies, they simply won't arise at an early hour. By "early hour," we don't necessarily mean two hours before daybreak, but rather early enough for you to keep class, work, and personal commitments. If arising at 10:00 A.M. consistently allows you to keep those commitments, there is little reason for you to be concerned about not getting up at 7:00 A.M. Enjoy those three extra hours of sleep, you lucky devil! Unfortunately, many classes and jobs begin long before 10:30, so most people are forced to get out of bed earlier than they would like in order to keep their commitments and meet their daily objectives.

Although getting out of bed at the appropriate hour certainly sets the stage for effective time use, the battle is not completely won at that point. Students still miss classes and appointments, they still spend more time in the student center than they intend, and they still sequence their activities in a time-consuming fashion.

Because the behaviors included in time management tend to interact, it may be appropriate to formulate several different goals in this area. For instance, you may want to set a time for getting to bed, a time for getting up, and other goals relating to being on time for classes and using your time efficiently. Since these goals are quite interdependent, you could hardly attain one if you exclude the others. For example, if you habitually get to bed late, you can't expect consistently to arise at an early hour. (Those rare individuals who thrive on four or five hours of sleep are exempt from this last statement.) For your goals to be functional, they must also be specific — arise by 7:00 A.M. four out of five days, leave for work by 7:40 A.M., be at class five minutes before it begins, spend no more than thirty minutes a day in the student center.

After establishing some time-related goals, you will want to record any time use that might affect attainment of those goals. Instead of recording around the clock, you may need to record your use of time only for certain hours during the day. There may be a number of hours during which you have minimal flexibility in what you do — hours at work, time spent in class, and travel time to and from your job and classes. Perhaps there are certain hours that you are already organizing quite well. Thus, you will need to record only that portion of the day in which you have some flexibility and in which your time management is suspect. The time chart described in Chapter 8 could be used for this purpose.

Graphing your baseline data may increase their diagnostic value. One behavior manager (Walters, 1977) graphed her time investment in three areas — recreational, domestic, and academic. Appropriate recreational activities were graphed in green, appropriate domestic activities in red, and appropriate academic activities in blue. Her graph allowed her to see immediately imbalances among the three areas. Also, by adding the three time investments each day and then subtracting that total from her sixteen waking hours, she could determine the amount of time she was devoting to no particular purpose.

Occasionally you will find that recording how you use your time leads to immediate improvement in time management, thus precluding the need for other self-management procedures. This is what happened to one student (Jason, 1975) who was having a problem getting up in the morning because he had difficulty falling asleep at night. To compensate for sleep he missed at night, he had been taking daytime naps. As his initial self-management intervention, he recorded the approximate number of minutes it took him to fall asleep, the time he woke up, and the amount of napping time. By the seventh week he no longer took daily naps. By the tenth week he was asleep by 12:30 A.M. five nights out of seven. Six months later he reported that his sleeping problems had not recurred, and all this was accomplished simply by recording the target behaviors.

Most likely, your baseline assessment will point to some changes that would immediately improve your time management. You may realize that several behaviors presently engaged in separately could be grouped together without undermining any of them. You could do any number of domestic tasks while watching TV: file your nails, wash dishes, pick up clothing, dust furniture. You may discover that you spend considerable time waiting for others or driving from store to store trying to find needed items. Thus you may decide that whenever an errand is likely to involve some waiting time — going to the dentist, seeing your landlord, picking up your children — you will take something to work on while you wait. (We've written portions of this book while waiting to play tennis.) You may also decide to use the Yellow Pages and make sure that a store has the desired item and for an acceptable price before going to that store. You may start combining several errands into one trip and then make that trip at the time of day when the stores and streets are least crowded.

If your goal is getting to work on time, your baseline analysis may suggest several changes in setting events. One student (Taylor, 1974) whose self-management project dealt with this goal made four specific changes in her setting events: (1) getting to bed by 11:00 P.M., (2) setting the alarm clock outside the bedroom door (not closing the bedroom door), (3) turning on the overhead light when shutting off the alarm, and (4) raising the room temperature so that shivering in the cold would not deter her from getting up. Another student (Miller, 1974), whose target behavior was leaving home by 7:45 A.M. in order to get to work on time, used "readiness tasks" done the night before as setting events. These readiness tasks consisted of (1) preparing clothes, (2) preparing lunches, (3) getting books and materials together, and (4) having a quick breakfast available. Doing these tasks the previous evening set the stage for an early departure the next morning.

You can usually enhance time management by using written reminders. For example, you might write notes to yourself and leave them in obvious places — use a memo magnet on the refrigerator door, put a note under the coffee pot, or tape a note to a door at eye level. (Use a paper that is a different color from the door, or use a brightly colored pen so that you can't miss seeing the note.) You might also leave yourself a note at the place where you'll be when you need to do a particular task. In order to keep each day's work in perspective, you might clip a weekly schedule of necessary domestic activities such as grocery shopping, banking, and appointments to the visor of your car or to your bicycle, or keep it in your coat pocket. A master schedule will allow you to focus on each day's tasks with the assurance that remaining tasks have their place on your long-term schedule.

Although a written schedule may be imperative in the early stages of time management, it does not ensure that you will fully utilize your capabilities throughout the day. Tennov (1977) has suggested that each person has rather consistent daily cycles. For example, you may have a period during your waking hours when your mental energy is at a peak and another period when you find it difficult to do anything requiring much concentration. Tennov has classified capability into five levels, with Level One representing peak energy and Level Five the lowest point of mental energy. Astute scheduling requires that you first monitor your capability levels in order to determine which levels occur at various

Table 12.1
How to be your superself

Time of day	Marie's level	Original schedule	Superself schedule
Early morning	one, two (her best)	X[a] Straightening bedrooms, X cleaning kitchen, laundry, X planning meals, ironing, X preparing lunches for children	Writing school paper, studying, doing regular homework assignments
Late morning	two, three (very good)	X Shopping for groceries, X general housecleaning, X shopping, watching TV	Attending classes, library work, reading textbook assignments
Midday to early afternoon	three, four (average)	O[b] Attending classes, visiting friends, O reading in the library	Straightening bedrooms, cleaning kitchen, laundry, ironing, preparing next day's lunches for the children, shopping
Late afternoon	four (slightly under par)	Preparing dinner, O reading	Preparing dinner, talking with the children, light housecleaning, grocery shopping
Evening	four, five (slightly to very under par)	Working at the drugstore, O doing homework, watching TV	Working at the drugstore, watching TV with the family, sewing, reading a novel

[a]X = Underemployment
[b]O = Overemployment
SOURCE: Reprinted from November 15, 1977, issue of *Family Circle Magazine.* © 1977 The Family Circle, Inc.

periods in the day. Then you can match task assignments to energy levels. Unless you do so, you will sometimes be overemployed (trying to do a very difficult task when your mental energy is low) and other times underemployed (doing mundane tasks when your energy level is high). (See Table 12.1.)

As for every other area of self-management, effective time use is more likely to be maintained if it results in pleasant consequences. One time manager (Loving, 1973) used a combination of immediate reinforcers, intermediate reinforcers, and long-range reinforcers. Each morning that he arose by the specified time he would have breakfast with his wife (immediate reinforcer). For each week that he met his performance standards, he would have dinner out (intermediate reinforcer). For each two weeks that he met his performance standards, he would earn one lesson in piloting an airplane (long-range reinforcer). You might also

Anything to wake up!

A student was having trouble with time management because he wasn't able to get up in the mornings. He had attended only about half his classes in eighteen months. His problem was causing him periods of depression and leading to serious doubts about his career goals and even about staying in college. He had tried unsuccessfully for a year to change his behavior pattern. An alarm clock did not awaken him. His wife tried calling him from her job to rouse him, but since the telephone was near his bed, he would fall asleep again after the call.

He went to a therapist who suggested some self-management procedures. At the therapist's suggestion he agreed to set two loud alarm clocks and place them in opposite corners of the room. Consequently he would have to get out of bed to turn them off and, hopefully, be wide enough awake to stay up. He was to terminate all reinforcing activities, such as television and reading at midnight, and to be in bed within a half-hour. He was also to grant himself several rewards when he stayed up in the morning after turning off the alarms.

After the first night, however, he did not set the alarms and turn off the lights. Perhaps the rewards were not sufficiently reinforcing, or perhaps once was not enough for the rewards to give the desired effect. In his desperation he made another contract, this one enlisting the aid of his wife. Since he thought a shower might awaken him, he was to take a shower as soon as he got out of bed and then reward himself for taking the shower. If he stayed in bed, after fifteen minutes his wife would splash water on his face every two minutes until he got up to take his shower! Fortunately she never had to execute this cruelty, and he began to collect his external payoffs. Because of his showering in the morning, he was alert throughout the day. At the end of the thirty-five weeks he had had no relapse and no periods of depression.

Adapted from Passman, R. H. 1977. The reduction of procrastinative behaviors in a college student despite the "contingency-fulfillment problem": The use of external control in self-management techniques. *Behavior Therapy 8*, 95–97.

---

consider rewarding yourself for changing setting events. For instance, if your target behavior is getting up at a certain time, you might also reward yourself for going to bed at a specified time, for setting the alarm clock, and for adjusting the room temperature. If your target behavior is arriving on time, you might reward yourself for leaving the previous location on time.

There are a great many natural consequences that serve to maintain good management. The additional work that you accomplish with efficient time use may be quite gratifying. Other people are certain to react more positively when you keep appointments and arrive on time. Many relationships go awry because one individual is habitually late; such tardiness often produces unverbalized resentment from the other person. However, when you consistently arrive on time, you convey respect for others — a message that is likely to be reciprocated. When you're able to use your time efficiently, you'll also have a sense of control over your life — a very rewarding feeling to most people.

Household management

Many students suffer from chaos in their living quarters. If your residence is typically messy, you may be embarrassed when friends drop in unexpectedly, you may frequently lose important papers or objects (your wallet, your door keys or car keys, your telephone, your dog . . .), and you may even dread returning home at night. You may also find that the disarray of your apartment undermines serious study. The task of finding appropriate materials and a spot to spread out those materials may quickly squelch any impulse to study.

The overall goal of household management is to arrange your furniture and materials in a way that is aesthetically appealing to you, permits you to find things when you need them, and facilitates other desired activities. However, household management doesn't end at this point. You have probably been seized with at least one or two attacks of "spring cleaning"; by the time the attack passes, you have your abode in immaculate order. Now comes the difficult part — maintaining some semblance of order in the coming days and weeks. Performing the tasks necessary to maintain order on a *daily* basis is a challenge that few people meet.

Ongoing household management entails many different behaviors: picking up extraneous materials from the floor, putting materials away, vacuuming or sweeping the floor, washing dishes, buying groceries, preparing food, dusting furniture, washing clothes, cleaning windows, and possibly caring for children. Actually, taking care of one's habitat can be a never-ending venture. There is always something that could be done around the house. We're not suggesting that you always be working when you're at home or that you should feel guilty about tasks not yet done. An important step is to identify which household duties are essential on a daily basis and which ones have priority. For example, with an empty pantry and dinner time approaching, it might be more imperative to do your grocery shopping than to dust the furniture. A clear delineation of priorities will allow you to do those things most essential to household management without feeling guilty about tasks remaining to be done.

Achieving your household priorities will probably require the development of a "game plan" that identifies necessary changes in setting events and reinforcement contingencies. Among the changes made by one student (Conner, 1977) were: (1) moving the coffee table out of the living room to reduce both clutter and pick-up time for that room, (2) setting the kitchen timer and ironing for a short time each day, and (3) buying a file in which to store all incoming bills and letters. If you live with someone, we suggest that you make a list of each person's daily chores and display that list where it can't be missed. The list may simultaneously serve as a setting event (reminder) for domestic activity and as a recording system if it has a column for checking the completion of daily activites.

A possible deterrent to doing certain household tasks (such as setting the machine dial for washing clothes, cooking quiche Lorraine) is not knowing how to do them. Much time would be saved in the long run if the person who knows how to do the various tasks (but will not necessarily be doing them) would write out simple instructions on a card and display that card in the place where the task is to be done. The card system might be especially useful if you are hiring domestic help. One person prepared detailed descriptions of all domestic tasks on separate cards that could be used repeatedly. For any given day, instead of preparing a new list of tasks for the domestic worker, she simply took the appropriate cards from her domestic file.

You may want to get your place organized and functioning smoothly, but be overwhelmed by the prospect of even starting such a venture. One starting point is to buy something especially attractive to go in your domicile. A beautiful painting, new curtains, or a new stereo system just wouldn't look right in a topsy-turvy setting. Some individuals feel they need a special prod in the form of a party or a visit from relatives. A scheduled party may be the impetus you need to initiate a massive clean-up campaign. However, keep the party tame, or you may have a more formidable task of cleaning up after the festivity than before!

Although scheduled visits from friends or relatives can provide the motivation needed to organize your habitat, unexpected visits and phone calls can undermine effective household management. If your surprise visitor is a dear friend whom you haven't seen in five years, drop what you're doing and enjoy that person's presence. However, if your visitor falls in the "not so special, more frequent" category, it's best to maintain your domestic momentum. You can inform such visitors that they are welcome to stay but that you've got some straightening to do while you talk. If you have visitors that fall in the chronic category, you can invite them to join you in some domestic activity such as folding clothes, washing dishes, and making up beds. Some visitors tend to stay for excessive periods; don't encourage their conversation by continuing to ask questions. Unless they are inveterate talkers, they will soon wind down if you're not actively pursuing the conversation. This principle would also hold true in dealing with lengthy phone calls. Don't forget that when visitors drop in at inopportune times or stay too long, you have a perfect right to indicate that you have work to do (you can enumerate the specific tasks) and that they should come back (or call back) at another time.

If part of your household management involves child-care responsibilities, consider the possibility of doubling up with other parents who have children similar in age to yours. Because children sometimes entertain each other, you may find it easier to keep two children than one. Perhaps you can work out an arrangement with other parents to keep their child one afternoon if they keep yours the next afternoon. You can also usually assume that if you invite a neighbor's child to spend the night with your child, the neighbor will reciprocate. Then you will have a chance to stay out until the wee hours of the morning (a privilege that parents of preadolescents don't frequently have) instead of leaving the party prematurely to get your baby sitter home.

Since most household tasks cannot be considered inherently reinforcing, you may need to provide a steady diet of external payoffs. For instance, you might reward yourself after you pick up all your clothes, then after you've got your clothes in the washer, and then after the clothes have been dried and put away. Another approach would be to reward yourself after each thirty minutes of appropriate domestic activity. As your reward, you could take ten minutes to do something that you especially enjoy. You may also want to reward yourself with points that can be redeemed for back-up reinforcers. The area of housework is one in which people typically have few misgivings about the propriety of tangible payoffs.

Although domestic activity has little intrinsic reinforcement value, it does allow you simultaneously to engage in some rather exciting fantasy. You can do domestic work with your mind far removed from the scene of the action. We suggested in Chapter 3 that you identify scenes that are especially pleasant to you. Armed with these scenes, you can take on your domestic work while fantasizing to your heart's content. Thus, when pleasant imagery begins to divert your attention from tasks requiring your complete attention, remember that you will have ample time to engage in such imagery during your domestic work. Is there any chance that pairing domestic activity with pleasant imagery could make domestic work something to which you would look forward? . . . No, that's asking too much.

Keeping a clean and organized household for several weeks doesn't make you immune to relapses. All people experience periods when they let things go around the house. A relapse may result from the development of serious problems in other areas discussed in the text. Thus, effective management in those areas should have a redeeming effect on household management. However, when relapses have occurred for whatever reason, there is still the problem of re-establishing your momentum. After a regression you may have difficulty admitting to yourself that you need to return to the fundamentals of domestic self-management. Re-establishing momentum in almost any activity is often more difficult than was initiating that momentum. However, your initial experiences with the strategies described in this section will indicate which strategies work for you. Start with these as you attempt to reclaim lost momentum.

Money management

Because many college students don't have a lot of extra money, they need to be especially effective in this area of management. Poor money management may cause you constantly to be in debt and unable to take advantage of some significant opportunities, such as attending a concert or going out on the town with a date. We've known several students whose money management was so poor that their creditors were constantly prodding them to pay up. These students were barely able to stay one step ahead of collection agents. This kind of situation can cause a great deal of tension and frustration, which of course will reduce your efficiency in other areas of responsibility.

Record keeping is unusually important in managing your money. During baseline, you should record all of your spending — the amount you spend and what you spend it for. If your expenditures follow a monthly pattern because you are paid monthly, you should establish a baseline for a whole month. If you record your spending patterns for only a week, you could get a very unrealistic picture of that spending. Imagine, for example, the potential difference between your spending the week after payday and the week before payday. Your baseline, of course, will indicate that certain spending is fixed (such as rent, utilities, laundry) but that considerable spending may fall in the incidental and impulsive category. It is from this latter category that you will gain considerable latitude in adjusting your expenditures.

Your game plan in money management will almost always involve the preparation of a budget. Use your baseline record and, if available, your financial records for the past several months to determine how much you have been spending in various areas — food, cleaning supplies, paper products, and personal-health and grooming items (all things you buy in a grocery store); housing; transportation; utilities; insurance;

medical costs; clothing; laundry and dry cleaning; entertainment; fixed monthly payments on loans or large purchases.

Scrutinize each area to determine where and how you can cut down — ride a bus or get into a car pool; take your lunch; go to matinees instead of more expensive evening performances; use several of the widely publicized procedures for lowering utility bills. For example, if you drink lots of water when you're home, the most economical practice is to keep a bottle of water in the refrigerator rather than letting the water run each time until it gets cold. And what about a dripping faucet? A slow drip will waste about fifteen gallons a day and a fast drip twenty-five gallons a day (Harris, 1975). Try to find ways to reduce impulse spending, such as planning your menus in advance and buying only items needed for the menus. Avoid certain stores in which the temptation is greatest to buy unneeded items — or just stay out of stores except when your schedule calls for shopping. Draw up a list of nonperishable items that you regularly use and stock up on these items when they're on sale. If credit cards are your downfall, put them in a safe place for a while instead of having them constantly with you. Cut your expenses in as many categories as possible when you're making out your new budget.

Of all the areas in which tangible payoffs might be used, money management appears the most promising. After preparing a budget and a list of ways to save money, give yourself a specified amount of credit for abiding by your budget and practicing money-saving ideas. The credit earned can be cashed in later for the money needed to attend that concert or to take that trip between quarters. Following your budget and money-saving list practically insures that the funds will be available to make good on your reinforcement contingencies.

Concluding thoughts

You've probably found very little in this chapter to excite your imagination. Frankly, we seldom get overstimulated at the prospect of vacuuming the house, washing clothes, or doing grocery shopping. Like most individuals, we have a natural inclination to delay such activities until we find ourselves in a bind, faced with a mammoth task. To spend time analyzing our behaviors in these areas is likewise not one of our high-priority activities. *However*, we do enjoy having lots of leisure time, interacting with our friends, and being professionally productive. The way we manage the domestic sphere can profoundly affect the time and resources available for more important pursuits. That's the message of this chapter.

References

Conner, B. 1977. Organizing household tasks. Unpublished class project, University of Tennessee.

Harris, B. C. 1975. Time saving kitchen tips. *House and Garden 147*, 144–145.

Jason, L. 1975. Rapid improvement in insomnia following self-monitoring. *Journal of Behavior Therapy and Experimental Psychiatry 6*, 349–350.

Loving, S. 1973. Arising early in the day. Unpublished class project, Michigan State University.

Miller, R. 1974. Departing for work on time. Unpublished class project, University of Tennessee.

Passman, R. H. 1977. The reduction of procrastinative behaviors in a college student despite the "contingency-fulfillment problem": The use of external control in self-management techniques. *Behavior Therapy 8*, 95–97.

Taylor, S. L. 1974. Getting to work on time. Unpublished class project, University of Tennessee.

Tennov, D. 1977. How to be more efficient every hour of the day. *Family Circle 90*(12), 22 ff.

Walters, C. 1977. Time management. Unpublished class project, University of Tennessee.

Whitman, T. L., and Dussault, P. 1976. Self control through the use of a token economy. *Journal of Behavior Therapy and Experimental Psychiatry 7*, 161–166.

Chapter 13
A familiar aspiration:

Helping others become self-directing

No word is oftener on the lips of men than
Friendship, and indeed no thought is more
familiar to their aspirations.

HENRY D. THOREAU

The wish to share friendship is not only a common but a beautiful aspiration.[1] A companion impulse is the desire to be genuinely helpful to all those with whom you have contact. What does it mean to be a friend or to give help to another human being? Though there are many ways you can help another, you could make few contributions more valuable than helping that person to become self-directing.

You may have close acquaintances right now who appear to be managing their lives very badly. They may seem exceedingly dependent, lack social skills, frequently express worries, or seldom fulfill personal and professional commitments. Although these people may exhibit all sorts of deficiencies, we're not recommending that you jump in and start altering their behavior, even if "you know best." Such interference would surely meet with resentment. Adults have a right to choose their own behaviors so long as those behaviors don't infringe upon the rights of others. Children, too, should be given increasing opportunities to assume responsibility for themselves.

There are times, however, when you should intervene in others' lives. We know there are times that we can't even manage our lives effectively unless we help others out of their dilemma. The problems of our colleagues, friends, students, and family affect us in innumerable ways. A day seldom passes when those closest to us don't reach out for help. They may seek our attention, our counsel, our approval, or our love. They may ask us for help directly, but more likely they will seek our assistance in subtle ways. Their subdued countenance may really be saying, "Ask me what's wrong."

The manner in which you help others is an issue of extreme importance. Assistance improperly given may ease the pain of the moment but render the other person less able to deal with future problems. That assistance may cause the person to be more dependent on your advice and approval, rather than being more self-directive. This chapter gives special attention to strategies that parents, teachers, counselors, and friends can employ in helping others develop self-management skills. The major emphasis is on what parents and teachers can do to assist children in becoming self-directed.

Why teach others to be self-directing?

The behaviors of others can often be changed more quickly and efficiently through external control than through self-control. Just think of

[1]Ron Carlini, a doctoral student in psychology at the University of Tennessee, served as editorial consultant for this chapter. Ron is presently working as a school psychologist in the Knox County Public Schools.

Avoid thinking about what you're going to say as others describe a problem.

the difficulty involved in training children to clean up their rooms, to do their homework, and to prepare their own snacks. However, most adults consider the payoffs worth the investment of time and energy. A major payoff of teaching a child to be self-directing is that the child will become less dependent on you and others. People who always need to be told how to approach or solve a problem will never achieve their full potential, and this dependency will eventually undermine even the most promising relationships. Consider the potential benefits of increasing the independent behaviors and decreasing the dependent behaviors listed in Table 13.1.

Children who are allowed to manage their own behaviors may also work harder than children whose behaviors are externally controlled. Lovitt and Curtiss (1969) found that children exhibited higher rates of academic behaviors when they were allowed to choose their own reinforcers and the ways in which they could earn them than when these decisions were made by the teacher — even when the self-selected conditions were identical to those previously or subsequently provided by the teacher. Thus it appears that self-direction can accentuate behavioral change.

Self-management strategies also avoid some of the other problems that may plague attempts to modify behavior. In externally controlled programs, individuals sometimes perform the target behavior only in the presence of those who administer the contingencies, only in the situations in which the contingencies are administered, and only for as long as the contingencies are administered (O'Leary and Kent, 1973). When

Table 13.1
Independent-dependent checklist

(I)[a]	1.	Turning in assignments early.
(I)	2.	Proposing a task for oneself.
(I)	3.	Bringing relevant additional material to class (such as books, magazines, a craft).
(I)	4.	Beginning work on assignments without being asked or directed to do so.
(I)	5.	After finishing assigned work, initiating other appropriate activity without being asked to do so.
(I)	6.	Making some improvement in the classroom environment without asking or being told to do so.
(I)	7.	Voting in the minority when all group members can see the hand count.
(I)	8.	Accepting blame for personal misdeeds ("I allowed myself to get upset," "I failed to listen to your directions.").
(D)	9.	Asking for approval ("Look at my paper," "Is this okay?" "Is this what you want?").
(D)	10.	Copying assignments from other students.
(D)	11.	Asking other students to see their work.
(D)	12.	Borrowing materials from other students.
(D)	13.	Blaming others for personal misdeeds ("He made me do it," "You didn't tell me. . .").

[a]Graduate students in educational psychology at the University of Tennessee judged these items as reflecting either independent (I) or dependent (D) behavior on the part of elementary school students.

the individuals themselves are in charge of the contingencies, the target behavior is more likely to generalize. Self-management programs also allow the individual to take personal credit for the change. This kind of change has been found to persist to a greater degree than a change attributed to an external agent (Davison and Valins, 1969).

Parent and teacher use

The goal of teachers and parents is to teach children how to control the environmental events affecting their behavior. This goal can best be reached by a gradual transfer of responsibility. You can start children on this path by having them operate under an externally managed system in which they are consistently reinforced for appropriate behavior. Glynn (1970) found that a class of ninth-grade girls that had been reinforced in a capricious manner was less productive under a subsequent self-management phase than a class that had been rewarded in a consistent manner. This study suggests that the ability to benefit from self-

The role of self-attribution

In treating a group of subjects who complained of insomnia, Davison, Tsujimoto, and Glaros (1973) used a treatment package composed of chloral hydrate (a drug used to induce sleep), self-produced relaxation, and specific suggestions for regulating sleep schedules. After the treatment phase, half the subjects were told that they had received an optimal dosage of chloral hydrate; the other half were told that the dosage had been too weak to have been effective. In reality, all subjects had received exactly the same dosage.

Chloral hydrate was then dropped from the treatment package but the relaxation and scheduling procedures were continued. The subjects who had been told that the drug had been too weak to change their sleep patterns maintained their improvement in sleeping habits to a significantly greater degree than the subjects who believed that their dosage had been optimally effective in making them sleep. Apparently the belief that they were responsible for their increased sleep enhanced control over sleep among the first group of subjects.

Adapted from Davison, G. C., Tsujimoto, R. N. and Glaros, A. G. 1973. Attribution and the maintenance of behavior change in falling asleep. *Journal of Abnormal Psychology 82,* 124–133.

management is strongly influenced by an individual's previous experience with external management.

Consistently applied external contingencies generate a sense of order that contributes to successful self-management. Once this order has been established, self-management procedures can be used to maintain behavioral gains initially developed through external management (Glynn et al., 1973; Frederiksen and Frederiksen, 1975). External programs are most successful in facilitating self-management when the reinforcement is contingent on the product of the child's activities rather than on *task-relevant behavior** (Marholin and Steinman, 1971). Emphasizing the product of the child's work puts more stress on independent behavior because this approach does not require the teacher's continual monitoring.

An initial transitional step between external control and self-control is self-monitoring. In this phase the responsibility for recording the target behavior is given to the individual. Although self-monitoring by itself will not always maintain long-term behavioral change, it does make the individual more aware of the target behavior and of environmental events preceding and following it. Self-monitoring has been effectively used with a wide range of behaviors, including such rare responses as

*Terms set in italics and followed by an asterisk are defined in the Glossary.

Calming the class bully

Jerry was the class bully. Not a day would go by when he wouldn't punch at least five or six children. Ms. Jones, the teacher, wanted to get Jerry to decrease this behavior, and she saw self-recording as the first step. Ms. Jones began by modeling the recording behavior. She had a punching bag in the corner of the room that she and the children could use when they became angry. She told the class (and made sure that Jerry was listening) that she wanted to know how many times she became angry and hit the bag each day. She taped a card on the wall next to the punching bag and explained that she was going to put a mark on the card each time she hit the bag. For the next week or so, Ms. Jones would call to the attention of the class (especially of Jerry) that she was marking the card immediately after punching the bag. She put a bar graph on the board to represent the frequency of the behavior. As a result of recording this behavior, her bag punching decreased rapidly. She explained to the class that keeping track of a behavior can make people more aware of what they are doing and thus help them control themselves.

It wasn't long before several well-bruised students suggested that Jerry keep track of his "mean spells." Ms. Jones said that since she had already done something like this, she would help Jerry keep track of his punching episodes. She pinned a card to Jerry's shirt on which she made a special green mark after every occurrence of the behavior. After several days of this, she gave Jerry the special green pencil and told him to mark the card himself every time he punched another child. If Jerry failed to make the mark immediately after the episode, Ms. Jones reminded him to do so. When Jerry's recording became quite reliable, she told him that she would no longer remind him to make the marks. Instead, she would keep her own count of the behavior and compare it to Jerry's count at the end of the day. She praised him if his total was the same as hers. When Jerry's count was consistent with hers for a period of several days, Ms. Jones gave him total responsibility for the recording of the behavior. At the last accounting, Jerry not only had become an astute self-recorder but also was the major advocate of nonviolence in the class.

the head jerks and barks associated with Gilles de la Tourette's Syndrome (Hutzell et al., 1974). Ballard and Glynn (1975) have shown that elementary-school children are quite capable of monitoring their own academic behaviors. For example, they recorded the number of sentences, the number of different describing words, and the number of different action words in stories they wrote.

As a teacher or parent, you may have reservations about the *reliability of self-recording* * by children. Some studies (Azrin and Powell, 1968; Ober, 1968) have shown children to be quite reliable in self-recording, while other studies (Fixsen et al., 1972; Risley and Hart,

1968) have seriously questioned that reliability. Fortunately, self-recording need not necessarily be reliable to have a facilitative impact on children's behavior. Broden, Hall, and Mitts (1971) reported on an eighth-grade girl who had requested help from the school counselor in order to improve her performance in a history class. The girl was asked to self-record her study activity, and without her knowledge this activity was also recorded by an observer. An interesting finding of the experiment was the discrepancy between the girl's and the observer's estimates of the percentage of time spent studying each day. The variations ran as high as 29 percentage points. However, despite the unreliability of the girl's self-recording, she achieved the desired change. Thus, it appears that self-change can occur even when self-monitoring is not very reliable.

We do believe, however, that training in the recording of behavior is essential and that reliability can be enhanced by the following strategies. A beginning step is to model the recording behavior. If you want to show Vernon how to keep track of his verbal outbursts, have him observe you keeping a count of those outbursts. Gradually the responsibility for recording can be transferred from you to the child. As Vernon assumes responsibility for recording his outbursts, give him immediate feedback regarding the accuracy of his recording, that is, when he has failed to record an outburst, tell him immediately, not fifteen minutes later. Rewards can also be used to increase reliability. In this case reward the child only when the child and the observer agree that the behavior has occurred, or penalize the child for records that fail to match the observer's.

Your next step might be to encourage the child to select and apply reinforcers for desired performances. The sooner you can involve your children or students in this process, the better. We suggest that you initially prepare a list of various reinforcers from which the children could choose (see Table 13.2). In this way you will probably have some activities that are reinforcing to everyone. Playing games, talking quietly with friends, listening to music, reading comic books, and watching TV are but a few of the many consequences that might be considered. It is certainly appropriate to ask the children what privileges should be added to the list.

As children assume responsibility for selecting their own reinforcers, they can also begin assuming responsibility for administering them according to agreed-upon rules. A common fear at this point is that children will take the reward without doing the prescribed work. You can deal with this probability by using much the same methods that we outlined for increasing reliability in self-monitoring. First, expose the child to a model who will administer the consequences according to these standards. The model could be a parent, a teacher, or another child.

Table 13.2
Children's reinforcement survey

	Dislike	Don't really care	Like	Like very much
Do you like painting?	____	____	____	____
Do you like making things out of wood?	____	____	____	____
Do you like to sing?	____	____	____	____
Do you like to read comic books?	____	____	____	____
Do you like to watch cartoons?	____	____	____	____
Do you like having an outdoor recess?	____	____	____	____
Would you like to be the winner of a contest?	____	____	____	____
Do you like to watch TV?	____	____	____	____
Do you like traveling to faraway places for vacation?	____	____	____	____
Do you like to go to the movies?	____	____	____	____
Do you like to play with model cars and airplanes?	____	____	____	____
Do you like to play baseball?	____	____	____	____
Do you like to play football?	____	____	____	____
Do you like to play basketball?	____	____	____	____
Do you like to play kickball?	____	____	____	____
Do you like to play with dolls?	____	____	____	____
Do you like to go camping?	____	____	____	____
Do you like listening to music?	____	____	____	____
Do you like go-carts?	____	____	____	____
Do you like minibikes?	____	____	____	____
Do you like going shopping?	____	____	____	____
Do you like to eat out in restaurants?	____	____	____	____
Do you like having a birthday and getting presents?	____	____	____	____
Do you like repairing things that are broken?	____	____	____	____
Do you like going on field trips in school?	____	____	____	____
Do you like being the teacher's helper?	____	____	____	____

SOURCE: This scale is a modified version of an unpublished "Children's Reinforcement Survey Schedule" developed by Joseph Cautela of the Department of Psychology at Boston College.

Self-control comes to the first grade

Mr. Smith was having real problems with his first graders during their seat work. They would begin on task, but their attention would soon be diverted to talking with each other and playing with items in their desks. Mr. Smith disliked constantly having to remind the children to get back to work. He turned to Ms. Gray, the other first-grade teacher in the school, who described the type of system she employed in her class. She assigned seat work in each subject by writing the assignments on the board. When the particular assignment was finished according to specified standards, the child was allowed to play at a table in the back of the room until time for the next lesson. The table held the most desirable toys and games in the class. Children who did not finish their work had to remain in their seats and continue working.

Things seemed to be working pretty well in Ms. Gray's class, so Mr. Smith decided to give the system a try. He began by explaining to his children what was to happen and by showing them Ms. Gray's class in action. At the prearranged time, Mr. Smith's class saw the children in Ms. Gray's room working diligently in their seats and then one by one hurrying to the toy table to play.

Mr. Smith began the program in his room by checking to see whether the seat work was completed according to the prescribed standards. If it was, the children were praised and sent to the toy table; and if it was not, the children were told to remain in their seats and finish the work. After several weeks of having their work checked by Mr. Smith, the children became quite accurate in knowing when they had completed their work and were eligible to visit the toy table. At this point the responsibility for deciding when they could go to the table was given to the children. Things generally went well during this period, but a few children still did not finish their work. These children either remained in their seats and played with something on their desks or wandered over to the table without finishing the work.

Mr. Smith went back to Ms. Gray for help. "Oh, I forgot to tell you something," said Ms. Gray. She explained that some children need additional assistance in working toward a goal. Other teachers had found that resistance to rule breaking is increased when a child is taught to verbalize instructions directing attention away from distracting stimuli (such as things on the desk) and toward the rewarding consequences of continued work (toy table). With Ms. Gray's assistance, Mr. Smith developed the following instructions that were learned and rehearsed by the children who were having difficulty:

I can't go back to the toy table until I finish my work.

I'm not going to think about anything now except my work.

The sooner I finish my work the more time I will have at the fun table.

All lived happily ever after.

Second, gradually transfer the responsibility for administering the consequences to the child. Third, reinforce the child for administering the consequences appropriately. Fourth, teach the child to verbalize self-instructions that would be helpful in resisting distractions from the desired task. Mischel and Patterson (1976) found that self-instructions directed toward inhibiting distractions, while focusing attention on the rewarding consequences of continued work, helped children abide by the reinforcement conditions. The instructions for resisting temptation were as follows (p. 944):

When Mr. Clown Box says to look at him and play with him, then you just say, "No, I'm not going to look at Mr. Clown Box." So that's what you can do. He says, "Look," and you say, "No, I'm not going to look at the clown box."

If you thought that Mr. Smith was trying to get his students to talk to themselves when you read "Self-control comes to the first grade" (page 273), you were absolutely right. Self-directed language may be an important tool in helping others control their own behaviors. The rationale for a self-instructional program comes from the work of the Russian psychologists Luria (1961) and Vygotsky (1962). Luria proposed three stages in the voluntary control of motor behavior. In the first stage, the speech of others, usually adults, directs the child's behavior. In the second stage, the child's own speech becomes the regulator of that behavior. Finally, the child's covert or inner speech assumes the regulatory role. Luria's approach is now being used with a number of different behaviors.

Research has shown that individuals can be trained to make self-statements that can control behaviors ranging from test anxiety to schizophrenic "crazy talk" (Meichenbaum and Cameron, 1974). Blackwood (1970) taught students to control their disruptive behavior by verbalizing fluently the consequences of that behavior. These students first read a paragraph describing their behaviors and the attending consequences, then they copied the paragraph, then paraphrased it, then wrote it in their own words from memory, and finally described the content of the paragraph.

Once the individuals have grown proficient in the self-administration of reinforcement contingencies, they are ready to begin developing their own rules of reinforcement. Felixbrod and O'Leary (1973) have found self-determined contingencies to be as powerful as those that are externally determined. The reinforcement standards self-determined by one group of children were externally imposed upon a second group of children. A third group performed in the absence of external rewards. The performance of the children in the self-determined group was greater than that of the children in the no-reinforcement group. There was no

"Having your cake . . ."

Dr. Robinson was a man with two problems. He had a secretary, Linda, who never had enough time to type insurance forms for his patients and a son, Mike, who never had enough spending money. After giving Mike his poker money for the third week in a row and having Linda threaten to look for another job if she didn't get some help, Dr. Robinson had an idea. Why not have Mike earn his extra money by typing the insurance forms for Linda? Mike could decide how much he would be paid for this job.

Well, the idea sounded good but Dr. Robinson had seen Mike work with a typewriter. His last history term paper looked as if it had been typed on a Gutenberg during the blackout! "But perhaps," thought Dr. Robinson, "if I go about it the right way I can establish an adequate standard." Dr. Robinson began by having Linda show Mike how to complete the form by doing a few herself. Dr. Robinson then went over all ten entries on the form and told Mike exactly what was to go in each blank. He specified how the name, address, and so on were to be typed. He also specified the criteria for an acceptably completed form: It had to have all the correct information in the correct slots with no misspellings and no typographical errors. According to the standards established, one error would be enough to invalidate the form.

With this preparation, Mike took a set of forms and went home. The completed forms were to be checked by Linda to determine whether they met the established standards. Mike decided on fifty cents for each correctly completed form. After a period of time Mike's accuracy rate was near 100 percent and he became his own checker. He was then allowed to withdraw fifty cents from petty cash for each completed insurance form without the supervision of Dr. Robinson or Linda.

significant difference in the performance levels under the self-determined and externally imposed conditions. It was found, however, that in the absence of social surveillance the children in the self-determined condition became progressively more lenient in their criteria for reinforcement. Therefore, you will periodically need to check on the reinforcement contingencies under which your self-directed children are operating.

Several measures can be taken to increase the likelihood of children's developing appropriate reinforcement standards. First, expose the child to a model (such as you, or another child) who uses acceptable performance standards. McMains and Liebert (1968) found that the achievement standards that a child set for himself in a bowling game were strongly influenced by the standards he observed in others. Thus, if you expect the child to set stringent standards, make sure the model sets stringent standards (Brownell et al., 1977). Second, reinforce the child for developing adequate standards. Your approval may serve quite well in this regard. Third, periodically check the reinforcement standards which the child has established. Occasional surveillance may be enough to maintain appropriate self-selection of reinforcement criteria.

The final transitional step takes one into total self-application of the self-management model. You can prepare your children and students for this phase in three ways. The first way is by presenting role models, particularly yourself. There is probably no strategy that has more potential for helping others develop self-management skills. When others see payoffs in your life that are attractive to them *and* see you employing self-management procedures to achieve those payoffs, you will be an effective role model. The second way to foster self-application is by exposing children to the full range of techniques described in Chapters 2 and 3. In this way you can provide them with the tools necessary for building the behaviors they deem desirable. Third, you can provide social support for the self-application of any or all of the self-management procedures. The survival of initial self-management applications depends on strong external support.

Counselor applications

Like parents and teachers, counselors also have much opportunity to help others become self-directing. The counselor can best achieve that goal by establishing a self-management framework similar to that described in Chapters 2 and 3. The initial objective is to help clients put their goals into behavioral terms. People tend to describe their problems in a vague and global way. Individuals want to feel better about themselves, they want to improve relationships, and they want to reduce personal discomfort. However, these goals need to be described in a specific and observable fashion if the counselor and the client are to determine a direction for counseling. Even if a client's concern is something as tangible as getting a job, that goal must be broken down into a sequence of specific behaviors that should lead to employment. The counselor is next concerned with having the client keep some type of diary regarding the occurrence of the specified behavior. Such a procedure makes the client aware of the frequency of the behavior and of the situations in which it occurs.

Most of the counselor's attention is directed toward indications by the clients that they are dealing with the problem. The counselor resists the natural tendency to focus on clients' expressions of heartbreak, confusion, disorganization, and self-pity, an approach that would probably reinforce self-defeating behaviors and prevent the clients from working toward a resolution of their problems. The counselor also resists the clients' expectations for advice and ready-made solutions. Advice is probably the most sought-after but the least used commodity in the universe! The counselor's major job is to help clients generate specific plans and strategies that they can use to reach their goals. The ultimate goal of counseling is to teach clients how to be their own counselors.

After using the client's diary to get an idea of the frequency and situational determinants of the behavior, the counselor is ready to help the client to develop a precise monitoring system and to gather baseline data. The importance of a baseline cannot be overemphasized to the client. It will provide a point of comparison for documenting behavioral change or the lack of it. The counselor will then assist the client in developing and implementing the appropriate self-management strategies. The steps of the model in Chapter 2 and the appropriate covert alternatives from Chapter 3 should be explained to clients so that they can then decide which, if any, of these strategies to employ. From that point on, the counselor's role is to help the clients through difficult periods in the application of the chosen strategy.

Application with friends

You may never be a parent, a teacher, or a counselor, but you will certainly have many chances to help others on a friendship basis. You can most easily help friends become self-directed by serving as an effective role model. However, others can appreciate the benefits of your self-management more readily than they can embrace the self-control strategies used to achieve these benefits. The fact that you have lost weight, stopped smoking, completed your work, or interacted effectively may be obvious, but without some input from you, others may not know why these changes have occurred. If a change relates to a dimension of life that is important to the other person, that person will probably comment on that change. This comment will give you a chance to talk about the self-management procedures that led to the change. In a word, you could thank your friend for noticing the improvement and then briefly outline what you did to achieve your goal. The accent is on *briefly*, because a dissertation on self-management might turn your friend off quite quickly.

The main thing to communicate is that you dealt with your behavior systematically. You want your friend to know that you were able to identify and control those factors that affected your behavior. The next step is largely up to the other person. If that person wants details regarding your self-management strategies, you can explain them or refer your friend to reading materials.

Perhaps the most important skill you can develop as a friend is active listening (see Chapter 10). Your listening permits the individual to explore the problem and to seek a solution. Listening, in effect, reflects the belief that others have the potential for resolving their own difficulties. It is essential to give your friends your complete attention. Anything less communicates a superficial regard for them and their problems. You must allow them to speak without constant interruption. As you listen to them describing their problems, avoid the temptation to reflect on similar problems in your own life. Otherwise you will be inclined to stop listening and wait for a chance to relate your experiences. Also, avoid thinking about what you're going to say as they describe a problem. You're not going to help others solve their problems when you do not hear what they are saying.

However, giving your total attention does not mean that you remain speechless. You will probably interject several brief comments along the way. These comments should be directed toward understanding what the other person is trying to say. Paraphrasing is one of the most effective ways of accomplishing that goal. You might begin a paraphrase with "You believe . . . ," "You feel . . . ," "You think . . . ," "In other words you . . ." The paraphrase should be brief and represent the crux of what the other person is saying.

Paraphrasing lets other people know that you have listened or understood. If you have misunderstood, paraphrasing provides a means of correcting that error. It also allows you to reflect back to others the subtle thoughts and feelings they are expressing. You will sometimes have a more accurate perception of what others are saying than will those people themselves. Once they have clarified their own thoughts and feelings, they should be in a better position to make a decision concerning the problem.

Some people can talk extensively about a problem and yet refuse to deal with it. We obviously feel that most personal problems could best be solved via the self-management model described in Chapter 2. Beyond simply serving as a role model, how do you get other people to use a self-management approach in dealing with their problems? First, through paraphrases and approval, you can selectively reinforce verbal behaviors that are consistent with the concepts of self-management. For example, careful listening may give you the opportunity to reflect: "You see your problem as being . . ." "You and John cannot agree about . . ." "Your job seems to pose the greatest problem when you . . ." "Your boss has asked you to . . . but you feel that . . ." From the person's own behavior, you have pieced together a rough description of the target behavior.

Similarly, when other people begin to discuss ways of dealing with their problems, you can give special attention to comments that relate to setting events and reinforcement contingencies. These people are, in essence, defining their own problems and moving toward solutions. Introducing the self-management model at this point would help them integrate and focus their efforts.

You can also, as a friend, provide the needed support and approval for the individual's use of any or all of the self-management techniques. As mentioned earlier, this approval is absolutely essential in the early phases of a program. Just remember to reinforce the slightest improvement or progress. When you share goals with friends, you can work out mutual setting events and reinforcement conditions.

Concluding thoughts

It's hard to be turned on to an approach without becoming a bit evangelical. Because self-management represents such potential for personal growth, the evangelical spirit is probably defensible in this area. The major damage that we see in self-management evangelism is the danger that characterizes all evangelical movements — intolerance for other viewpoints. As useful as the recording of behavior and the changing of setting events and the administering of reinforcement contingencies might be, some people prefer not to analyze their lives in these terms. Respect this right. If you are willing to hear about their life styles, they will be more inclined to explore your self-management approach. But remember — no approach should be presented as the *sine qua non*. Let us also keep in mind that although the influence we have on others is enormous, the ultimate decision to change remains with the individual, which is the way it should be.

References

Azrin, N. H., and Powell, J. 1968. Behavioral engineering: The reduction of smoking behavior by a conditioning apparatus and procedure. *Journal of Applied Behavior Analysis 1*, 193–200.

Ballard, K. D., and Glynn, T. 1975. Behavioral self-management in story writing with elementary school children. *Journal of Applied Behavior Analysis 8*, 387–398.

Blackwood, R. O. 1970. The operant conditioning of verbally mediated self-control in the classroom. *Journal of School Psychology 8*, 251–258.

Broden, M., Hall, R. V., and Mitts, B. 1971. The effect of self-recording on the classroom behavior of two eighth grade students. *Journal of Applied Behavior Analysis 4*, 191–199.

Brownell, K. D., Collette, G., Ersner-Hershfield, R., Hershfield, S. M., and Wilson, G. T. 1977. Self-control in school children: Stringency and leniency in self-determined and externally imposed performance standards. *Behavior Therapy 8*, 442–455.

Davison, G. C., and Valins, S. 1969. Maintenance of self-attributed and drug-attributed behavior change. *Journal of Personality and Social Psychology 11*, 25–33.

Davison, G. C., Tsujimoto, R. N., and Glaros, A. G. 1973. Attribution and the maintenance of behavior change in falling asleep. *Journal of Abnormal Psychology 82*, 124–133.

Felixbrod, J. J., and O'Leary, K. D. 1973. Effects of reinforcement on children's academic behavior as a function of self-determined and externally imposed contingencies. *Journal of Applied Behavior Analysis 6*, 241–250.

Fixsen, D. L., Phillips, E. L., and Wolf, M. M. 1972. Achievement place: The reliability of self-reporting and peer reporting and their effect on behavior. *Journal of Applied Behavior Analysis 5*, 19–30.

Frederiksen, L. W., and Frederiksen, C. B. 1975. Teacher-determined and self-determined token reinforcement in a special education classroom. *Behavior Therapy 6*, 310–314.

Glynn, E. L. 1970. Classroom applications of self-determined reinforcement. *Journal of Applied Behavior Analysis 3*, 123–132.

Glynn, E. L., Thomas, J. D., and Shee, S. M. 1973. Behavioral self-control of on-task behavior in an elementary classroom. *Journal of Applied Behavior Analysis 6*, 105–113.

Hutzell, R. R., Platzek, D., and Logue, P. E. 1974. Control of symptoms of Gilles de la Tourette's syndrome by self-monitoring. *Journal of Behavior Therapy and Experimental Psychiatry 5*, 71–76.

Lovitt, T. C., and Curtiss, K. 1969. Academic response rate as a function of teacher- and self-imposed contingencies. *Journal of Applied Behavior Analysis 2*, 49–53.

Luria, A. 1961. *The role of speech in the regulation of normal and abnormal behavior.* New York: Pergamon Press.

McMains, M. J., and Liebert, R. M. 1968. Influence of discrepancies between successively modeled self-reward criteria on the adoption of a self imposed standard. *Journal of Personality and Social Psychology 8*, 166–171.

Marholin, D., and Steinman, W. M. 1977. Stimulus control in the classroom as a function of the behavior reinforced. *Journal of Applied Behavior Analysis 10*, 465–478.

Meichenbaum, D. H., and Cameron, R. 1974. The clinical potential and pitfalls of modifying what clients say to themselves. In M. J. Mahoney and C. E. Thoresen (eds.), *Self-control: Power to the person.* Monterey, Calif.: Brooks/Cole.

Mischel, W., and Patterson, C. J. 1976. Substantive and structural elements of effective plans for self-control. *Journal of Personality and Social Psychology 34*, 942–950.

Ober, D. C. 1968. Modification of smoking behavior. *Journal of Consulting and Clinical Psychology 32*, 543–549.

O'Leary, K. D., and Kent, R. 1973. Behavior modification for social action: Research tactics and problems. In L. Hamerlynck, L. Handy, and E. Mash (eds.), *Behavior change: Methodology, concepts, and practice.* Champaign, Ill.: Research Press, 69–96.

Risley, T. R., and Hart, B. 1968. Developing correspondence between the nonverbal and verbal behavior of preschool children. *Journal of Applied Behavior Analysis 1*, 267–281.

Vygotsky, L. 1962. *Thought and language.* New York: Wiley.

Epilogue

Now that you have concluded the book, it would be nice if we could get together over a cup of coffee to discuss where you go from here. Since that will not be possible unless we have a chance meeting, let us simply offer a few parting thoughts. Most people have the potential for resolving most of their personal problems. We hope this text has provided the techniques for you to actualize that potential. Until you have consistently applied these techniques, you cannot judge the extent to which self-management can affect your life.

However, self-management is more than just a collection of techniques; it is a life style, a way of looking at yourself and at life. We may not have discussed the behaviors of greatest importance to you or the setting events and reinforcement contingencies necessary to alter your target behaviors; but if our message has taken hold, you now can assume these responsibilities for yourself. You can describe your problems in behavioral terms, and you can rearrange the environment to produce the behaviors you desire.

Do not conclude from our book that you need to spend the rest of your life recording and charting behavior. Behavior recording is most indispensable when you're just beginning self-management endeavors. When the self-management approach becomes habitual, you can analyze and resolve many problems without putting anything on paper. For example, we used a multitude of self-management strategies in revising this book. However, very few of these were ever formalized. From our previous writing experiences, we knew what setting events and reinforcers were necessary to maintain writing behaviors. These were applied abundantly, but inconspicuously, throughout the project.

Although we are committed to partaking of life's happier moments, we realistically accept life's insolubles. The song "If I Ruled the World" reflects our sentiments about such problems. However, most of our time is devoted to problems over which we have some control. It is our ability to deal with these problems that primarily determines the quality of life. Our thesis is that people must be true to themselves before they can be true to others. Live the fullest life you can and you will have something to contribute to the rest of us.

Glossary

Aerobics An exercise scheme developed originally for the Air Force by Kenneth H. Cooper. It includes gradual training programs in eight different areas for achieving cardiovascular conditioning. The scheme, which has a point system for monitoring exercise levels, would fit very nicely into our self-management model.

Applied behavior analysis The systematic examination of how environmental events affect behavior in real-world settings, such as the home, the school, and the community. This type of behavior analysis is in contrast to the study of behavior in highly controlled laboratory situations. Many principles of behavior modification first formulated from laboratory research have, however, proved quite workable in applied settings.

Back-up reward A reward that can be obtained by cashing in other items such as points, physical tokens, stars, and money. Back-up rewards give value to such items as points, which can be given immediately for desired behavior. For example, you might award yourself one point for each five minutes of study. Subsequently you could cash in a specified number of points for a night out. If back-up rewards prove effective in strengthening target behaviors, they can legitimately be called back-up reinforcers.

Contingency A behavioral condition under which a reinforcer or punisher is administered. For example, if you require yourself to engage in a specific amount of exercise before you attend a certain theatrical performance, the exercise requirement would constitute a reinforcement contingency (that is, condition for reinforcement). On the other hand, if you flip yourself with a rubber band whenever you have a specified thought, having that thought would be considered the contingency (condition) for self-punishment.

Contracting A process whereby two or more persons agree to do or not to do certain things. Contracts usually specify appropriate and inappropriate behaviors and the consequences of each. For example, one person might agree to grant a special privilege to another person if that person smokes fewer than five cigarettes a day for a period of a week.

Extrinsic reinforcement Reinforcement that is part of a person's external environment, as opposed to reinforcement coming from inner thoughts and feelings. Money, food, and praise are examples of extrinsic reinforcement. What is external may eventually be internalized. For example, you might start praising yourself for behaviors for which you have been externally praised.

Gilles de la Tourette's Syndrome A rare behavioral disorder characterized by multiple motor tics, unprovoked loud utterances, and compulsive swearing. The cause of the disorder is largely unknown.

High-probability behavior A behavior in which an individual frequently engages when there are no external consequences for engaging in that behavior. Such behavior can be used to reinforce low-probability or infrequent behavior by making access to the high-probability behavior (such as socializing) contingent upon performing the low-probability behavior (studying). See Premack principle.

Imagery Mental images; used in conjunction with covert strategies such as covert reinforcement and covert sensitization. The mental image of a behavior or situation should include all the sensations of the actual behavior or situation.

Incompatible behavior A behavior that is inconsistent with and cannot occur simultaneously with another behavior. Cooperation, for example, is incompatible with aggression. One way to reduce aggression in a given setting would be to reinforce cooperative behavior.

Internal kinesthetic feedback Sensory feedback regarding your muscle movement, which indicates whether a behavior has been executed appropriately. In this case, appropriateness is defined primarily in terms of process. For example, when tennis players feel a sense of rhythm in their strokes, internal kinesthetic cues suggest that they are stroking the ball correctly. Because of these cues, experienced tennis players can usually determine from the moment of impact whether a ball has been hit correctly.

Locus of control The perceived origin of the events in one's life. Individuals with an internal locus of control perceive themselves as being responsible for those events, while those with an external locus of control see themselves as being the victims of fate and governed by circumstances beyond their control.

Personality inventory A scale or "test" that purports to measure a particular set of personal characteristics. Personality inventories are aimed primarily at helping individuals gain insight into their own actions and are not considered tests in the sense of having right and wrong answers.

Positive reinforcer Any stimulus that strengthens (maintains or increases) the behavior it follows. What constitutes a positive reinforcer may vary from person to person and from time to time. Positive reinforcers usually take the form of approval, pleasant activities, and tangible payoffs. Events that serve as positive reinforcers often are called simply "reinforcers."

Premack principle Given two behaviors of different probabilities, the more probable behavior can be used to reinforce the less probable. For example, the individual who infrequently studies but frequently socializes could reinforce study by making socializing contingent upon study. In other words, first work, then play.

Process behaviors Responses that either facilitate or hinder achievement of desired outcomes. It is these behaviors (such as snacking, socializing) that contribute to a behavior product (overweight, incomplete academic assignments) and that should receive primary attention in behavior management rather than products themselves.

Programmed materials Instructional materials that are arranged in small segments, from easiest to most difficult, in order to insure maximum success for the learner. Typically, on each segment the learner must respond overtly (for example, fill in a blank) before proceeding to the next segment. The learner also receives immediate feedback by comparing the response with the correct response.

Reliability of self-recording The extent to which self-recorded data agree with an external observer's records of the same behavior. For example, a person might self-record the frequency of "uhs" and have an external observer concurrently record the same response. If the self-recording is reliable, the two counts will be very similar. Reliability is usually expressed in terms of percentage of agreement.

Satiation   A strategy of repeatedly indulging in a reinforcing activity until the activity is no longer reinforcing. For example, some people have found that smoking one cigarette after another can cause them to tire of cigarettes. In using this strategy, you must be sure that you reach satiation; otherwise the behavior may become even more resistant to change.

Self-reward   Administering a reward to oneself. Typically, the individual also controls the requirements for the reward. However, these requirements may be highly consistent with contingencies that initially were externally imposed. Praising yourself, awarding yourself tokens, or allowing yourself to partake of a particular privilege are examples of self-reward.

Statistically significant   A mathematical indicator that a given outcome is a function of the technique employed rather than a result of chance. An outcome is typically reported as statistically significant if the chances are no more than 5 out of 100 that the outcome might have occurred by chance alone.

Symptom   Any sensation, behavior, or occurrence thought to be indicative of a larger problem. Some psychologists suggest that behaviors are symptoms (signs) of internal events (thoughts, feelings). For example, some believe that overeating, excessive sleep, and alcoholism are indicators of a much larger problem, such as a feeling of rejection. Behaviorists, however, generally contend that symptoms are real problems and that individuals can be helped by dealing directly with behavior.

Target behavior   The behavior an individual aspires to alter with a behavior-management plan.

Task-relevant behavior   Any behavior oriented toward achieving a desired objective. A goal of behavioral self-management is to decrease responses such as anxiety and repetitive thoughts that compete with task-relevant behavior.

Thought stopping   Process used to inhibit the recurrence of unwanted thoughts. The approach initially involves thinking an unwanted thought from ten to twenty times daily for several days and shouting "stop!" to end each trial. After a few days of practice, you can maintain control by covertly shouting "stop" each time the thought occurs.

Token economy   A system in which tokens (such as points, poker chips) are given as immediate reinforcers for appropriate behavior. A specified number of tokens can subsequently be cashed in for back-up reinforcers.

Treatment period   The phase of a self-management project in which you apply a strategy to change a behavior. This phase is usually preceded by a baseline assessment of the behavior.

Ultimate aversive consequence   The long-range punitive effect of engaging in an undesirable behavior. Obesity, loss of friendship, and cancer may be the ultimate aversive consequences of overeating, sarcasm, and smoking, respectively. Thinking about personally meaningful ultimate aversive consequences may reduce undesired actions.

Index